American
GOVERNMENT
NINTH EDITION

Using
MicroCase®
ExplorIt

Barbara Norrander
University of Arizona

Michael Corbett
Ball State University

 **WADSWORTH**
CENGAGE Learning™

Australia • Brazil • Japan • Korea • Mexico • Singapore • Spain • United Kingdom • United States

WADSWORTH
CENGAGE Learning

**American Government: Using MicroCase®
ExplorIt, Ninth Edition**
Barbara Norrander and Michael Corbett

Executive Editor: David Tatom

Associate Development Editor:
Rebecca Green

Editorial Assistant: Cheryl Lee

Technology Project Manager:
Michelle Vardeman

Consulting Editor: Julie Aguilar

Marketing Manager: Janise Fry

Marketing Assistant: Teresa Jessen

Advertising Project Manager:
Nathaniel Michelson

Project Manager, Editorial Production:
Christy Krueger

Print Buyer: Judy Inouye

Permissions Editor: Stephanie Lee

Production Service: Brent Veysey

Cover Designer: Garry Harman

For product information and technology assistance, contact us at
Cengage Learning Customer & Sales Support, 1-800-354-9706

For permission to use material from this text or product,
submit all requests online at **cengage.com/permissions**
Further permissions questions can be e-mailed to
permissionrequest@cengage.com

Library of Congress Control Number: 2005930048

ISBN-13: 978-0-534-60231-4

ISBN-10: 0-534-60231-2

Wadsworth
25 Thomson Place
Boston, MA 02210
USA

Cengage Learning products are represented in Canada by Nelson Education, Ltd.

For your course and learning solutions, visit **academic.cengage.com**

Purchase any of our products at your local college store or at our preferred online store
www.ichapters.com

Printed in Canada
3 4 5 6 7 10 09 08

CONTENTS

Acknowledgments v

Preface vii

Getting Started. ix

Part I   **Foundations** 1

Exercise 1   "One Nation": Uniting a Diverse People 3

Exercise 2   Federalism: "A More Perfect Union". 25

Exercise 3   "Of the People": An Interested and Informed Public 45

Part II   **Freedom: Civil Liberties and Civil Rights** 63

Exercise 4   Civil Liberties: Free Speech 65

Exercise 5   Civil Rights: Equality 83

Part III   **Government and the Individual**. 101

Exercise 6   Public Opinion and Political Socialization 103

Exercise 7   The Media 119

Exercise 8   Political Participation 133

Exercise 9   Political Parties 151

Exercise 10   Elections 165

Exercise 11   Interest Groups and PACs 177

Part IV   **Institutions** 193

Exercise 12   The Congress 195

Exercise 13   The Presidency 213

Exercise 14   The Bureaucracy 231

Exercise 15   The Courts 245

                Appendix: Variable Names and Sources A1

ACKNOWLEDGMENTS

Michael Corbett and I assumed co-authorship of *American Government: Using MicroCase ExplorIt* with the seventh edition. Mike led the way in our efforts, having the expertise in creating interesting and challenging exercises in data analysis through his other publications using the MicroCase software. Sadly, Mike succumbed to cancer at the conclusion of the seventh edition, and his assistance on the current edition was greatly missed. Mike was a gifted teacher of political science, not only to his students at Ball State University, but to thousands of students nationwide through his textbooks and workbooks. He and his contributions will be sorely missed by the profession.

The current edition also owes much of its format to the six editions that proceeded Mike's and my involvement in the project. Through the years, this book had many "authors" who helped to shape the topics and assignments. Further, the contributions of instructors who were willing to try something new need to be acknowledged. Because so many people who teach American government really care, the computer-based approach to "hands-on" learning incorporated in this workbook can continue to contribute to the education of succeeding cohorts of students.

David Tatom of Wadsworth Publishing should be credited for his continued support of the MicroCase series of workbooks. As always, Julie Aguilar, MicroCase Technology Program Manager, provided invaluable assistance in the handling of the data sets and the MicroCase program. Brent Veysey was the production coordinator. Rebecca Green of Wadsworth Publishing oversaw the project. The contributions of Julie, Brent, and Rebecca were essential for the successful completion of this updated version.

I would like to acknowledge the contribution of Rodney Stark at the University of Washington, who first developed the format used in this series of introductory workbooks. His leadership in making real data analysis accessible to students has transformed the way many teach introductory social science courses. Special thanks goes to Matt Bahr, who oversaw much of the development, organization, and cleaning of the data files for this project.

I would like to thank a number of individuals and institutions who provided us with the data files upon which most of these exercises are based. The inclusion of selected variables from the American National Election Study would not have been possible without the generous help and permission of Nancy Burns and Donald R. Kinder and the National Election Studies, Institute for Social Research at the University of Michigan. I also thank the Inter-university Consortium for Political and Social Research for their permission to use the NES data. Special thanks goes to Tom W. Smith at the National Opinion Research Center for his continued direction and administration of the General Social Survey. Many of the international variables are based on the World Values Survey, for which I must thank Ronald Inglehart at The Institute for Social Research, University of Michigan. Professor Inglehart's book *Modernization and Postmodernization: Cultural, Economic and Political Change in 43*

Societies (Princeton, 1997) provided the inspiration for a number of examples in this workbook. The Center for the American Woman and Politics at the Eagleton Institute of Politics at Rutgers University also provided very useful data.

Finally, I would like to thank the following individuals who have contributed to this edition or previous editions: Gary Aguiar, Texas A&M International University; John B. Ashby, Northern Michigan University; Lindsey Back, Morehead State University; Martha Bailey, Southern Illinois University at Edwardsville; Hal Barger, Trinity University; Devin Bent, James Madison University; John Berg, Suffolk University; Milton Boykin, The Citadel; Robert Bradley, Illinois State University; Chalmers Brumbaugh, Elon College; Jeri Cabot, College of Charleston; Sara B. Crook, Peru State College; Roy Dawes, Gettysburg College; Robert J. Duffy, Rider College; Leonard Faulk, SUNY at Fredonia; William Flanigan, University of Minnesota; Richard Fulton, Northwest Missouri State University; Tucker Gibson, Trinity University; John Hibbing, University of Nebraska–Lincoln; Randolph Horn, Samford University; Laurence F. Jones, Angelo State University; Nancy Kindred, McNeil High School; Karen King, Bowling Green State University; Jonathan Knuckey, University of Central Florida; Nancy Kral, North Harris Montgomery College District; Jim Lemke, Coker College; Roger C. Lowery, University of North Carolina at Wilmington; Peter Maier, University of Wisconsin–Milwaukee; Theresa Marchant-Shapiro, Union College; Suzanne M. Marilley, Capital University; David McLaughlin, Northwest Missouri State University; Scott L. McLean, Quinnipiac College; Lawrence W. Miller, Collin County Community College; Francie Mizell, Dekalb College; William J. Murin, University of Wisconsin–Parkside; Dale A. Neuman, University of Missouri–Kansas City; G. R. Patterson, Porterville College; Kelly D. Patterson, Brigham Young University; Richard Pride, Vanderbilt University; Ron Rapoport, College of William and Mary; James Reed, College of St. Benedict; William Rosburg, Kirkwood Community College; Ralph Salmi, California State University–San Bernardino; David Schultz, University of Minnesota; Randy Siefkin, Modesto Jr. College; Valerie Simms, Northeastern University; J. Donald Smith, Cornell College; Joseph Stewart, University of New Mexico; Christopher Stream, University of Idaho; Eric Uslaner, University of Maryland–College Park; Jeff Walz, Concordia University–Wisconsin; Robert Weber, St. John's University; Matthew E. Wetstein, San Joaquin Delta College; Peter Wielhouwer, Spelman College; Harvey Williams, Christopher Newport College; Nancy Zingale, University of St. Thomas; Gary Zuk, Auburn University.

Barbara Norrander
Tucson, Arizona

PREFACE

The purpose of *American Government: Using MicroCase ExplorIt* is to let you discover many basic aspects of the American government and political system for yourself. There is nothing make-believe or "only educational" about this package. You will have access to the highest-quality data files available to professional researchers. The "facts" you discover are not someone's opinion—they accurately describe the real world.

You will browse the best and latest information available on questions such as

- To what extent are Americans interested in (and informed about) politics? What kinds of people are more interested and informed?

- Who participates in politics? What kinds of people are more likely to vote? Are nonvoters different from voters in terms of political views?

- In comparison with people in other nations, to what extent do Americans support civil liberties and civil rights? Would most Americans allow atheists or others who hold unpopular views to express those views?

- How do political parties function? How do Americans become party members? How are third parties handicapped in the United States?

- What kinds of people are elected to Congress? Where do they get their campaign money? Does it make any difference whether a member of Congress is a Democrat or a Republican?

- How can we explain which presidents cast the most vetoes and which presidents see more of their vetoes overridden by Congress?

- What do Americans think about the government? Do Americans generally trust the government and see it as responding to public preferences, or are Americans cynical about the government? How do Americans evaluate government institutions such as the U.S. Congress and the Supreme Court?

Discovering answers to these questions won't hurt a bit, even if you have never used a computer. The software is so easy to use that you will pick up everything you need to know in a few minutes.

What's New in the Ninth Edition

What's New in the Ninth Edition

As before, the data sets are extensive, current, and from the best sources available. The ninth edition uses the 2002 General Social Survey and the 2004 National Election Study. Both data sets include an extensive list of questions, allowing students to analyze topics beyond those examined in the exercises. The congressional data set has been updated to the 108th Congress and includes information on individual votes, interest group ratings, campaign expenditures, and personal and political information on each representative. Updates have been added to the data set on the 50 states, especially new information from the 2000 Census.

With this edition, both the MicroCase program and the data sets can be downloaded and installed from a website. A card is packaged with this book that contains a single-use PIN code. Using the PIN code the student will register online and can then download the software as often as he or she needs during the course of the school year.

GETTING STARTED

INTRODUCTION

Political science is an empirical science. The goal of this workbook is to help you learn how to use data to explore the world of political science and how to investigate new ideas and conduct research to test these ideas.

Each exercise in this workbook has two sections. The first section discusses a particular area of American government and demonstrates how data are used to support, augment, and test the ideas proposed. It is possible to read this section without using your computer. However, all of the graphics in the text can be created on your computer by following the ExplorIt Guide, which is described later in this section. Ask your instructor whether you should follow along the first section of each exercise with a computer.

The worksheet section allows you to follow up on these ideas by doing your own research. You will use the student version of ExplorIt to complete these worksheets.

When you finish this workbook, you'll know what political scientists actually do!

SYSTEM REQUIREMENTS

The minimum computer requirements are

- Windows 98, ME, 2000, XP
- Pentium II 233MHz
- 32MB RAM (64MB recommended)
- 800x600, 16-bit high-color display
- 8x CD-ROM drive
- 20MB of hard drive space (if you want to install it)

Macintosh Note: This software was designed for use with a PC. To run the software on a Macintosh, you will need PC emulation software or hardware installed. Many Macintosh computers in the past few years come with PC emulation software or hardware. For more information about PC emulation software or hardware, review the documentation that came with your computer, check with your local Macintosh retailer, or try the website: http://macs.about.com.

NETWORK VERSIONS OF STUDENT EXPLORIT

A network version of Student ExplorIt is available at no charge to instructors who adopt this book for their course. We strongly recommend installing the network version if students may be using this software on lab computers. The network version is available from the Instructor Companion page for this book at http://politicalscience.wadsworth.com.

INSTALLING STUDENT EXPLORIT

A card has been packaged with this book. This card contains a PIN code and a website address from which you can download the Student ExplorIt software needed to complete the exercises in this book. You must have this card to obtain the software and only one person may use this card.

To install Student ExplorIt to a hard drive, you will need to follow the instructions on the card to register for access. Once you are on the download screen, follow these steps in order:

1. Select DOWNLOAD to begin downloading the software.

2. You will then be selected with a choice:

   a. Run this program from its current location. This is the recommended option and this option will allow the installation to begin as soon as the file is downloaded to your computer.

   b. Save this program to disk. This option will allow you to save the downloaded file to your computer for later installation. This option also provides you a file that will reinstall the software in the event this is needed. If you select this option, you will then need to specify where to save the file. Be sure to select a location where you can easily find the file. This file is named STU602312.exe. Once the file has downloaded, locate the downloaded file and open or double-click the file name.

3. A security warning may appear next. Select [Yes].

4. The next screen will display the name of this book. Click [OK] to continue.

5. The next screen shows where the files needed for the installation will be placed. We strongly recommend you accept the default location, but if desired, you can specify a new location. Click [Unzip] to begin the install.

6. During the installation, you will be presented with several screens, as described below. In most cases you will be required to make a selection or entry and then click [Next] to continue.

The first screen that appears is the License Name screen. Here you are asked to type your name. It is important to type your name correctly, since it cannot be changed after this point. Your name will appear on all printouts, so make sure you spell it completely and correctly! Then click [Next] to continue.

A Welcome screen now appears. This provides some introductory information and suggests that you shut down any other programs that may be running. Click [Next] to continue.

You are next presented with a Software License Agreement. Read this screen and click [Yes] if you accept the terms of the software license.

The next screen has you Choose the Destination for the program files. You are strongly advised to use the destination directory that is shown on the screen. Click [Next] to continue.

7. The Student ExplorIt program will now be installed. At the end of the installation, you will be asked if you would like a shortcut icon placed on the Windows desktop. We recommend that you select [Yes]. You are now informed that the installation of Student ExplorIt is finished. Click the [Finish] button and you will be returned to the opening Welcome Screen. To exit completely, click the option "Exit Welcome Screen."

STARTING STUDENT EXPLORIT

There are two ways to run Student ExplorIt: (1) from a hard drive installation or (2) from a network installation. Both methods are described below.

Starting Student ExplorIt from a Hard Drive Installation

If Student ExplorIt is installed to the hard drive of your computer (see earlier section "Installing Student ExplorIt"), locate the Student ExplorIt "shortcut" icon on the Windows desktop, which looks something like this:

To start Student ExplorIt, position your mouse pointer over the shortcut icon and double-click (that is, click it twice in rapid succession). If you did not permit the shortcut icon to be placed on the desktop during the install process (or if the icon was accidentally deleted), you can follow these directions to start the software:

Click [Start] from the Windows desktop.

Click [Programs].

Click MicroCase.

Click Student ExplorIt - AG.

After a few seconds, Student ExplorIt will appear on your screen.

Starting Student ExplorIt from a Network

If the network version of Student ExplorIt has been installed to a computer network, double-click the Student ExplorIt icon that appears on the Windows desktop to start the program. You will need to enter your name each time you start the network version. Anything you print from software will display the name you enter and the current date. (*Note:* Your instructor may provide additional information that is unique to your computer network.)

MAIN MENU OF STUDENT EXPLORIT

Student ExplorIt is extremely easy to use. All you do is point and click your way through the program. That is, use your mouse arrow to point at the selection you want, and then click the left button on the mouse.

The main menu is the starting point for everything you will do in Student ExplorIt. Look at how it works. Notice that not all options on the menu are always available. You will know which options are available at any given time by looking at the colors of the options. For example, when you first start the software, only the Open File option is immediately available. As you can see, the colors for this option are brighter than those for the other tasks shown on the screen. Also, when you move your mouse pointer over this option, it becomes highlighted.

EXPLORIT GUIDES

Throughout this workbook, "ExplorIt Guides" provide the basic information needed to carry out each task. Here is an example:

> ➤ Data File: **STATES**
> ➤ Task: **Mapping**
> ➤ Variable 1: **11) POP2003**
> ➤ View: **Map**

Each line of the ExplorIt Guide is actually an instruction. Let's follow the simple steps to carry out this task.

Step 1: Select a Data File

Before you can do anything in Student ExplorIt, you need to open a data file. To open a data file, click the OPEN FILE task. A list of data files will appear in a window (e.g., COLONIAL, NES, GSS, etc.). If you click on a file name once, a description of the highlighted file is shown in the window next to this list. In the ExplorIt Guide shown above, the ➤ symbol to the left of the Data File step indicates that you should open the STATES data file. To do so, click STATES and then click the [Open] button (or just double-click STATES). The next window that appears (labeled File Settings) provides additional information about the data file, including a file description, the number of cases in the file, and the number of variables, among other things. To continue, click the [OK] button. You are now returned to the main menu of Student ExplorIt. (You won't need to repeat this step until you want to open a different data file.) Notice that you can always see which data file is currently open by looking at the file name shown on the top line of the screen.

Step 2: Select a Task

Once you open a data file, the next step is to select a program task. Six analysis tasks are offered in this version of Student ExplorIt. Not all tasks are available for each data file, because some tasks are appropriate only for certain kinds of data. Mapping, for example, is a task that applies only to ecological data, and thus cannot be used with survey data files.

In the ExplorIt Guide we're following, the ➤ symbol on the second line indicates that the MAPPING task should be selected, so click the Mapping option with your left mouse button.

Step 3: Select a Variable

After a task is selected, you will be shown a list of the variables in the open data file. Notice that the first variable is highlighted and a description of that variable is shown in the Variable Description window at the lower right. You can move this highlight through the list of variables by using the up and down cursor keys (as well as the <Page Up> and <Page Down> keys). You can also click once on a variable name to move the highlight and update the variable description. Go ahead–move the highlight to a few other variables and read their descriptions.

If the variable you want to select is not showing in the variable window, click on the scroll bars located on the right side of the variable list window to move through the list. See the following figure:

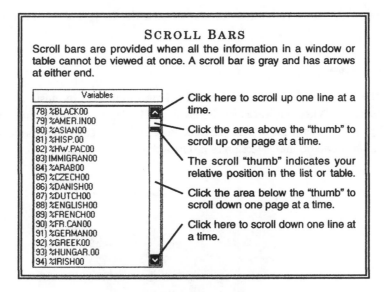

By the way, you will find an appendix at the back of this workbook that contains a list of the variable names for key data files provided in this package.

Each task requires the selection of one or more variables, and the ExplorIt Guides indicate which variables should be selected. The ExplorIt Guide example here indicates that you should select 11) POP2003 as Variable 1. On the screen, there is a box labeled Variable 1. Inside this box, there is a vertical cursor that indicates that this box is currently an active option. When you select a variable, it will be placed in this box. Before selecting a variable, be sure that the cursor is in the appropriate box. If it is not, place the cursor inside the appropriate box by clicking the box with your mouse. This is important because in some tasks the ExplorIt Guide will require more than one variable to be selected, and you want to be sure that you put each selected variable in the right place.

To select a variable, use any one of the methods shown below. (*Note:* If the name of a previously selected variable is in the box, use the <Delete> or <Backspace> key to remove it–or click the [Clear All] button.)

- Type the **number** of the variable and press <Enter>.

- Type the **name** of the variable and press <Enter>. Or you can type just enough of the name to distinguish it from other variables in the data—POP2 would be sufficient for this example.

- Double-click the desired variable in the variable list window. This selection will then appear in the variable selection box. (If the name of a previously selected variable is in the box, the newly selected variable will replace it.)

- Highlight the desired variable in the variable list, then click the arrow that appears to the left of the variable selection box. The variable you selected will now appear in the box. (If the name of a previously selected variable is in the box, the newly selected variable will replace it.)

Once you have selected your variable (or variables), click the [OK] button to continue to the final results screen.

Step 4: Select a View

The next screen that appears shows the final results of your analysis. In most cases, the screen that first appears matches the "view" indicated in the ExplorIt Guide. In this example, you are instructed to look at the Map view–that's what is currently showing on the screen. In some instances, however, you may need to make an additional selection to produce the desired screen.

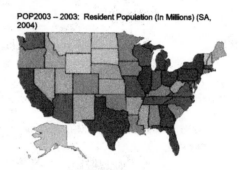

POP2003 -- 2003: Resident Population (In Millions) (SA, 2004)

(OPTIONAL) Step 5: Select an Additional Display

Some ExplorIt Guides will indicate that an additional "Display" should be selected. In that case, simply click on the option indicated for that additional display. For example, this ExplorIt Guide may have included an additional line that required you to select the Legend display.

Step 6: Continuing to the Next ExplorIt Guide

Some instructions in the ExplorIt Guide may be the same for at least two examples in a row. For instance, after you display the map for population in the example above, the following ExplorIt Guide may be given:

> Data File: **STATES**
> Task: **Mapping**
> ➤ Variable 1: **14) URBAN00**
> ➤ View: **Map**

Notice that the first two lines in the ExplorIt Guide do not have the ➤ symbol in front of the items. That's because you already have the data file STATES open and you have already selected the MAPPING task. With the results of your first analysis showing on the screen, there is no need to return to the main menu to complete this next analysis. Instead, all you need to do is select URBAN00 as your new variable. Click the [🔁] button located in the top left corner of your screen and the variable selection screen for the MAPPING task appears again. Replace the variable with 14) URBAN00 and click [OK].

To repeat: You need to do only those items in the ExplorIt Guide that have the ➤ symbol in front of them. If you start from the top of the ExplorIt Guide, you're simply wasting your time.

If the ExplorIt Guide instructs you to select an entirely new task or data file, you will need to return to the main menu. To return to the main menu, simply click the [Menu] button at the top left corner of the screen. At this point, select the new data file and/or task that is indicated in the ExplorIt Guide.

That's all there is to the basic operation of Student ExplorIt. Just follow the instructions given in the ExplorIt Guide and point and click your way through the program.

Additional Shortcuts

There are some additional ways to navigate through the software that you may find helpful.

- If you are frequently switching between 2–4 data files, using the Windows 2000 or higher operating system, you can quickly change files from any screen by clicking [File] on the drop-down menu. The last four files opened will appear at the bottom of the drop-down list. You can select the desired file from this list, the file will open automatically, and you will be returned to the main menu to select the desired task.

- Again, by clicking [File] on the drop-down menu, you can select [Open] to open any data file from any screen. When you open a new file, you will automatically return to the main menu.

- To switch to a different statistical task, instead of returning to the main menu, select [Statistics] from the drop-down menu and select the desired task. *Note:* if you select a task that is not enabled on the main menu, a message box will open alerting you that this task is not available.

- You can open a list of variables in the open file at any time by pressing the <F3> key.

ONLINE HELP

Student ExplorIt offers extensive online help. You can obtain task-specific help by pressing <F1> at any point in the program. For example, if you are performing a scatterplot analysis, you can press <F1> to see the help for the SCATTERPLOT task.

If you prefer to browse through a list of the available help topics, select Help from the pull-down menu at the top of the screen and select the **Help Topics** option. At this point, you will be provided a list of topic areas. A closed-book icon represents each topic. To see what information is available in a given topic area, double-click on a book to "open" it. (For this version of the software, use only the "Student ExplorIt" section of help; do not use the "Student MicroCase" section.) When you double-click on a book graphic, a list of help topics is shown. A help topic is represented by a graphic with a piece of paper with a question mark on it. Double-click on a help topic to view it.

If you have questions about Student ExplorIt, try the online help described above. If you are not very familiar with software or computers, you may want to ask a classmate or your instructor for assistance.

EXITING FROM STUDENT EXPLORIT

If you are continuing to the next section of this workbook, it is not necessary to exit from Student ExplorIt quite yet. But when you are finished using the program, return to the main menu and select the [Exit Program] button that appears on the screen.

Part I

FOUNDATIONS

Exercise 1   "One Nation": Uniting a Diverse People

Exercise 2   Federalism: "A More Perfect Union"

Exercise 3   "Of the People": An Interested and Informed Public

America has always been a large and very diverse place—even before it became a nation.

In 1776, at the start of the American Revolution, the 13 colonies covered 4 times the area of France and 17 times the area of England—of all European nations at that time, only Russia had a greater land area. And, although the total population of the 13 colonies was a bit less than 4 million, that was not a small population for the time. The population of England then was only slightly more than 7 million and was concentrated in an area about the size of Pennsylvania, while the American colonists were spread across an extremely diverse range of climates and terrains. Moreover, the American people themselves differed greatly from one place to another, from mountaineers and merchants to sailors and slaves.

Thus, from the very start, the physical and human features of the United States have posed political challenges. How can such a large and diverse society be governed fairly, effectively, and democratically? More than two centuries of efforts to solve these fundamental questions provide the foundations of the American government.

In the first three exercises, you will explore aspects of these foundations.

"ONE NATION": UNITING A DIVERSE PEOPLE

I pledge allegiance to the flag of the United States of America and to the Republic for which it stands, one Nation . . .

THE PLEDGE OF ALLEGIANCE,
FRANCIS BELLAMY, 1892

Tasks: Mapping, Historical Trends
Data Files: COLONIAL, STATES, COUNTY, HISTORY

In the beginning the "United States" were hardly united in any important sense of the word. Initially each "state" was a British colony administered independently by a governor and other officials sent from Britain. Even the perils of the Revolutionary War did not bring much unity. General George Washington often lacked troops and supplies because individual colonies often failed to keep their promises to provide them. Following the war, efforts to create a nation initially resulted in a very weak union of the 13 "states" under the provisions of the Articles of Confederation. The Articles established a national legislature having one house to which states could send up to seven delegates, but each state had only one vote. There was no president, and each state had its own courts. Real power remained in the individual states, and the national legislature was able to do very little. However, a series of political and economic crises led to growing support for a stronger central government. Eventually this resulted in the Constitutional Convention, which gathered in Philadelphia in 1787 and created the federal system that has been in operation since the Constitution was ratified by the states—Rhode Island being the last state to do so, on May 29, 1790.

All things considered, it was relatively easy to merge the original 13 colonies into a nation because they were similar in so many ways. For example, the overwhelming majority of citizens in each state were native English speakers of British ancestry (English, Scottish, Welsh, and Irish).

In a standard textbook, a statement like this might be followed by an instruction directing you to look at a printed map to show you the percentage of the population of British ancestry in each of the colonies. In fact, such a map appears on the next page of this book. But what makes this workbook different from an ordinary textbook is that *you* are able to generate a map of *any* item included in the COLONIAL, NATIONS, COUNTY, or STATES data files—whether it be a map of British ancestry in the American colonies or the unemployment rate in the 50 states today. And once a map is on your computer screen you can do a lot of other things to it, which you will discover as you proceed through this exercise.

➤ *Data File:* **COLONIAL**
➤ *Task:* **Mapping**
➤ *Variable 1:* **3) %BRITISH**
➤ *View:* **Map**

%BRITISH – 1790: Percent of White Population of British Ancestry

If you want to reproduce this graphic on the computer screen using ExplorIt, review the instructions in the *Getting Started* section. For this example, you would open the COLONIAL data file, select the MAPPING task, and select 3) %BRITISH for Variable 1. The first view shown is the Map view. (Remember, the ➤ symbol indicates which steps you need to perform if you are doing all examples as you follow along in the text. So, in the next example, you only need to select a new view—that is, you don't need to repeat the first three steps because they were already done in this example.)

In this map of the nation in 1790, the states appear in several colors from very dark to very light. The darker a state, the higher the percentage of its citizens who were of British ancestry. The states shown in the lightest color have the lowest percentage. Now let's look at the actual percentages.

Data File: **COLONIAL**
Task: **Mapping**
Variable 1: **3) %BRITISH**
➤ *View:* **List: Rank**

RANK	CASE NAME	VALUE
1	Massachusetts	89.0
2	North Carolina	86.5
3	Virginia	84.9
4	South Carolina	84.7
5	Georgia	84.4
6	Vermont	84.3
7	Rhode Island	78.8
8	Maryland	77.9
9	Delaware	74.3
10	Maine	72.5

As indicated by the ➤ symbol, if you are continuing from the previous example, select the [List: Rank] button. The number of rows shown on your screen may be different from that shown here. Use the cursor keys and scroll bar to move through this list if necessary.

Massachusetts was the highest, with 89 percent of its population in 1790 being of British ancestry. North Carolina was number two (86.5 percent). Moving down this list we discover that Pennsylvania was the lowest, but even it had a substantial majority (54.9 percent) of British origins. Let's note that there were many colonists from other nationalities as well, such as the French, the Germans, the Swedish, and the Dutch. Further, keep in mind that there were parts of the continent that would later become part of the United States that were heavily French or Spanish (e.g., Louisiana, Florida). Keep in mind also that a substantial percentage of the population consisted of slaves, who were, of course, from Africa. However, the important point here is that the population of the original thirteen colonies was primarily from a British background, and this had a great impact on the prospects of establishing a unified nation with a national identity.

4

Political scientists frequently refer to "variables" when they do research. For example, they might describe the percent British as an "interesting variable." A **variable** is anything that varies or takes different values among the things or units of analysis being studied. In this case these things or units are the states in 1790. And the percent British is something that varies among them. But not just any feature of states is a variable. For example, each of the states had a population. Therefore, having a population is not a variable (it does not vary). But a different number of people lived in each state, and therefore the size of each state's population is a variable: We can rank states from the smallest to the largest. Similarly, the population of each state differed (or varied) in terms of what percentage of the total was of British ancestry. Other pertinent variables include the geography and climate of these states, their histories, the percentage who belonged to churches, the size of the average farm, and the number of bars and taverns per 10,000 population—all characteristics on which the states differ are variables.

When we study individuals, we also are interested in variables: age, sex, race, weight, education, income, party affiliation, favorite TV shows, and so on—all the ways in which people differ from one another are variables.

Sometimes political scientists seek variables that reveal the greatest amount of difference. However, for the moment, our interest is in showing that there was little variation among the original states on some variables, that in these ways the states were very similar. So let's examine another such variable.

Data File: **COLONIAL**
Task: **Mapping**
➤ Variable 1: **4) % PROT.**
➤ View: **Map**

% PROT. – 1776: Percent of Church Members Who Are Protestants

If you are continuing from the previous example, use the [⤺] button to return to the variable selection screen. Select variable 4) % PROT. as the new Variable 1.

This map shows the percentage of all church members in each state who were Protestants in 1776.

Data File: **COLONIAL**
Task: **Mapping**
Variable 1: **4) % PROT.**
➤ View: **List: Rank**

RANK	CASE NAME	VALUE
1	Massachusetts	100.0
1	South Carolina	100.0
1	New Hampshire	100.0
1	Rhode Island	100.0
1	North Carolina	100.0
1	Connecticut	100.0
1	Maine	100.0
1	Vermont	100.0
1	Georgia	100.0
10	Virginia	99.8

The states were even more similar in terms of religion than ethnicity. In only six states were there any Roman Catholics, and even Maryland, initially the only colony that admitted Catholics, was overwhelmingly Protestant (84.4 percent). In fact, the great majority of Americans of Irish ancestry were Irish Protestants; it was not until the 1840s that substantial numbers of Irish Catholics began to arrive.

While the overwhelming majority of the colonists were Protestants, there was substantial diversity among these Protestants—a diversity that had strong implications for the development of the new nation and its Constitution and continues to be important in American politics today. "Protestantism" in the colonies ranged from Puritans to Methodists to a rational religion based on ideas coming out of European Enlightenment. Nevertheless, the common Protestant background helped to forge a coalition of traditional and nontraditional religious groups to carry out the American Revolution.

THE LEGACY OF SLAVERY

However, the original states were extremely different in one important way—a difference that would long haunt American political history: slavery.

Data File: **COLONIAL**
Task: **Mapping**
➤ Variable 1: **5) # SLAVES**
➤ View: **Map**

SLAVES – 1790: Number of Slaves

Here the variable is the number of slaves in each state as recorded by the first U.S. Census, conducted in 1790.

Data File: **COLONIAL**
Task: **Mapping**
Variable 1: **5) # SLAVES**
➤ View: **List: Rank**

RANK	CASE NAME	VALUE
1	Virginia	293427
2	South Carolina	107094
3	Maryland	103036
4	North Carolina	100572
5	Georgia	29264
6	New York	21324
7	New Jersey	11423
8	Delaware	8887
9	Pennsylvania	3737
10	Connecticut	2759

Virginia had 293,427 slaves in 1790 (out of a total population of 748,308). South Carolina was second with 107,094. However, in 1790 slavery was not restricted to the southern states. In 1774 Rhode Island was the first colony to abolish slavery, but did not free those currently in bondage, requiring only that their children be born free (which is why in 1790 there were still 952 slaves in Rhode Island). In 1780 Massachusetts outlawed slavery with no exemptions, which is why no slaves were found in that state by the time of the first census (at that time, Maine was part of Massachusetts). That same year Pennsylvania abolished slavery but exempted current slaves, which is why there still were 3,737 slaves in 1790. Connecticut abolished slavery, with exemptions, in 1784. Notice that there were many slaves in New York and New Jersey in 1790. That's because these states did not outlaw slavery until 1799 and 1820, respectively. All importation of slaves into the United States was prohibited by federal law in 1808, but it would take a civil war to free the slaves already here.

As new states came into the Union, repeated battles arose as to whether slavery would be legal or prohibited in each. The first severe conflict arose in 1820 when Missouri applied for statehood as a "slave" state. Because that would have created a majority in the Senate from states permitting slavery, Missouri's admission was opposed by northern senators. The "Missouri Compromise" admitted Missouri as a slave state, but balanced its Senate membership by at the same time admitting Maine as a "free" state. The compromise also drew a line across the nation and proposed that in the future all new territory north of this line would be free and all south of it slave. This line, just south of the border between Pennsylvania and Maryland, was known as the Mason-Dixon line. The compromise did not last and, as the nation expanded westward, conflicts over slavery grew increasingly heated.

➤ *Data File:* **STATES**
   ➤ *Task:* **Mapping**
➤ *Variable 1:* **7) SLAVE/FREE**
   ➤ *View:* **Map**

SLAVE/FREE -- 1860: Slave States = Dark; Free States = Light

The ➤ symbol on the Data File line indicates that you must return to the main menu and open a new data file—STATES.

In 1860, 15 states did not yet exist, so these states were neither slave nor free. Since these states have no data, they are the same color as the background on this map. On the ranking screen, the value of this variable for each of these states will be blank. West Virginia was part of Virginia prior to the Civil War and is shown as a slave state on this map.

Here the variable shows the split between slave and free states in 1860. Fifteen states had slavery, 19 states were free: The balance had been tipped by the admission of Kansas, Oregon, and California as free states. No wonder that the future of slavery became the dominant issue in the 1860 presidential election. There were four major candidates. First to be nominated was John Bell of Tennessee, running as the candidate of the Constitutional Union Party, which took a moderate stand on slavery. The second was Abraham Lincoln, the nominee of the new, antislavery Republican Party. That year the Democratic Party split over the issue of slavery, the southern faction adopting a platform supporting the right to own slaves while the northern faction took a much more circumspect position on the issue. The northern faction nominated Stephen A. Douglas for president, and the southern Democrats chose John C. Breckinridge of Kentucky, the current vice president. As the campaign developed and slavery became the main issue, many southern leaders made it clear that the South would secede if Lincoln won.

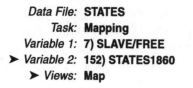

Data File: **STATES**
Task: **Mapping**
Variable 1: **7) SLAVE/FREE**
➤ Variable 2: **152) STATES1860**
➤ Views: **Map**

SLAVE/FREE -- 1860: Slave States = Dark; Free States = Light

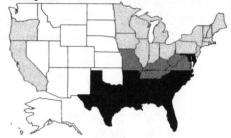

STATES1860 -- 1860: Electoral Votes: Lincoln=Light;Douglas or Bell=Medium; Breckinridge=Dark

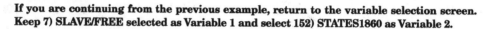

If you are continuing from the previous example, return to the variable selection screen. Keep 7) SLAVE/FREE selected as Variable 1 and select 152) STATES1860 as Variable 2.

Notice how similar these maps are. Lincoln won a close election by carrying 18 of the free states, some by very narrow margins (he won California by 711 votes out of a total of 119,868). Douglas took Missouri and part of New Jersey; Bell took Virginia, Kentucky, and Tennessee; and Breckinridge carried 11 slave states.[1]

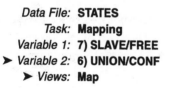

Data File: **STATES**
Task: **Mapping**
Variable 1: **7) SLAVE/FREE**
➤ Variable 2: **6) UNION/CONF**
➤ Views: **Map**

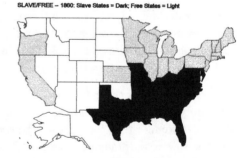

SLAVE/FREE -- 1860: Slave States = Dark; Free States = Light

---

[1] This happened because New Jersey voters at the time cast ballots for individual electors rather than the presidential candidates. Four electors supporting Lincoln were elected, and three electors supporting Douglas were chosen.

If you are continuing from the previous example, replace Variable 2, 152) STATES1860, with 6) UNION/CONF.

Following Lincoln's election, the South made good on its threats to secede, South Carolina being the first to do so, and the Civil War ensued. This map shows the states that remained in the Union (light colored) and those that joined the Confederate States. (West Virginia split from Virginia in opposition to the Confederacy.) By the time the war ended, 444,964 soldiers (North and South) had died to determine whether this would be two nations or one. In fact, the Civil War was the bloodiest war in American history—407,316 Americans were killed in World War II, 116,708 in World War I, 58,168 in the Vietnam War, 293 in the Gulf War of 1991. By mid-2005, over 1,700 American troops had been killed in fighting in Iraq and Afghanistan.

Although the Civil War settled the issue of slavery, it did not resolve issues concerning the position of African Americans, especially in the South, and continuing concerns about race and bitter memories of the war shaped the politics of the South for the next century.

While African Americans gained the right to vote in 1870 with the passage of the 15th Amendment, Southern states soon began to engage in tactics to disenfranchise these former slaves. Intimidation and violence were used to prevent blacks from voting. In addition, Southern states imposed poll taxes and literacy tests to make it difficult to register to vote. Blacks could not afford to pay the poll taxes, and literacy test were administered and judged by white officials. As a result, few African Americans living in the South were able to register to vote. This was true up to the early 1960s, 100 years after the Civil War.

Data File: **STATES**
Task: **Mapping**
➤ *Variable 1:* **222) BLK REG'60**
➤ *View:* **Map**
➤ *Display:* **Legend**

BLK REG'60 – 1960: Percent of Blacks Registered to Vote in Southern States (SA, 1978)

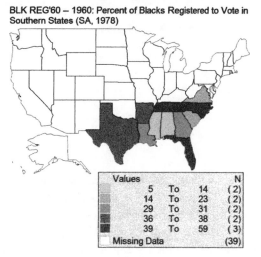

Values			N
5	To	14	(2)
14	To	23	(2)
29	To	31	(2)
36	To	38	(2)
39	To	59	(3)
Missing Data			(39)

This map shows the percentage of African Americans registered to vote in 1960 in 11 southern states. Look at the legend for the map. Southern states with the lowest level had between 5 and 14 percent of their African American citizens registered to vote. Southern states with the highest levels had between 39 and 59 percent registered. Now, let's switch views to look at the rankings of these 11 southern states.

Data File: **STATES**
Task: **Mapping**
Variable 1: **222) BLK REG'60**
➤ View: **List: Rank**

RANK	CASE NAME	VALUE
1	Tennessee	59
2	Florida	39
2	North Carolina	39
4	Arkansas	38
5	Texas	36
6	Louisiana	31
7	Georgia	29
8	Virginia	23
9	South Carolina	14
10	Alabama	14
11	Mississippi	5

The list of rankings shows that Tennessee had the highest percentage of its African American citizens registered to vote at 59 percent. In sharp contrast, only 5 percent of blacks living in Mississippi were registered to vote. One way to summarize the average level of African American registration in 1960 for these southern states is to look for the median value. The median value is the value for the case (here, state) which ranks exactly in the middle of all others. With 11 states, the median value would be the value for the 6th ranked state. This state would have five states ranked above it and five states ranked below it. Looking at the rankings, the 6th case is Louisiana, where 31 percent of African Americans were registered to vote. On average, 31 percent of southern blacks were registered to vote in 1960, or in other words, about one-third of southern blacks were eligible to vote.

Let's compare this to the average percentage of southern whites registered to vote.

Data File: **STATES**
Task: **Mapping**
➤ Variable 1: **223) WHT REG 60**
➤ View: **List: Rank**

RANK	CASE NAME	VALUE
1	North Carolina	92
2	Louisiana	77
3	Tennessee	73
4	Florida	69
5	Alabama	64
5	Mississippi	64
7	Arkansas	61
8	Georgia	57
8	South Carolina	57
10	Virginia	46
11	Texas	43

Looking at these rankings, we can see that 92 percent of whites in North Carolina were registered to vote in 1960, while only 43 percent of whites in Texas were registered to vote. Let's once again figure out the median value. Sometimes, cases have the same values and so they share the same ranking. In this listing, both Alabama and Mississippi have the same percentage of whites registered to vote, and both are listed as having the 5th rank. Notice that the next case, Arkansas, is ranked as 7th. The 6th ranking is missing because it is shared with the 5th ranking for Alabama and Mississippi. The median value for the 11 southern states would be the 6th rank case, or here, the value shared by Alabama and Mississippi. Thus, the average percentage of whites registered to vote in southern states in 1960 was 64 percent, or approximately two-thirds. Whites were twice as likely to be registered to vote as African Americans in 1960.

With African Americans prevented from voting, the southern electorate for the last half of the 19th century and the first half of the 20th century was composed primarily of whites. These white southerners always voted Democratic, holding Republicans responsible for Lincoln and the Civil War. These southern Democrats, however, were conservative on a host of issue and especially on civil rights issues. Nevertheless, they could be counted on to vote for the Democratic candidate for president. As a result, for several generations, political commentators referred to "the Solid South," noting that every Democratic presidential candidate could count on these votes and could win by just breaking close to even elsewhere.

The Solid South began to soften during the years of the Eisenhower administration of the 1950s, and it appears that the 1960 presidential election was the last time that a non-southern Democratic presidential candidate could count on most of the old Solid South. The dark states on the following map are the ones carried by Kennedy, who did well in the South.

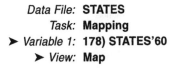

STATES'60 -- 1960: Dark States Won by Kennedy (Dem.), Light States Won by Nixon (Rep.)

In the 1964 presidential election landslide, the Democratic candidate, Johnson, won all but six states, but five of these six states were in the South. Perhaps because Johnson steered the 1964 Civil Rights Act through Congress, he did worse in the South than in the rest of the country. Thus, the crumbling of the Solid South was evident in 1964. This crumbling continued in 1968 when the Democratic candidate, Humphrey, did worse in the South than anywhere else. The migration of southern voters to the Republican Party was not yet evident, however, because of the third-party candidacy of Alabama's George Wallace, who carried five southern states and received a substantial percentage of the votes in some other southern states.

The end of the Solid South was very evident in the 1972 election. Not only did the Republican candidate, Nixon, win by a landslide, but, as the following map shows, he did better in the South than anywhere else.

Data File: **STATES**

Task: **Mapping**

➤ Variable 1: **187) NIXON'72**

➤ View: **Map**

NIXON'72 -- 1972: Percent Voting for Richard M. Nixon (Republican)

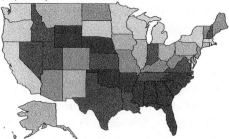

Notice that the majority of the darkest colored states, where Nixon received the largest percentage of the vote in 1972, are in the South.

Data File: **STATES**

Task: **Mapping**

Variable 1: **187) NIXON'72**

➤ View: **List: Rank**

RANK	CASE NAME	VALUE
1	Mississippi	78.2
2	Georgia	75.3
3	Oklahoma	73.7
4	Alabama	72.4
5	Florida	71.9
6	South Carolina	70.8
7	Nebraska	70.5
8	North Carolina	69.5
9	Wyoming	69.0
10	Arkansas	68.9

Additional values may be scrolled on the screen.

In a year when he carried every state except Massachusetts, it was Mississippi that gave Nixon his largest margin, followed by Georgia, Oklahoma, Alabama, Florida, and South Carolina.

Finally, the legacy of slavery was no longer a dominant feature of American presidential politics. The Democratic Party could no longer expect automatic support from white southern voters for its presidential candidates.

➤ Data File: **HISTORY**

➤ Task: **Historical Trends**

➤ Variables: **27) SOUTH.DEM**

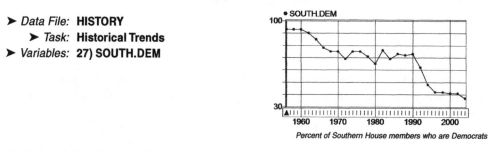

Percent of Southern House members who are Democrats

The ➤ symbol on the Data File line indicates that you must return to the main menu and open a new data file—HISTORY.

The percentage of southern members of the House who are Democrats has declined from over 90 percent in 1956 to only 37 percent after the 2004 elections.

DIVERSITY IN THE AMERICAN POPULATION

Americans today have a variety of faces. As a nation of immigrants, the composition of the American population has changed much since the days of the original 13 states. During the first 50 years of U.S. history, most immigrants were English-speaking Protestants. In the 1840s large numbers of Irish Catholics, fleeing the potato famine, came to the United States. In the later half of the 19th century, increasing numbers of southern and eastern Europeans arrived, speaking a variety of languages and participating in a diversity of religions– Protestants, Catholics, Orthodox Christians, and Jews.

The changing ethnic, religious and class backgrounds of newer immigrants often fostered tensions between them and native-born Americans. At times, discriminatory laws were passed, such as the 1879 California provision prohibiting Chinese immigrants from owning land or, at the national level, the 1882 Chinese Exclusion Act that bannned further immigration of working-class Chinese. National immigration laws in the early 20th century imposed country quotas for new immigrants which greatly favored migration from northern Europe countries while severely limiting immigration from Asia, Africa, and southern and eastern Europe. These country quotas were not lifted until 1965.

Now, let's look at the trends in immigration over the 20th century.

Data File: **HISTORY**
Task: **Historical Trends**
➤ *Variables:* **78) %FOREIGN B**

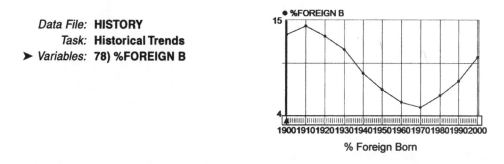

% Foreign Born

Notice first the values listed on the vertical axis which provide the range of values for these data. All of the values will fall between 4 percent of the U.S. population being foreign born to 15 percent of the U.S. population being foreign born. Now let's look at the trend line. Notice that the percentage of immigrants was highest in the early 20th century. In 1910, 14.4 percent of Americans were born in another country, the second-highest rate in American history after the 14.8 percent in the 1890 census. Immigration rates fell in the mid-20th century, with the lowest percent of foreign-born residents occurring in 1970. Since 1970, the percent of foreign-born residents has increased, though the rate remains lower than found at the beginning of the 20th century. These newest immigrant groups come increasingly from Latin America and Asia.

America today is composed of a wide variety of racial, ethnic, and religious groups, as well as considerable variation in wealth, educational attainment, and occupations. Let's explore which areas of the country are home to different racial and ethnic groups in America. We could compare U.S. states to see where these different groups of Americans live. However, the U.S. Census Bureau provides us with breakdowns for the more than 3,000 counties in the United States, so let's look at these.

The legacy of slavery may mean that even today we would see the largest percentages of African Americans in southern states.

➤ *Data File:* **COUNTY**
➤ *Task:* **Mapping**
➤ *Variable 1:* **11) %BLACK**
➤ *View:* **List: Map**

Indeed, the highest concentrations of African American citizens are found in the southern states.

Let's see where the largest Hispanic populations are found.

Data File: **COUNTY**
Task: **Mapping**
➤ *Variable 1:* **59) %HISPANIC2**
➤ *View:* **Map**

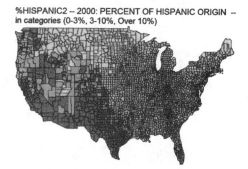

%HISPANIC2 -- 2000: PERCENT OF HISPANIC ORIGIN --
in categories (0-3%, 3-10%, Over 10%)

This map is very different. Here we see that people of Hispanic origin are more likely to live in the southwestern part of the United States. Counties with the darkest colors have Hispanic populations greater than 10 percent. (To examine the actual percentage for a given county, use variable %HISPANIC.)

Do American Indians tend to live in one region of the United States?

Data File: **COUNTY**
Task: **Mapping**
➤ *Variable 1:* **13) %AMER.IND2**
➤ *View:* **Map**

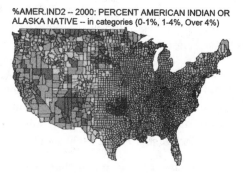

%AMER.IND2 -- 2000: PERCENT AMERICAN INDIAN OR
ALASKA NATIVE -- in categories (0-1%, 1-4%, Over 4%)

Whereas the South is widely populated by African Americans, and the Southwest has large percentages of people of Hispanic origin, American Indian populations tend to be concentrated in particular counties west of the Mississippi. In fact, there are many instances where a county having a high percentage of American Indians borders a county with a very low percentage of American Indians—this often reflects the location of Indian reservations.

Finally, let's see where Asian Americans live. This time, we will return to looking at the 50 states.

> *Data File:* **STATES**
> *Task:* **Mapping**
> *Variable 1:* **27) %ASIAN**
> *View:* **List: Map**
> *Display:* **Legend**

%ASIAN -- 2000: Percent Asian (Census)

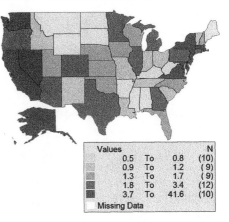

Values			N
0.5	To	0.8	(10)
0.9	To	1.2	(9)
1.3	To	1.7	(9)
1.8	To	3.4	(12)
3.7	To	41.6	(10)
Missing Data			

High numbers of Asian Americans live on the West Coast and in northeastern states such as New York and New Jersey. However, the legend for the map indicates that the percentage of Asian Americans in most states falls at 3.4 percent or less. Where might the highest number of Asian Americans live? We could ask to see the state rankings by changing the view to "List: Rank." However, most of us might expect the largest number of Asian Americans to live in Hawaii. If you move your computer mouse over the Hawaiian Islands at the bottom left of the map and left-click, the MicroCase program will show you the value for Hawaii. Turns out we were right. Hawaii is ranked first for the largest percentage of Asian Americans with 41.6 percent of Hawaiians having an Asian background.

Thus far we have learned how the faces of Americans have changed since the first 13 states came together to form the United States in the 1790s. We also saw how historical patterns, such as slavery, continue to affect American politics through the 20th century. We have discovered these patterns by using the mapping procedure in the MicroCase program. We have learned how to create maps, view rankings (and pick out the median case), and highlight specific states to view their values and rankings. We also learned how to interpret trend lines. There is much more to discover about the faces of Americans and the politics of today.

Your turn.

WORKSHEET

NAME:

COURSE:

DATE:

REVIEW QUESTIONS

Based on the first part of this exercise, answer True or False to the following items:

1. The early colonies were relatively easy to merge into a nation because they were similar in many ways.   T   F

2. The original colonies were more similar in terms of religion than they were in ancestry.   T   F

3. The 1960 presidential election was the last time that a non-southern Democratic candidate could count on the votes of most of the old Solid South.   T   F

4. The percentage of southern members of the House of Representatives who are Democrats has steadily declined over the past 40 years.   T   F

5. Most African Americans have moved out of the southern states.   T   F

6. A smaller percentage of Americans were foreign born in the 1970s than today.   T   F

7. The counties with the largest percentages of American Indians tend to be found in the eastern half of the United States.   T   F

EXPLORIT QUESTIONS

You will need to use the Explorit software for the remainder of the questions. Make sure you have already gone through the *Getting Started* section that is located prior to the first exercise. If you have any difficulties using the software to obtain the appropriate information, or if you want to learn additional features of the MAPPING task, use the on-line help (F1).

THE CHANGING SOUTH

Earlier we saw that one of the legacies of slavery was the "Solid South," where conservative white southerners voted Democratic in presidential elections through the first half of the 20th century. However, this Democratic "Solid South" began to break apart in the 1960s, and in the 1972 presidential election, Republican candidate Richard Nixon won all the southern states (and all but one of the rest of the states). Perhaps, the Democratic Party could recapture some of the southern vote when its candidate is from the South. In 1976, Jimmy Carter, the former governor of Georgia, was the Democratic candidate. Let's see how many southern states he won.

➤ *Data File:* **STATES**
    ➤ *Task:* **Mapping**
➤ *Variable 1:* **188) STATES'76**
➤ *Variable 2:* **2) BIG REGION**
    ➤ *View:* **Map**

STATES'76 -- 1976: Dark States Won by Carter (Dem.), Light States Won by Ford (Rep.)

BIG REGION -- Large Regions as Defined by the Census

To create this map using ExploreIt, open the STATES data file, select the MAPPING task, select 188) STATES'76 as Variable 1 and 2) BIG REGION as Variable 2.

8. Jimmy Carter won almost all of the southern states in 1976.   T   F

Twenty years later, the Democratic presidential candidate was Bill Clinton from Arkansas.

     Data File: **STATES**
        Task: **Mapping**
➤ *Variable 1:* **198) STATES'92**
➤ *Variable 2:* **2) BIG REGION**
     ➤ *View:* **Map**

9. Bill Clinton won almost all of the southern states in 1992.   T   F

10. Even when running a southern candidate, the Democratic
Party today may not recapture the southern vote.   T   F

The southern legacy of a Solid South for the Democratic Party has changed over the years. Let's look for other changes in southern politics.

In the preliminary portion of this exercise, we saw that African Americans were prevented from registering to vote up through 1960. After a long, hard battle, the civil rights movement succeeded in removing the barriers preventing African Americans from registering to vote in the South. Has this changed the registration rates of blacks?

> Data File: **STATES**
> Task: **Mapping**
> Variable 1: **224) BLK REG'76**
> ➤ View: **List: Rank**

11. What was the lowest percentage of African Americans registered to
vote in a southern state in 1976? _____ %

12. What was the highest percentage of African Americans registered to
vote in a southern state in 1976? _____ %

Now let's compare this to the percentage of whites registered to vote in these states.

> Data File: **STATES**
> Task: **Mapping**
> ➤ Variable 1: **225) WHT REG'76**
> ➤ View: **List: Rank**

13. What was the lowest percentage of whites registered to vote in
a southern state in 1976? _____ %

14. What was the highest percentage of whites registered to vote in a
southern state in 1976? _____ %

15. In 1960, whites were twice as likely as African Americans to be
registered to vote. Does this pattern still hold in 1976? Yes   No

One final change in southern politics is where African Americans have gained political office. The number
of African Americans elected to national, state or local offices has grown over the past 40 years. In 1970,
African Americans filled 1,469 elected positions in the United States. In 2001, there were 9,061 African
Americans in elected government posts. In which states are African Americans more likely to be elected
to office? One hypothesis would predict fewer African Americans elected to public office in southern
states because of a history of discrimination. On the other hand, many African Americans continue to live
in the South, providing a base of support for African American candidates. Let's see which pattern actually exists.

> Data File: **STATES**
> Task: **Mapping**
> ➤ Variable 1: **63) BLK OFF**
> ➤ View: **Map**

16. The highest numbers of elected African American officials are found
in the southern states. T   F

DIVERSITY OF THE AMERICAN POPULATION

Hispanics are now the largest minority group in the United States. This growth comes from families already living in the U.S. and from recent immigrants. How have these changes affected American politics? One factor would be a growth in the number of elected officials who are Hispanic. In 1985, 3,147 government posts were held by Hispanics. By 2003, Hispanics had been elected to 4,432 political offices. Where would you expect to find the largest numbers of elected officials who are Hispanic? One hypothesis would suggest that most Hispanic officials would be found in the areas where many Latinos live.

> Data File: **STATES**
> Task: **Mapping**
> ➤ Variable 1: **64) HISP OFF**
> ➤ Variable 2: **29)%HISPANIC**
> ➤ View: **Map**

17. These two maps look similar. Latino officials tend to be found in states
with higher Latino populations.   T   F

Besides being a nation of immigrants, the United States is a nation where people move frequently. People move from town to town and from state to state. This internal migration could be offsetting–the same number of people move in as move out of a town, state, or region of the country. Another possibility is that a pattern exists in this movement, such that some states gain population while others lose population. Let's see if there are any regional patterns to population growth over the past decade.

> Data File: **STATES**
> Task: **Mapping**
> ➤ Variable 1: **13) POPGROW00**
> ➤ Variable 2: **2) BIG REGION**
> ➤ View: **Map**

Changes in the population are not evenly distributed across all 50 states. Some states have grown faster than others.

18. Which of the following regions have seen the largest growth in population
between 1990 and 2000?

     a. East and Midwest

     b. Midwest and South

     c. South and West

     d. East and West

One of the political consequences of changes in population growth is that representation in the U.S. House of Representatives is based on the population size of each state. Every 10 years the seats in the

U.S. House are reapportioned based on the new census figures. Some states gain seats and some states lose seats.

> Data File: **STATES**
> Task: **Mapping**
> ➤ Variable 1: **60) HSE CHG**
> ➤ View: **List: Map**
> ➤ Display: **Legend**

Use the number (N) listed for each value in the Legend to answer the following questions.

19. How many states lost two seats in the House of Representatives?   _____

20. How many states lost one seat in the House of Representatives?   _____

21. How many states gained one seat in the House of Representatives?   _____

22. How many states gained two seats in the House of Representatives?   _____

23. States gaining seats in the House of Representatives tend to be located in which part of the country?

    a. East and Midwest

    b. Midwest and South

    c. South and West

    d. East and West

24. Most of the states losing seats in the House of Representatives tend to be located in which parts of the country?

    a. East and Midwest

    b. Midwest and South

    c. South and West

    d. East and West

<u>WHAT HAVE WE LEARNED?</u>

In this portion of the exercise, you will be asked to summarize the materials covered in previous sections. You also will be asked to speculate on the political consequences of the patterns uncovered in the data.

I.　How did slavery affect U.S. politics in the 100 years after the Civil War (1860s to 1960s)? In particular, how did it shape politics in the South? Over the past 40 years, much has changed in the South. How have these changes affected politics in the South and the nation?

II.　Citizens of the first 13 states shared many similarities in their backgrounds. Today, the United States consists of a variety of ethnic and racial groups. What are some of the regional patterns of concentration for African Americans, Hispanics, Asian Americans, and Native Americans? How might these regional patterns influence American politics?

III.　Americans move from state to state and region to region. As a result, some states grow faster than others. In recent years, which areas of the country are growing the fastest and which are growing more slowly? Besides changing the distribution of seats in the U.S. House of Representatives, what might be some other political consequences to uneven population growth among the states?

WHAT ELSE CAN BE EXPLORED?

The analyses in this exercise merely scratch the surface of the topics that can be explored concerning the diversity of citizens in the United States. The COUNTY, STATES, and HISTORY files contain many more variables that describe the American population. Listed below are just a few topics that you might want to do further research with these data.

1. With the COUNTY file you can explore more about the ethnic background of Americans. The file contains the ancestry of the population of each county, e.g., the percent of British ancestry, the percent of Mexican ancestry, or the percent of Arab ancestry. What might be some political implications of varying settlement patterns for different groups of Americans?

2. U.S. states differ on a number of dimensions. The STATES file contains data on such factors as urbanism, income, educational levels, age distributions, and employment. You can look at each of these traits with a separate map, or you might want to compare two at one time by listing one as Variable 1 and a second trait as Variable 2. How could variations in these factors affect politics in the 50 states?

3. With the HISTORY file you can explore more about the changing U.S. population including trends in population age, educational levels, and urbanization. How is politics today different from politics 100 years ago due to such changes in the population?

FEDERALISM: "A MORE PERFECT UNION"

We the People of the United States, in Order to form a more perfect Union, establish Justice, insure domestic Tranquility, provide for the common defence, promote the general Welfare, and secure the Blessings of Liberty to ourselves and our Posterity, do ordain and establish this Constitution for the United States of America.

PREAMBLE TO THE CONSTITUTION,
SEPTEMBER 17, 1787

Tasks: Mapping, Scatterplot, Historical Trends
Data File: STATES, HISTORY

From the start, Americans had two basic concerns about the structure of their government. First, they wished to retain as much local authority as possible—each state had its particular concerns, interests, and local culture that it wished to protect. Second, they wished to have sufficient centralized authority so as to regulate relations among the states and provide for the common interests—defense, for example. The first attempt failed—the Articles of Confederation maximized the independence of the states, but failed to provide sufficient central authority. So, the Constitutional Convention tried a different approach. The result was called **federalism**, a system of government wherein two or more levels of government have formal authority over the same geographic area and the same citizens. That is, unlike most European nations, which concentrate nearly all power in a central government, a great deal of power was reserved for local governments—state, county, and city. But, unlike the previous confederation, the federal government was given substantial powers to enforce laws and policies nationwide. These powers were specifically spelled out in the Constitution. In addition, the Bill of Rights, the first ten amendments to the Constitution that were adopted at the end of 1791, further specified limits on the powers of governments and noted:

Amendment X

The powers not delegated to the United States by the Constitution, nor prohibited by it to the States, are reserved to the States respectively, or to the people.

Despite these provisions, the federal and local governments exist in a state of mutual tension, pulling and pushing for greater control. During the two centuries since the federal government was created, it has gained a great deal more power than was intended by those who drew up the Constitution and the power of the individual states has been curtailed.

THE GOVERNMENTS OF THE UNITED STATES

One consequence of federalism is that the United States has lots of governments. We have one national government and 50 state governments.Yet, the largest number of governments is found at the local level. Today, over 87,000 local governments exist in the United States! Found at the local level are city governments, county governments, school districts, and a host of special districts covering such things as fire protection, water supplies, and waste removal. Let's look where we find these local governments.

> ➤ *Data File:* **STATES**
> ➤ *Task:* **Mapping**
> ➤ *Variable 1:* **143) LOC GOVTS**
> ➤ *View:* **Map**

LOC GOVTS -- 2002: Number of Local Governments (SA, 2004)

If you want to reproduce this graphic on the computer screen using ExplorIt, review the instructions in the *Getting Started* section. For this example, you would open the STATES data file, select the MAPPING task, and select 143) LOC GOVTS for Variable 1. The first view shown is the Map view. (Remember, the ➤ symbol indicates which steps you need to perform if you are doing all examples as you follow along in the text. So, in the next example, you only need to select a new view—that is, you don't need to repeat the first three steps because they were already done in this example.)

On this map, the darker a state, the larger the number of local governments found. We can also look at the exact number of local governments in each state, from the most to the least, by asking to view the rankings.

> *Data File:* **STATES**
> *Task:* **Mapping**
> *Variable 1:* **143) LOC GOVTS**
> ➤ *View:* **List: Rank**

RANK	CASE NAME	VALUE
1	Illinois	6903
2	Pennsylvania	5031
3	Texas	4784
4	California	4409
5	Kansas	3887
6	Ohio	3636
7	Minnesota	3482
8	Missouri	3422
9	New York	3420
10	Indiana	3085

Illinois has the largest number of local governments at 6,903. Pennsylvania is next with 5,031, followed by Texas with 4,784. Only the first 10 states are listed above, but with the MicroCase program you can scroll down the rankings list to view all 50 states. If you do so, you will see that Hawaii has the fewest local governments at only 19.

Part I: Foundations

One might wonder if states with more people have more governments. This might be the case if sheer numbers produce more demands for government services. For example, a large number of school children might require many more school districts. However, other factors may also come into play. One reason Hawaii has such a low number of local governments is that it is the only state to have a statewide school system, rather than the local school districts found in the other states. But let's start by looking for any overlap between state population size and the number of local governments.

Data File: **STATES**
Task: **Mapping**
Variable 1: **143) LOC GOVTS**
➤ Variable 2: **10) POPULATION**
➤ View: **Map**

LOC GOVTS -- 2002: Number of Local Governments (SA, 2004)

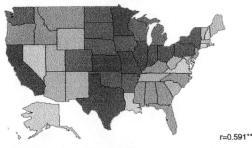

r=0.591**

POPULATION -- 2000: Resident Population (In Millions)(Census)

The two maps have some similarities. States such as New York, Illinois, Texas, and California rank in the highest categories in both maps–these are large-population states with a large number of local governments. Yet, other states present a mixed pattern. For example, Minnesota ranks in the top category for number of local governments, with 3,482, but ranks in the middle category in terms of population. Meanwhile, Arizona has approximately the same population as Minnesota, but ranks in the second lowest category for number of local governments, with 638. Thus, while the maps are similar, they are not identical. That means that population size is only one of a number of factors that "explains" the number of local governments. Other potential factors might be regional variations in preferences for local versus state authority, differences between urban and rural states, or whether a state has a wealthier or poorer citizenry. The advantage of using data sets along with a software program such as MicroCase is that you can test out these alternative explanations.

FEDERAL TAX POLICY

Each level of government needs money to operate. Thus, as Americans we are faced with a national income tax, state taxes that are often in the form of an additional income tax or a sales tax (or both), and local taxes which frequently include property taxes. The federal government, however, has the greatest ability to raise taxes. The federal government spends some of this money directly on federal programs, such as defense or space exploration; some of the money is directed toward individual citizens, such as Social Security checks; and some of the money is transferred to state and local governments in the form of grants.

Let's begin by looking at the historical trends for how the federal government raises its money.

➤ Data File: **HISTORY**
➤ Task: **Historical Trends**
➤ Variables 1: **101) INC TAX GD**
       103) SOC SEC GD
       104) EXCISE GD

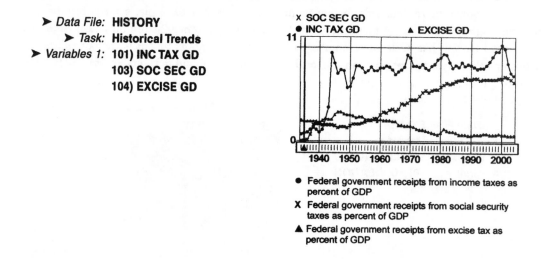

● Federal government receipts from income taxes as percent of GDP

X Federal government receipts from social security taxes as percent of GDP

▲ Federal government receipts from excise tax as percent of GDP

This graph looks at the amount of money raised from the federal income tax, Social Security tax, and excise taxes. Money amounts over time can be misleading, because inflation means that a dollar today is worth less than a dollar 10 years ago. Thus, money values over time are frequently "standardized" in some manner. In this case, money values are standardized by comparing the amount of money raised by the federal government with each tax type to the size of the nation's economy at the time. The size of the nation's economy is measured by a statistic known as the Gross Domestic Product, or GDP. Thus, values given in this graph are the amounts of money raised by each tax as a percentage of the total size of the U.S. economy. For example, in 2004, the federal government raised nearly $850 billion from individual income taxes, but the size of the U.S. economy was nearly $12 trillion. Thus, the federal income tax as a percentage of GDP was 7 percent.

Until the 20th century, virtually all federal revenues came from customs duties on imports from abroad and from excise taxes on alcohol and tobacco, while state and local revenues came mainly from property taxes. There were neither federal nor state income taxes. During the Civil War the federal government imposed an income tax (with a minimum rate of 3 percent and a maximum rate of 5 percent). This tax was cancelled after the end of the war. In 1894 President Grover Cleveland, the newly elected Democrat, pushed an income tax law through Congress. It was held to be unconstitutional by the Supreme Court, thus requiring backers of the tax to amend the Constitution (the 16th Amendment) in order to tax incomes. Begun in 1913, the federal income tax rates soon rose far beyond the "maximum limits" promised when the amendment was adopted.

Returning to the historical trends graph, the income tax rose significantly during World War II and has remained the largest source of U.S. federal funds since that time. Excise taxes, the mainstay of the federal government in the 19th century, have become an increasingly small component of the federal coffers. Finally, Social Security is an increasing component of the money raised (and spent) by the federal government.

Since the income tax is the major source of money for the federal government, let's see how the payment of this tax is distributed across the 50 states.

> ➤ *Data File:* **STATES**
> ➤ *Task:* **Mapping**
> ➤ *Variable 1:* **76) INCOME TAX**
> ➤ *View:* **Map**

INCOME TAX -- 2001: Federal Income Tax Per Capita (SA, 2004)

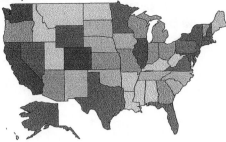

Not surprisingly, the average resident in some states pays far more in federal income taxes than does the average resident in some other states.

> *Data File:* **STATES**
> *Task:* **Mapping**
> *Variable 1:* **76) INCOME TAX**
> ➤ *View:* **List: Rank**

RANK	CASE NAME	VALUE
1	Connecticut	6222
2	New Jersey	4821
3	Massachusetts	4768
4	New York	4285
5	New Hampshire	3870
6	Maryland	3684
7	Colorado	3624
8	Illinois	3569
9	Washington	3507
10	California	3454

People in Connecticut pay the most federal income tax (an average of $6,222 per person), followed by residents of New Jersey ($4,821). People in Mississippi pay the least ($1,568), only one-fourth of what people in Connecticut pay. Now let's examine family incomes in the states.

> *Data File:* **STATES**
> *Task:* **Mapping**
> ➤ *Variable 1:* **20) FAMILY$**
> ➤ *View:* **Map**

FAMILY$ -- 2000: Median Family Income (2000 Inflation-Adjusted Dollars) (Census: C2SS)

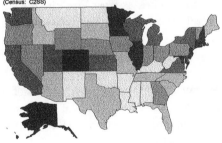

RANK	CASE NAME	VALUE
1	New Jersey	65182
2	Connecticut	64369
3	Maryland	62437
4	Massachusetts	61560
5	Alaska	60124
6	New Hampshire	58470
7	Hawaii	58159
8	Minnesota	57847
9	Colorado	55756
10	Illinois	55198

No surprise. Connecticut and New Jersey also are among the states with the highest median family incomes and Mississippi is among the lowest here too.

Obviously, per capita income tax payments reflect income. States where people earn the most are states where people pay the most income tax. That is confirmed by this map of median family income, which closely resembles the map of per capita income taxes. And that statement raises this issue: How much alike must two maps be in order for them to be "alike"?

In Exercise 1 you were asked to compare many maps of the United States and to say which ones were very similar and which ones were very different. You no doubt found it easy to notice when two maps were very much alike. But, as you examined maps that were less alike, you must have found it more difficult to say how much alike they were.

As it turns out, there is a simple method for determining precisely how much alike are any two maps. It was invented about 100 years ago in England by Karl Pearson. Once you see how he did it, you will find it easy to apply.

Let's begin with these two maps of income taxes and family income.

To see Pearson's method, we can draw a horizontal line across the bottom of a piece of paper. We will let this line represent the map of median family income. So, at the left end of this line we will write 34,465, which indicates West Virginia, the state with the lowest income. At the right end of the line we will write 65,182 to represent New Jersey as the state with the highest income.

34,465   65,182

Now we can draw a vertical line up the left side of the paper. This line will represent the map of per capita income tax. At the bottom of this line we will write 1,568 to represent Mississippi, the state with the lowest income tax. At the top we will write 6,222 to represent Connecticut, the state with the highest income tax.

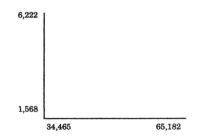

Now that we have a line with an appropriate scale to represent each map, the next thing we need to do is refer to the distributions for each map in order to learn the value for each state and then locate it on each line according to its score. Let's start with New Jersey. Since it is the state with the highest median income, we can easily find its place on the horizontal line. We will make a small mark at 65,182 to locate New Jersey. Next, New Jersey has a per capita federal income tax of $4,821. So, we make a mark on the vertical line about where we think that 4,821 would be. This point will be roughly three-fourths up the vertical line. Now we draw a line up from the mark for New Jersey on the horizontal line and draw another out from the mark for New Jersey on the vertical line. Where these two lines meet (or intersect), we draw a dot. This dot represents the combined map locations of New Jersey—it represents both the per capita income tax and the median family income for this state.

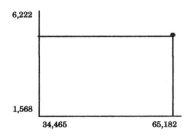

Now let's locate Connecticut. To find Connecticut on the horizontal line (also known as the X-axis), estimate where 64,369 is located and make a mark at that spot. Connecticut's tax rate is easy to find because it is the highest: 6,222. So, make a mark at 6,222 on the vertical line (also known as the Y-axis). Now we draw a line up from the horizontal line and draw another line across from the mark on the vertical line. Where these two lines intersect, we put a dot to represent Connecticut for both per capita income tax and median family income.

When we have followed this procedure for each state, we will have 50 dots located within the space defined by the vertical and horizontal lines representing the two maps. What we have done is to create a **scatterplot**. Fortunately, you don't have to go to all this trouble. ExplorIt will do it for you.

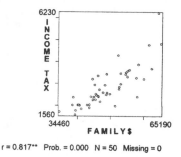

r = 0.817** Prob. = 0.000 N = 50 Missing = 0

Data File: **STATES**
➤ Task: **Scatterplot**
➤ Dependent Variable: **76) INCOME TAX**
➤ Independent Variable: **20) FAMILY$**

Notice that the SCATTERPLOT task requires two variables.

Special feature: When the scatterplot is showing, you may obtain information on any dot by clicking on it. A little box will appear around the dot, and the values of 20) FAMILY$ (or the X-axis variable) and of 76) INCOME TAX (or the Y-axis variable) will be shown.

Each of these dots is a state.

Once Pearson had created a scatterplot, his next step was to calculate what he called the **regression line**.

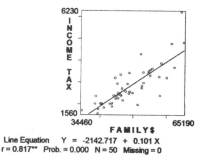

Line Equation   Y = -2142.717 + 0.101 X
r = 0.817** Prob. = 0.000 N = 50 Missing = 0

Data File: **STATES**
Task: **Scatterplot**
Dependent Variable: **76) INCOME TAX**
Independent Variable: **20) FAMILY$**
➤ View: **Reg. Line**

To show the regression line, select the [Reg. Line] option from the menu.

The regression line represents the best effort to draw a straight line that connects all of the dots. It is unnecessary for you to know how to calculate the location of the regression line—the program does it for you.

To see how the regression line would look if the maps were identical, all you need to do is examine the scatterplot for identical maps. So, if you create a scatterplot using FAMILY$ as both the dependent and independent variables, you will be comparing identical maps and the dots representing states will all be on the regression line like a string of beads.

However, since the maps for income tax and income are only very similar, but not identical, most of the dots are scattered near, but not on, the regression line. Pearson's method for calculating how much alike are any two maps or lists is easy, once the regression line has been drawn. What it amounts to is measuring the distance out from the regression line to every dot.

Data File: **STATES**
Task: **Scatterplot**
Dependent Variable: **76) INCOME TAX**
Independent Variable: **20) FAMILY$**
➤ View: **Reg. Line/Residuals**

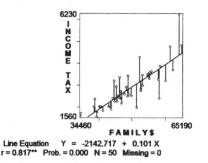

Line Equation Y = -2142.717 + 0.101 X
r = 0.817** Prob. = 0.000 N = 50 Missing = 0

To show the residuals, select the [Residuals] option from the menu.

See all the little lines. If you added them all together, you would have a sum of the deviation of the dots from the regression line. The smaller this sum, the more alike are the two maps. For example, when the maps are identical and all the dots are on the regression line, the sum of the deviations is 0.

In order to make it simple to interpret results, Pearson invented a procedure to convert the sums into a number he called the **correlation coefficient**. The correlation coefficient varies from 0.0 to 1.0. When maps are identical, the correlation coefficient will be 1.0. When they are completely unalike, the correlation coefficient will be 0.0. Thus, the closer the correlation coefficient is to 1.0, the more alike the two maps or lists. Pearson used the letter r as the symbol for his correlation coefficient.

Look at the lower left of the screen above and you will see r = 0.817**. This indicates that the maps are extremely similar. (The meaning of the asterisks will be explained a bit later.)

Correlation coefficients can be either positive or negative. This correlation is positive: Where incomes are higher, people pay higher income taxes. That is, as one rises so does the other—they tend to occur in unison. But when we examine a new scatterplot, the whole picture changes radically.

Data File: **STATES**
Task: **Scatterplot**
Variable Dependent: **76) INCOME TAX**
➤ Variable Independent: **22) %POOR**
➤ View: **Reg. Line**

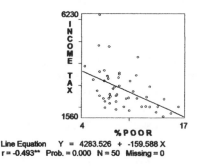

Line Equation Y = 4283.526 + -159.588 X
r = -0.493** Prob. = 0.000 N = 50 Missing = 0

This time we are measuring the wealth (or lack thereof) by the percent of a state's residents who live below the poverty line. A high measure on the percent poor variable indicates a state with less wealth. Remember, that our measure of income tax paid is measured where higher values indicate higher levels of payment. Thus, we would expect that as the number of poor increased in a state, the level of income tax payments should go down. We expect a negative correlation, since a high value on percent poor should match up with a low value on level of income tax paid. In fact, that is what happens with the correlation coefficient equaling -0.493**.

The point of calculating correlation coefficients is not simply to say how alike or unalike two maps are. Indeed, the point of comparing two maps usually is not motivated by artistic concerns, but is done in search of links, or connections, between variables. Moreover, only when such links exist can we propose that there is a causal relationship between them. Thus, implicit in our first two uses of the scatterplot technique was the assumption that one variable might be the cause of the other.

No one would really think it is just an accident that there is an extremely high correlation between income and income taxes. Rather, it seems likely that one is a cause of the other—that people must pay high income taxes because they have high incomes. In similar fashion, it seems likely that income tax rates are lower where more people are poor.

Whenever social scientists become interested in a variable, the first thing they generally ask is what causes it to vary. And the first test of any proposed answer to such a question is to demonstrate the existence of a correlation between the variable to be explained and its proposed cause. In this instance we have demonstrated that income may be a cause of the level of taxes they pay since the two variables are highly correlated. By itself correlation does not establish that a causal relationship exists. But without a correlation, there can be no causal relationship between two variables.

That helps explain the distinction between independent and dependent variables. In the SCATTERPLOT task, the software first asks for the dependent variable and then asks for the independent variable. If we think something might be the cause of something else, then we say that the cause is the independent variable and that the consequence (or the thing being caused) is the dependent variable. Put another way, the dependent variable *depends on* the independent variable.

Now, suppose that someone suggests that states with a fast-growing population also might be gaining wealth and therefore paying more in federal income taxes. We can measure how fast a state is growing by the percent of change in the state's population between the 1990 and 2000 censuses. By comparing the change in a state's population (used as the independent variable) to the level of income taxes paid (used as the dependent variable), we can test whether the assumption about population growth and taxes paid holds true.

Data File:	**STATES**
Task:	**Scatterplot**
Variable Dependent:	**76) INCOME TAX**
➤ *Variable Independent:*	**13) POPGROW00**
➤ *View:*	**Reg. Line**

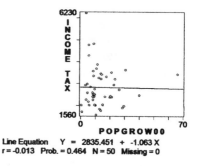

Line Equation   Y = 2835.451 + -1.063 X
r = -0.013   Prob. = 0.464   N = 50   Missing = 0

This is what a scatterplot looks like when two variables are not correlated. The points are scattered widely around the regression line. The lack of a pattern between population growth and level of income taxes paid is confirmed by the correlation coefficient, which equals -0.013. (Notice that there are no asterisks accompanying this coefficient.) The odds are very high that this very small correlation is nothing more than a random accident. Thus, we conclude that a state's population growth is not related to the amount of federal income taxes paid by its residents.

In Exercise 3 you will learn how political scientists calculate the odds as to whether or not a correlation is random. Here it is sufficient to know that many correlations are so small, we treat them *as if they were zero.* And the software automatically does that calculation for you and gives you the results. If you look back at the correlation between income and income tax, you will see that there are two asterisks following the value of r (r = 0.817**). Two asterisks means that there is less than 1 chance in 100 that this correlation is a random accident. One asterisk means that the odds against a correlation being random are 20 to 1. Whenever there are no asterisks following a correlation, the odds are too high that it could be random.[1] That's how we know that the correlation between population growth and income taxes paid is too small to matter—there are no asterisks. *Treat all correlations without asterisks as zero correlations.*

Keep in mind, however, that correlation and causation are not the same thing. It is true that without correlation there can be no causation. But correlations often occur between two variables without one being a cause of the other.

States vary on a whole host of demographic and political traits. Not all of these aspects would be related in a causal process. For example, states vary in the number of their citizens who have become U.S. Supreme Court justices. The largest number of states, 19, have had no Supreme Court appointments. The remaining states have been home to at least one justice, and New York has had 14 of its citizens appointed to the Supreme Court. One can think of a number of possible reasons for this variation in the home states of Supreme Court justices, such as how long a state has been part of the United States or how large is a state's population. However, it would take very convoluted logic to think of a reason why the number of Supreme Court justices from a state would affect the level of income taxes paid. Remember, a good number of these Supreme Court justices were appointed in the 1800s before a federal income tax existed. Nevertheless, the number of Supreme Court justices is correlated with the level of income taxes paid. Let's look at the maps.

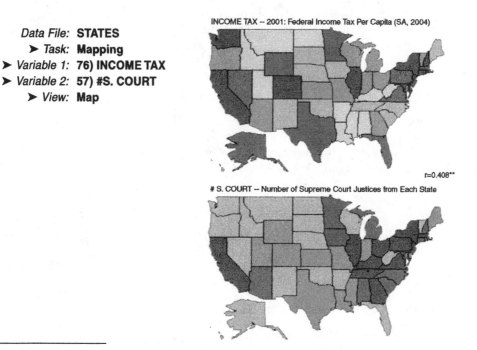

Data File: **STATES**
➤ *Task:* **Mapping**
➤ *Variable 1:* **76) INCOME TAX**
➤ *Variable 2:* **57) #S. COURT**
➤ *View:* **Map**

INCOME TAX -- 2001: Federal Income Tax Per Capita (SA, 2004)

r=0.408**

S. COURT -- Number of Supreme Court Justices from Each State

---

[1] As you'll find in the next exercise, statistical significance in survey data helps us to assess whether or not a relationship exists in the population from which the survey sample was drawn. In ecological data sets, such as the 50 states, statistical significance helps us determine whether the existing relationship is a result of chance factors.

The two maps are somewhat similar. Both New York and California rank in the highest category for both income taxes paid and number of Supreme Court justices. Idaho, Montana and North Dakota have not had a Supreme Court justice appointed from their citizenry (at least not up until early 2005), and all three states rank in the lowest category for per capita income taxes paid.

In fact, there is a moderate correlation between the two maps, with $r = 0.408$**. (The correlation coefficient given in the mapping program is identical to the one given in the scatterplot function.) The correlation between justices and income taxes paid also is statistically significant. However, correlation does not prove causality. In this case, no plausible explanation exists for why the number of Supreme Court justices appointed from a state over the country's 200-year history would influence the level of income taxes paid in 2001. Sometimes, two traits exist together without one causing the other.

Your turn.

REVIEW QUESTIONS

Based on the first part of this exercise, answer True or False to the following items:

1. If the correlation coefficient between two variables is large, it means that one variable is the cause of the other.　　　　　　　　　　　　T　　F

2. The correlation coefficient shown when two maps are on the screen is interpreted differently than the correlation coefficient that appears in the SCATTERPLOT task.　　　T　　F

3. A negative correlation coefficient confirms that two variables are not associated with one another.　　　　　　　　　　　　T　　F

4. When a correlation coefficient is not followed by any asterisks, we treat it as a zero correlation.　　　　　　　　　　　　T　　F

5. States where people have high median family incomes tend to be the same states where people pay the most in federal income taxes.　　　T　　F

EXPLORIT QUESTIONS

If you have any difficulties using the software to obtain the appropriate information, or if you want to learn additional features of the MAPPING or SCATTERPLOT tasks, refer to the online help.

FEDERALISM: MATCHING STATE POLICIES WITH STATE NEEDS

One of the arguments in favor of federalism is that it allows states to match their own governmental policies to their particular set of needs. Some states may want to spend more money on education. Some states may want to establish policies to attract more small businesses. Still other states may feel a greater need to combat the problem of crime. Let's explore this last category.

Let's first look at a mapping of the violent crime rate, and then we will compare this with a mapping of the money that states spend on corrections.

> ➤ Data File:　**STATES**
> ➤ Task:　**Mapping**
> ➤ Variable 1:　**127) VIOL.CRIME**
> ➤ View:　**Map**

6. This map shows the violent crime rate for the 50 states. While there is no absolutely clear-cut pattern here, which of the following statements is most accurate concerning the states with the highest crime rates? (Circle the letter of the most appropriate answer.)

    a. Many of the states with higher crime rates are in the Midwest.

    b. Many of the states with higher crime rates are in the South and Southwest.

    c. Most of the states with higher crime rates are in the Northeast.

Exercise 2: Federalism: "A More Perfect Union"　　　　　　　　37

7. If states with higher violent crime rates also have higher rates of spending on correction facilities (e.g., prisons), when we compare the maps for these two variables they should be

    a. similar to each other.

    b. opposite of each other.

    c. neither similar nor opposite.

    d. We can't predict what the maps will look like.

8. If states with higher violent crime rates have lower rates of spending on corrections, then these maps should be

    a. similar to each other.

    b. opposite of each other.

    c. neither similar nor opposite.

    d. We can't predict what the maps will look like.

Let's look at both maps so that we can see if the violent crime rate has any effect on how much a state spends on corrections.

> Data File: **STATES**
> Task: **Mapping**
> Variable 1:   **127) VIOL.CRIME**
> ➤ Variable 2:   **114) ST CORR**
> ➤ Views: **Map**

9. These maps are

    a. similar to each other.

    b. opposite of each other.

    c. neither similar nor opposite.

Sometimes it is difficult to determine how alike two maps are simply by looking at them. Let's use the SCATTERPLOT task to examine these same variables.

> Data File   **STATES**
> ➤ Task: **Scatterplot**
> ➤ Dependent Variable: **114) ST CORR**
> ➤ Independent Variable: **127) VIOL.CRIME**
> ➤ View: **Reg. Line**

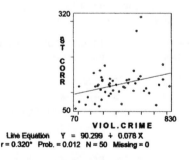

Line Equation   Y = 90.299 + 0.078 X
r = 0.320*   Prob. = 0.012   N = 50   Missing = 0

Note that the SCATTERPLOT task requires you to choose two variables. Make sure your screen matches the scatterplot shown above.

10. The states that have the highest rates of spending on corrections should appear as dots at the

    a. right of the scatterplot.

    b. left of the scatterplot.

    c. top of the scatterplot.

    d. bottom of the scatterplot.

    e. We cannot tell where these dots should be.

11. The states that appear as dots at the right of the scatterplot represent those that have the

    a. highest violent crime rates.

    b. lowest violent crime rates.

    c. highest rates of spending on corrections.

    d. lowest rates of spending on corrections.

    e. The location of the dots is not related to the value of the cases on either variable.

Special feature: When the scatterplot is showing, you may obtain the information on any dot by clicking on it. A little box will appear around the dot, and the values of 114) ST CORR (or the Y-axis variable) and of 127) VIOL.CRIME (or the X-axis variable) will be shown. The information also shows the value of the correlation coefficient with the high-lighted case removed. Ignore this new value of the correlation coefficient.

12. Identify the case that is highest on ST CORR: _____

13. What is its value on ST CORR (Y)?   _____

14. What is its value on VIOL.CRIME (X)?   _____

15. Identify the case that is highest on VIOL.CRIME: _____

16. What is its value on VIOL.CRIME (X)?   _____

17. What is its value on ST CORR (Y)?   _____

18. What is the correlation coefficient (r) for this scatterplot? (Remember to include any asterisks and begin with a 0 in front of the decimal point.)   _____

19. Is it statistically significant?   Yes   No

20. The results indicate that states with higher violent crime rates spend higher proportions of money on corrections.   T   F

Another way of examining the connection between the crime problem and the government's response to this problem is to check the connection between the violent crime rate and the number of police officers in the state and local governments. We could hypothesize that states with higher rates of violent crime would have more police officers (per 10,000 population).

        Data File: **STATES**

        Task: **Scatterplot**

➤ *Dependent Variable:*   **141) POLICE**

➤ *Independent Variable:*   **127) VIOL.CRIME**

       ➤ *View:*   **Reg. Line**

21. Write in the Pearson correlation (r) for this relationship.   r = _____

22. Is the relationship statistically significant?   Yes   No

23. In general, states that have higher crime rates have more police officers per 100,000 population.   T   F

24. Which state has the highest number of police officers per 100,000 population?   _____

FEDERAL GRANTS

A significant component of contemporary federalism in the United States is that the federal government transfers money to state and local governments through a series of grants. Some of these grants are designated for specific programs, while others are more general grants given to cover a broader policy area, such as education. Some of the grant money helps cover the cost of federal programs and mandates that are implemented by the states. States are advantaged by these grant programs with additional money added to their budgets. On the other hand, the federal government has greater influence on state policies through these grants. Sometimes the federal government uses a threat of holding back grant money to influence states to change their policies. For example, in the 1980s in an effort to reduce drunk-driving accidents among teenagers, the federal government threatened to reduce transportation grants to states that did not raise their minimum drinking age to 21. By the end of the 1980s, all states had done so.[2]

Federal grants for transportation are given to the states to support the Interstate Highway System and other major roads that are part of the National Highway System. Thus, we would expect that states with more such roadways would receive a larger transportation grant from the federal government. In other words, we expect a positive relationship between the eligible miles of roadway in a state and the size of the transportation grants.

>   Data File: **STATES**
> ➤ Task: **Mapping**
> ➤ Variable 1: **97) FED TRAN**
> ➤ Variable 2: **98) HIGHWAY**
> ➤ View: **Map**

25. Write in the Pearson correlation (r) for this relationship.   r = _____

26. Is the relationship statistically significant?   Yes   No

27. In general, states with more eligible highway miles receive larger transportation grants from the federal government.   T   F

A second major area of federal grants to the states is for food and nutrition programs, such as Food Stamps (a program that provides poorer families with vouchers to be used to buy food at grocery stores) and the WIC program (which provides pregnant women and young children with access to specific foods and dietary information).

---

[2] The U.S. Supreme Court approved of this federal tactic for changing states' minimum drinking age in the case of *South Dakota v. Dole* (1987).

28. One might expect that the lower the average family income in a state the higher the amount of federal grant money for food programs. Thus we are expecting a _____ relationship between average family income in a state and the level of federal grants for food programs.

    a. positive

    b. negative

             Data File: **STATES**

        ➤ *Task:* **Scatterplot**

➤ *Dependent Variable:* **92) FED FOOD**

➤ *Independent Variable:* **20) FAMILY$**

        ➤ *View:* **Reg. Line**

29. Write in the Pearson correlation (r) for this relationship.   r = _____

30. Is this relationship statistically significant?   Yes   No

31. Is this relationship in the positive or negative direction?   Positive   Negative

32. States where the average family earns more money receive smaller grants from the federal government to cover food and nutrition programs.   T   F

Another way to measure the economic well-being of a state's residents is with the proportion of families living in poverty. This time we would expect that the greater the number of poor families in a state the larger the amount of money from federal grants for food and nutrition programs.

33. Thus we are expecting a _____ relationship between the number of poor families in a state and the level of federal grant money for food and nutrition programs.

    a. positive

    b. negative

             Data File: **STATES**

           Task: **Scatterplot**

    Dependent Variable: **92) FED FOOD**

➤ *Independent Variable:* **22) %POOR**

        ➤ *View:* **Reg. Line**

34. Write in the Pearson correlation (r) for this relationship   r = _____

35. Is this relationship statistically significant?   Yes   No

36. Is this relationship in the positive or negative direction?   Positive Negative

37. States where a greater proportion of the families living in poverty receive _____ of federal grants for food and nutrition programs compared to other states.

    a. larger amounts

    b. smaller amounts

    c. the same amount

WHAT HAVE WE LEARNED?

I.   In this exercise we learned how to compare maps through the use of Pearson's r. We also learned to use this same statistic to analyze the distribution of points in a scatterplot. What does a Pearson's r tell you about the relationship between two variables? What does it mean for this relationship to be statistically significant? What does it mean when Pearson's r shows a positive relationship? What does it mean when Pearson's r is negative?

II.   The 50 states vary in the economic well-being of their residents. In some states the average family earns more money and fewer families live in poverty; in other states the average family earns less money and more families live in poverty. How does this variation in economic well-being influence the collection of federal income taxes and the distribution of federal grants for food and nutritional programs?

III.   Crime rates vary across the 50 states. How does this variation shape state policies?

<u>WHAT ELSE CAN BE EXPLORED?</u>

Many other aspects of modern federalism can be explored with the data in the STATES file.

1. More information is available on spending for a wide variety of state programs (education, health, welfare, highways, and corrections), as well as total state expenditures and debt. Are there aspects of a state or its citizenry which may account for variations in these state policies?

2. In this exercise we explored some aspects of the federal income tax. The STATES file also contains information on state tax policies: how much a state raises in income taxes, how much a state raises from a general sales tax, and whether a state has a lottery. Are there any patterns in how much and which types of taxes are used by the states?

3. The STATES file also contains information about local governments: how they raise revenue through local taxes, how much revenue comes from grants from the federal and state governments, and how much local governments spend and owe. Are there any patterns among these indicators of local government revenue and expenditures?

"OF THE PEOPLE": AN INTERESTED AND INFORMED PUBLIC

> *. . . government of the people, by the people, for the people . . .*
>
> ABRAHAM LINCOLN,
> GETTYSBURG ADDRESS,
> NOV. 19, 1863

Tasks: Mapping, Univariate, Cross-Tabulation, Auto-Analyzer
Data Files: NATIONS, NES

While not everyone would agree completely on the details of what we can loosely call democratic theory, there are certain ideas that most democratic theorists would agree on. Most would agree, for example, that a democratic government must be responsive to the will of the people and that it must act in accord with at least some definition of the public good. On the other side of this coin, democratic theory also makes certain assumptions about the citizen. In order for the government to represent the people, citizens must take an interest in public affairs and be adequately informed about them. (Democratic theory also assumes that citizens participate in politics, and we will return to political participation in Exercise 8.) Let's begin with interest in politics.

POLITICAL INTEREST ACROSS NATIONS

➤ *Data File:* **NATIONS**
➤ *Task:* **Mapping**
➤ *Variable 1:* **3) P.INTEREST**
➤ *View:* **Map**

P.INTEREST -- Percent Very or Somewhat Interested in Politics (WVS)

This map is based on public opinion polls conducted in 40 nations from 1991 through 1993. The same questions (translated into the local language) were asked in each poll. Here we see the percentage of people in each country who responded that they were very or somewhat interested in politics when asked "How interested would you say you are in politics?"

Data File:	NATIONS
Task:	Mapping
Variable 1:	3) P.INTEREST
➤ View:	List: Rank

RANK	CASE NAME	VALUE
1	Latvia	79
2	Czech Republic	75
3	Germany	74
4	South Korea	73
4	Bulgaria	73
4	Lithuania	73
7	Norway	72
8	Switzerland	66
9	Japan	62
9	Netherlands	62
9	China	62

People in Latvia were most apt to say that they were "very" or "somewhat" interested in politics, closely followed by the Czechs and the Germans. The Japanese (62 percent) and Chinese (62 percent) were slightly more interested in politics than were Americans, who were tied with Slovaks and Estonians at 59 percent, while 58 percent of Canadians were very or somewhat interested in politics. In contrast, in many nations, including Mexico, Italy, and India, only about a third of survey participants were interested in politics and in Romania only 18 percent were interested.

Data File:	NATIONS
Task:	Mapping
➤ Variable 1:	4) TALK POL.
➤ View:	Map

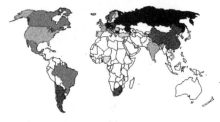

TALK POL. – Percent Who Often Talk about Politics with Their Friends (WVS)

This map shows variations across nations in the percentage who answered "often" to the question "When you get together with your friends, would you say you discuss political matters frequently, occasionally, or never?"

Data File:	NATIONS
Task:	Mapping
Variable 1:	4) TALK POL.
➤ View:	List: Rank

RANK	CASE NAME	VALUE
1	Latvia	47
2	Lithuania	45
3	Bulgaria	42
3	Estonia	42
5	Czech Republic	33
5	Belarus	33
5	Germany	33
8	Russia	31
9	Slovak Republic	30
10	Argentina	28

Again, Latvians rank highest, at 47 percent, in talking about politics. Indeed, people in the nations of Eastern Europe, once part of the Soviet bloc, do the most talking about politics. Only 14 percent of Americans frequently talk politics, and only 6 percent of the Japanese do.

➤ *Data File:* **NES**
➤ *Task:* **Univariate**
➤ *Primary Variable:* **75) GEN INT**
➤ *View:* **Pie**

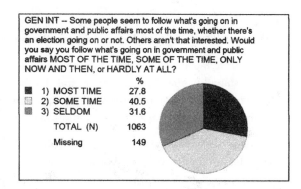

GEN INT -- Some people seem to follow what's going on in government and public affairs most of the time, whether there's an election going on or not. Others aren't that interested. Would you say you follow what's going on in government and public affairs MOST OF THE TIME, SOME OF THE TIME, ONLY NOW AND THEN, or HARDLY AT ALL?

		%
■	1) MOST TIME	27.8
▨	2) SOME TIME	40.5
▨	3) SELDOM	31.6
	TOTAL (N)	1063
	Missing	149

Note that this task uses a new data file.

Here are the results of a national survey of American adults conducted during the 2004 election. This opinion survey, known as the *National Election Study*, is conducted every two years during the national election campaigns by the Institute for Social Research of the University of Michigan. During the interview, each respondent was asked about his or her interest in politics. Twenty-eight percent of the interviewees indicated a high level of interest; the rest had less interest.

You probably take opinion polling for granted—you have been encountering survey findings in the news media as long as you can remember. Nevertheless, you may have wondered how it is possible to assess the distribution of political opinions among more than 280 million Americans, 150 million Russians, or more than 1 billion Chinese on the basis of interviews conducted with only 1,000 to 2,000 people. The answer is to be found in the **laws of probability**.

Just as a sophisticated gambler can calculate the odds involved in a particular bet, so too political scientists know how to calculate the odds that findings based on a sample of the population yield an accurate portrait of that population. And just as gamblers assume that they are participating in a random game (that the deck has not been stacked or the dice loaded), so too the odds on a sample being accurate depend on the sample being selected at random from the population.

Thus, the first principle of accurate polling is that people are selected by using **random sampling**. For example, interviewers conducting telephone polls often use random dialing software to place their calls. This produces a random sample of all telephones (including those with unlisted numbers) and therefore a random sample of households (except for the 1 percent having no phone). The most careful pollsters then randomly sample a person in each selected household.

If the sample is selected at random, we can use the laws of probability to calculate the odds that what we find accurately reflects the population from which the sample was drawn. These odds are determined by two factors: the size of the sample and the amount of variation on a trait or attitude in the population.

First of all, the sample must be **sufficiently large**. Obviously, we couldn't use a sample of two people as the basis for describing the American population—there is a very high probability that they both would be white. For this reason, survey studies include enough cases so that they can accurately reflect the population in terms of variations in such characteristics as age, sex, education, religion, and the like. The accuracy of a random sample is a function of its size: the larger the sample, the more accurate it is. Oddly enough, accuracy depends only on the size of the sample, not on the size of the sample relative to the size of the population from which the sample is drawn. Thus, a sample of 1,000 persons will yield an equally accurate description of the populations of Fargo, North Dakota, New York City, or the whole United States.

Good survey samples include at least 1,000 persons. The National Election Survey we are using in this exercise is based on 1,212 Americans, and therefore the results are very accurate.

Often, news reports of surveys of public opinion consist of the percentages in favor of or against something—usually something controversial. Unfortunately, too often these "surveys" are not based on randomly selected samples (as when people are invited to register their opinions by dialing an 800 number) or are based on samples that are far too small to be accurate.

The data we have examined thus far report the distribution of opinions of entire populations, for example, how interested are Russians, Canadians, or Americans in politics. However, often we wish *to compare* the opinions of various *groups* within the population. For example, are Americans more or less interested in politics depending on their region?

Data File: **NES**
➤ Task: **Cross-tabulation**
➤ Row Variable: **75) GEN INT**
➤ Column Variable: **9) REGION**
➤ View: **Table**
➤ Display: **Column %**

GEN INT   by   REGION
Cramer's V: 0.038

		REGION				
		EAST	MIDWEST	SOUTH	WEST	TOTAL
G E N I N T	MOST TIME	54	69	105	68	296
		29.3%	24.4%	28.6%	29.7%	27.8%
	SOME TIME	73	125	145	88	431
		39.7%	44.2%	39.5%	38.4%	40.5%
	SELDOM	57	89	117	73	336
		31.0%	31.4%	31.9%	31.9%	31.6%
	Missing	34	31	50	34	149
	TOTAL	184	283	367	229	1063
		100.0%	100.0%	100.0%	100.0%	

To construct this table, return to the main menu and select the CROSS-TABULATION task, then select 75) GEN INT as the row variable and 9) REGION as the column variable. When the table is showing, select the [Column %] option.

Here, region, as defined by the Bureau of the Census, is divided into four areas. The table reveals that people living in the West (29.7 percent) are more apt than people in other regions to say they are highly interested in politics. People in the Midwest are least apt to be interested (24.4 percent) with Easterners (29.3 percent) and Southerners (28.6 percent) falling in between.

Here, however, we must deal with a second limitation on the accuracy of survey results, one that has to do with the **magnitude of the difference** observed in the table. Simply put, if the difference between the percentaged results is high (e.g., 80 percent of Southerners are very interested in politics, compared to 30 percent of Westerners), then the odds that a difference actually exists in the full population are very good. But if the percentaged differences are small (30 percent of Southerners are very interested in politics, compared to 24 percent of Midwesterners), then there is an increased chance that these differences are simply due to randomness, rather than some actual difference in the population. Think about it this way. Suppose you have a bag containing 1,000 marbles. If after drawing out 100 of the marbles you find that 90 are black and 10 are white, you can be pretty confident in stating that there are many more black marbles remaining in the bag than white marbles. However, if you draw out 55 black marbles and 45 white marbles, you will be less confident in stating that there are more black marbles than white marbles remaining in the bag. Thus, in addition to the overall size of the sample, *the size of the difference within the population* must be considered. The larger the difference in the population, the greater the probability that this difference will be reflected in the sample.

These two limits apply because samples are based on the principle of random selection, and therefore they are subject to some degree of *random fluctuation*. That is, for purely random reasons there can be small differences between the sample and the population. Thus, whenever we examine cross-tabulations such as the one shown above, political scientists always must ask whether what they are seeing is a real difference—one that would turn up if the entire population were examined—or only a random fluctuation, which does not reflect a true difference in the population.

The small size of the regional differences observed above (on a sample this size) will always make an experienced analyst suspicious that it is merely the result of random fluctuations. Fortunately, there is a simple technique for calculating the odds that a given difference is real or random. This calculation is called a **test of statistical significance**. Differences observed in samples are said to be statistically significant when the odds against random results are high enough. There is no mathematical way to determine just how high is high enough. But, through the years, social scientists have settled on the rule of thumb that they will ignore all differences (or correlations) unless the odds are at least 20 to 1 against their being random. Put another way, social scientists reject all findings when the probability they are random is greater than .05, or 5 in 100. What this level of significance means is that if 100 random samples were drawn independently from the same population, a difference this large would not turn up more than 5 times, purely by chance.

There are two ways to see what the level of significance is for this table. If you want to know the exact probability of whether the results may be due to random fluctuations, you need to switch to the statistics view.

Data File:	**NES**
Task:	**Cross-tabulation**
Row Variable:	**75) GEN INT**
Column Variable:	**9) REGION**
View:	**Table**
➤ Display:	**Statistics (Summary)**

GEN INT   by   REGION

Nominal Statistics

Chi-Square: 3.068	(DF =	6; Prob. = 0.800)			
V:	0.038	C:	0.054		
Lambda:	0.000	Lambda:	0.000	Lambda:	0.000
(DV=9)		(DV=75)			

Ordinal Statistics

Gamma:	-0.009	Tau-b:	-0.006	Tau-c:	-0.007
s.error	0.039	s.error	0.027	s.error	0.028
Dyx:	-0.006	Dxy:	-0.007		
s.error	0.025	s.error	0.028	Prob. =	0.809

Ignore everything on this screen except for the first two lines of text. At the end of the first line you'll see "Prob. = 0.800." This value indicates that the odds these results are simply due to randomness are 800 in 1,000 (or about 8 in 10). Since social scientists require that these odds be less than 1 in 20 (.05), we know that the slight regional differences between those who were highly interested in politics might be due to random fluctuations.

There is another number on this screen that you'll find useful when doing cross-tabulation analysis. In the second row, locate the value "V = 0.038." The V stands for Cramer's V, which is a correlation coefficient developed for cross-tabulations. Cramer's V is similar to Pearson's r (see Exercise 2) in that its value varies from 0 to 1. If the relationship between these two variables was perfect (that is, if all people in the South indicated they were very interested in politics while all people in the West indicated they were not interested in politics), then this would be a value of 1. However, unlike Pearson's r, V does not indicate whether the relationship is positive or negative—the kind of relationship must be inferred from the table itself. Also, it should be noted that survey data produce much lower correlations than do data based on aggregates such as states or nations. For our purposes, let's use the following guidelines to assess the strength of Cramer's V.

- If V is between .00 and .10, the relationship is very weak or nonexistent.

- If V is between .10 and .25, the relationship is moderate.

- If V is over .25, the relationship is strong.

For this table, V is only .038. Thus, there is virtually no strength to this relationship. People from all regions of the country have the same level of interest in politics.

It's important to understand that Cramer's V assesses the strength of the relationship shown in the table, not the odds that the results are statistically significant. A difference could exist between the groups in the population, even when this difference is very small. Thus, we would conclude that the relationship between two variables is substantively insignificant (i.e., very small difference) even though the relationship in the sample is statistically significant (i.e., not due to random chance). In general, a difference of 5 to 10 percentage points in the sample is needed to conclude that there is a substantive difference in behavior between two groups of people.

However, sometimes a finding of no difference between groups may be an interesting finding, especially if one was expecting larger differences. For example, if one had hypothesized that Westerners would have significantly higher levels of political interest than Americans in other regions of the country, but the sample showed almost no difference between respondents from the different regions, this would be an interesting finding.

Here's something else to remember. Sometimes in large surveys like the NES, you'll see differences in tables of only 2 to 3 percentage points, yet they are statistically significant. Even if this difference does exist in the entire population, it's generally not worthy of note. Whenever you examine cross-tabulations in this book, always look at the actual difference in percentage points. If the difference is less than 5 or 10 percentage points, ask yourself whether it's substantively significant.

Hence, when doing cross-tabulation analysis, you should follow these steps. First, look at the table to see how large the observed differences are. Second, if you are testing a hypothesis, be sure that the percentages differ in the predicted direction. For instance, if you predict that men are more likely than women to be interested in politics, then the differences in the table should support this. Assuming you make it through the first two steps, the third step is to look at the actual strength of the relationship by examining the correlation coefficient (V). Finally, determine whether the results are statistically significant. It's in this final step that you apply the .05 rule described earlier.

The CROSS-TABULATION task in ExplorIt makes this process even easier by placing all the information needed on one screen. Return to the [Column %] option to view the table again. Notice that the value of V appears at the top of this screen too. If these results were statistically significant at the .05 level, one asterisk would appear after this value. If these results were significant at the .01 level (making the odds 1 in 100), two asterisks would appear. Since there are no asterisks following the V value, we know that these regional differences are too small to be statistically significant.

The following chart sums up the process of "Assessing a Relationship Between Variables in a Cross-Tabulation." If you need guidelines, just follow the steps in this chart.

ASSESSING A RELATIONSHIP BETWEEN VARIABLES IN A CROSS-TABULATION

Step 1: Determine whether the observed differences are worth noting. Example: Are the differences in political interest between men and women big enough to be important?

↓   ↓

The differences are only a   The differences are at least
few percentage points.   5–10 percentage points.

↓   ↓

Men and women are the same   Men and women may have different
in terms of political interest.   levels of political interest.

↓

Step 2: If testing a hypothesis, check whether the results are in the hypothesized direction. For example, if you hypothesized that men would have higher political interest than women, are the results in accord with this?

↓

Step 3: Examine the strength of the relationship by looking at the correlation coefficient, Cramer's V.

↓

Step 4: Determine whether the results are statistically significant.

↓   ↓

The significance level is .05 or less   The significance level is greater
—there is at least one asterisk next   than .05—there is no asterisk next
to Cramer's V.   to Cramer's V.

↓   ↓

The relationship is statistically sig- The relationship is not statistically
nificant. We decide that there is a   significant. We decide that there is
real relationship between the var-   no real relationship between the
iables in the population from which   variables in the population.
the sample was selected.

Let's examine another example.

Data File: **NES**
Task: **Cross-tabulation**
Row Variable: **75) GEN INT**
➤ Column Variable: **7) AGE**
➤ View: **Table**
➤ Display: **Column %**

GEN INT   by   AGE
Cramer's V: 0.192**

| | | AGE | | | | | |
		< 30 YEARS	30 TO 39	40-49	50-64	65 AND UP	TOTAL
G E N I N T	MOST TIME	31	31	64	97	73	296
		15.0%	18.1%	32.3%	32.3%	39.0%	27.8%
	SOME TIME	80	70	64	130	87	431
		38.6%	40.9%	32.3%	43.3%	46.5%	40.5%
	SELDOM	96	70	70	73	27	338
		46.4%	40.9%	35.4%	24.3%	14.4%	31.6%
	Missing	32	26	35	35	21	149
	TOTAL	207	171	198	300	187	1063
		100.0%	100.0%	100.0%	100.0%	100.0%	

Reading and comparing across the values for the first *row*, we discover that older people are more interested in politics than are younger people. Cramer's V is 0.192**, which is moderate in size. The two asterisks indicate that the odds are less than 1 in 100 that these age differences are random. We can have a lot of confidence that in this instance age really matters.

Does one's education level affect the level of interest he or she has in politics?

Data File: **NES**
Task: **Cross-tabulation**
Row Variable: **75) GEN INT**
➤ Column Variable: **4) EDUCATION**
➤ View: **Table**
➤ Display: **Column %**

GEN INT   by   EDUCATION
Cramer's V: 0.158**

| | | EDUCATION | | | | |
		NO HS DEGR	HS GRAD	SOME COLLE	COLL GRAD	TOTAL
G E N I N T	MOST TIME	20	65	78	133	296
		21.1%	21.4%	22.9%	41.2%	27.8%
	SOME TIME	35	131	138	127	431
		36.8%	43.1%	40.5%	39.3%	40.5%
	SELDOM	40	108	125	63	336
		42.1%	35.5%	36.7%	19.5%	31.6%
	Missing	16	51	43	39	149
	TOTAL	95	304	341	323	1063
		100.0%	100.0%	100.0%	100.0%	

We easily can see in the table that more educated people are more likely to be interested in politics than are less educated people. Once again the relationship is moderate (V = 0.158**) and the results are statistically significant at the .01 level, as indicated by the two asterisks. Let's examine another key demographic: union membership.

Data File: **NES**
Task: **Cross-tabulation**
Row Variable: **75) GEN INT**
➤ Column Variable: **11) UNION**
➤ View: **Table**
➤ Display: **Column %**

GEN INT   by   UNION
Cramer's V: 0.052**

| | | UNION | | | |
		YES	NO	Missing	TOTAL
G E N I N T	MOST TIME	55	240	1	295
		30.7%	27.3%		27.9%
	SOME TIME	77	353	1	430
		43.0%	40.1%		40.6%
	SELDOM	47	287	2	334
		26.3%	32.6%		31.5%
	Missing	28	119	2	149
	TOTAL	179	880	6	1059
		100.0%	100.0%		

The table shows that union members (30.7 percent) are more apt to be interested in political campaigns than are those not in unions (27.3 percent). Notice, however, there is only a 3-percentage-point difference between union members and those not in unions. This small difference does not have much substantive significance—even if the results were statistically significant. In this situation, both union members and those not in unions lack interest in politics and the difference between them is so small that it is not important. In this particular example, the summary statistics reiterate the weak relationship: Cramer's V is very slight (0.052), and the results are not statistically significant.

When political scientists study a particular behavior or attitude, they first examine the overall distribution (such as a pie chart) of that attitude. For example, one of the first things we looked at in this exercise was the percentage of Americans who indicate they are very interested in politics, what percentage have some interest, and so on. Next, political scientists look at the relationship between that variable and various demographic variables, such as age, education, gender, and so on. We did the same thing in this exercise using the technique of cross-tabulation to see how interest in politics is distributed in the population. This type of preliminary analysis provides a snapshot of the population with regard to the variable of interest.

For the next two examples, let's use the AUTO-ANALYZER task that is available on the main menu.

Data File: **NES**
➤ Task: **Auto-Analyzer**
➤ Variable: **75) GEN INT**
➤ View: **Univariate**

GEN INT -- Some people seem to follow what's going on in government and public affairs most of the time, whether there's an election going on or not. Others aren't that interested. Would you say you follow what's going on in government and public affairs MOST OF THE TIME, SOME OF THE TIME, ONLY NOW AND THEN, or HARDLY AT ALL?

	%
MOST TIME	27.8%
SOME TIME	40.5%
SELDOM	31.6%
Number of cases	1063

Among all respondents, 27.8% of the sample say they follow what's going on in public affairs most of the time.

To obtain these results, return to the main menu and select the AUTO-ANALYZER task. Then select 75) GEN INT as your analyzer variable and click [OK].

The first result that Auto-Analyzer provides is the *univariate* distribution for the variable you selected. As you can see, the percentages are the same as what we found earlier using the UNIVARIATE task from the main menu. As the textual summary indicates, among all respondents, 27.8 percent of the sample expressed very much interest in politics.

Data File: **NES**
Task: **Auto-Analyzer**
Variable: **75) GEN INT**
➤ View: **Education**

GEN INT -- Some people seem to follow what's going on in government and public affairs most of the time, whether there's an election going on or not. Others aren't that interested. Would you say you follow what's going on in government and public affairs MOST OF THE TIME, SOME OF THE TIME, ONLY NOW AND THEN, or HARDLY AT ALL?

	NO HS DEGR	HS GRAD	SOME COLLE	COLL GRAD
MOST TIME	21.1%	21.4%	22.9%	41.2%
SOME TIME	36.8%	43.1%	40.5%	39.3%
SELDOM	42.1%	35.5%	36.7%	19.5%
Number of cases	95	304	341	323

The higher the education, the more likely the individual is to say they follow what's going on in public affairs most of the time. The most significant difference comes between those with some college and those with college degrees.

The higher the education, the less likely the individual is to say they seldom follow public affairs. The most significant difference comes between those with some college and those with college degrees.

If continuing from the previous example, simply click the button [Education] to see the results.

These results are identical to what you would obtain if you cross-tabulated the variable GEN INT with EDUCATION. The only difference is that it is not necessary for you to percentage the table and a summary of the table is provided. As shown by the description, those with college degrees are more likely to be very much interested in politics. The difference is statistically significant.[1]

In the worksheets, you'll have a chance to explore several attitudes using the AUTO-ANALYZER task. You will also find this task useful in doing **exploratory analysis** for papers or projects you may work on for this and other classes.

Your turn.

---

[1] In some cases, the significance of V on the table and the significance given in Auto-Analyzer may be slightly different. The statistic V is used in the CROSS-TABULATION task and is based on chi-square, which summarizes the entire table. Auto-Analyzer relies on column-by-column comparisons in an attempt to uncover patterns of interest. In other words, these two tasks focus on slightly different aspects of the results.

NAME: _____

COURSE: _____

DATE: _____

REVIEW QUESTIONS

Based on the first part of this exercise, answer True or False to the following items:

1. There is very little difference in the public's interest in politics across the different countries of the world.　　　T　F

2. Cramer's V is similar to Pearson's r in that both are correlation coefficients.　　　T　F

3. The probability (significance) level assesses the strength of the relationship, while V indicates the odds that the results are due to random fluctuations.　　　T　F

4. Older people tend to have greater interest in politics than do younger people.　　　T　F

5. Cramer's V does not indicate whether a relationship is positive or negative. The kind of relationship must be inferred from the table itself.　　　T　F

6. A relationship between two variables can be *statistically significant* without being strong enough to be *substantively significant*.　　　T　F

7. In order for us to decide that a relationship is statistically significant, we want the significance level to be greater than .05.　　　T　F

EXPLORIT QUESTIONS

POLITICAL KNOWLEDGE

In the opening section of this exercise, we examined survey responses on how interested individual Americans were in politics, but how much do Americans actually know about politics? The NES asked respondents to identify the political offices held by Dennis Hastert, Dick Cheney, Tony Blair, and William Rehnquist. Respondents could identify all of these correctly, know the government positions of some of these individuals, or be unfamiliar with all of them. A variable was created to count the number of correct identifications, with the lowest category being those who knew none of these individuals or only one, the middle category includes those respondents who correctly identified two of the four political officials, and the highest category includes those respondents who knew the government position of three or more of these officials.

> ➤ *Data File:* **NES**
>   ➤ *Task:* **Auto-Analyzer**
> ➤ *Variable:* **111) KNOW**
>   ➤ *View:* **Univariate**

With the NES file open, select the AUTO-ANALYZER task, then select 111) KNOW as the analyzer variable.

Exercise 3: "Of the People": An Interested and Informed Public

The first table shows the distribution of this attitude in the entire sample.

8. What percent of the survey respondents know at least three of these public officials? _____%

Let's now look at the effect of some demographic characteristics on the person's level of information. In addition to looking at whether the results are statistically significant, you must look at the actual percentages to determine which differences are important.

> The AUTO-ANALYZER task has nine demographic characteristics, each represented by a separate option. By selecting one of these demographic options, you see not only the table showing the relationship between the analyzer variable and the selected demographic variable, but also a brief summary of the relationship.

Data File: **NES**
Task: **Auto-Analyzer**
Variable: **111) KNOW**
➤ View: **Region**

Look at the following patterns in the third row, 3-4 correct, to judge which groups have the highest levels of political knowledge.

9. Southerners are the most knowledgeable.   T   F

10. The regional difference on this variable is not statistically significant.   T   F

11. Westerners are the most knowledgeable.   T   F

> ➤ View: **Education**

12. The higher a person's education, the more knowledgeable the person.   T   F

13. This suggests that education may help create a more knowledgeable electorate.   T   F

> ➤ View: **Sex**

14. Males and females are equally knowledgeable.   T   F

15. Females are more knowledgeable than males.   T   F

16. Males are more knowledgeable than females, and the difference is statistically significant.   T   F

> ➤ View: **Income**

17. The higher the income, the more knowledgeable the individual.   T   F

18. The differences across the income groups are statistically significant.   T   F

> ➤ View: **Age**

19. Those over 65 are the most knowledgeable.   T   F

20. One of the most significant differences in gaining knowledge is between those under 30 and those 30 to 39.   T   F

Notice, however, that this AUTO-ANALYZER option is available only for basic demographic variables. In order to look at the effect of other variables on this attitude, you must use the CROSS-TABULATION task. Let's look at the effect of news orientation on how informed the individual is.

Data File: **NES**
➤ Task: **Cross-tabulation**
➤ Row Variable: **111) KNOW**
➤ Column Variable: **113) NEWS TYPE**
➤ View: **Table**
➤ Display: **Column %**

21. The relationship between political knowledge and type of news orientation is not statistically significant.   T   F

22. Those who use both television and newspaper are the most knowledge.   T   F

23. Those who use the newspaper are more knowledgeable than those who use television.   T   F

24. Those who use both television and newspaper are not much more informed than those who use the newspaper only.   T   F

Not all research is simply descriptive. Frequently, political scientists analyze data to test hypotheses. For example, most of us would hypothesize a link between an individual's interest and level of political knowledge: Those who are more interested will be more knowledgeable. We can use cross-tabulation to test this hypothesis.

Data File: **NES**
Task: **Cross-tabulation**
Row Variable: **111) KNOW**
➤ Column Variable: **75) GEN INT**
➤ View: **Table**
➤ Display: **Column %**

25. What is the value of V for this table?   V = _____

26. Is V statistically significant?   Yes   No

27. This table supports our hypothesis that those who are more interested will be more knowledgeable.   T   F

A RESPONSIVE GOVERNMENT?

A democracy requires a citizenry that is interested and informed about politics, but it also requires a government that listens to the public. How much faith do Americans have that government officials pay attention to their preferences?

> *Data File:* **NES**
> ➤ *Task:* **Univariate**
> ➤ *Primary Variable:* **106) GOVT ATTN**
> ➤ *View:* **Pie**

28. The largest percentage of Americans feels that the government pays _____ attention to what people think.

     a. a good deal of

     b. some

     c. not much

Does a person's political interest or political knowledge influence his or her opinion on how much attention the government pays to public preferences? Let's see.

> *Data File:* **NES**
> ➤ *Task:* **Cross-tabulation**
> ➤ *Row Variable:* **106) GOVT ATTN**
> ➤ *Column Variable:* **75) GEN INT**
> ➤ *View:* **Table**
> ➤ *Display:* **Column %**

29. What is the value of V for this table?   V = _____

30. Is V statistically significant?   Yes   No

31. What is the substantive strength of this relationship?

     a. The relationship is weak, V is between .00 and .10.

     b. The relationship is moderate, V is between .10 and .25.

     c. The relationship is strong, V is over .25.

32. People who are more interested in politics are more likely than others to feel the government pays attention to the public a good deal of the time.   T   F

> *Data File:* **NES**
> *Task:* **Cross-tabulation**
> *Row Variable:* **106) GOVT ATTN**
> ➤ *Column Variable:* **111) KNOW**
> ➤ *View:* **Table**
> ➤ *Display:* **Column %**

33. What is the value of V for this table?   V = _____

34. Is V statistically significant?   Yes   No

35. What is the substantive strength of this relationship?

     a. The relationship is weak, V is between .00 and .10.

     b. The relationship is moderate, V is between .10 and .25.

     c. The relationship is strong, V is over .25.

36. The more one knows about politics the more one feels the government
pays attention to public preferences a good deal of the time.   T   F

WHAT HAVE WE LEARNED?

I.   What are the steps to undertake when interpreting a table comparing answers from two questions on a public opinion survey? What does it mean when the relationship between these two questions is statistically significant? How does the MicroCase software tell you that a relationship is statistically significant? What are the methods to judge how large the relationship is between the two variables?

II.   What types of Americans are most likely to be interested in politics?

III. What types of Americans are more likely to be knowledgeable about politics?

WHAT ELSE CAN BE EXPLORED?

1. In this exercise, we explored Americans' attitudes on how responsive the government was to the public. The NES survey contains a number of similar evaluations of the government, including one on the trustworthiness of the government, 101) TRUST GOV; whether the government wastes tax money, 103) GOVT WASTE; whether politicians are usually crooked, 104) CROOKED?; whether public officials care about what people think, 105) DON'T CARE; and whether elections make the government pay attention to the people, 107) ELECT ATTN. Any one of these could be used as the row variable, with characteristics of survey respondents (e.g., education or race) used as the column variables.

2. The results of the 2000 presidential election hung in doubt for several weeks while Florida officials engaged in a variety of recounts of ballots due to the very close vote between Al Gore and George W. Bush. Whichever candidate won the Florida vote would become the next president of the United States. The recounting of ballots concluded when the Supreme Court ruled there was insufficient time for a recount that would meet the standards of equal protection and due process. Did this election outcome shake Americans' confidence in the electoral system? The NES question 18) ELEC FAIR asked respondents whether they felt the 2000 presidential election was decided in a fair or unfair way. What types of factors may have shaped Americans' reactions to the process by which the 2000 presidential election was decided? Views on the election's fairness will be the row variable in the tables, and characteristics or attitudes of survey respondents will be the column variables.

3. Regardless of how Americans feel about the current government, Americans are quite patriotic and proud to be Americans. Americans, however, can differ on the best way to demonstrate this patriotism. Some Americans express their pride in their reactions to the American flag. Which Americans have the most pride in the flying of the American flag? Pride in the flag, 55) FLAG FEEL, will be the dependent variable (i.e., the row variable), while individual traits and attitudes will be the independent variables (i.e., the column variables).

Part II

FREEDOM: CIVIL LIBERTIES AND CIVIL RIGHTS

Exercise 4   **Civil Liberties: Free Speech**

Exercise 5   **Civil Rights: Equality**

When people speak of the United States as a "free country," they have two basic kinds of freedom in mind. The first kind of freedom consists of what are called **civil liberties**. These include freedom of speech, press, religion, assembly, and petition. The Bill of Rights guarantees these freedoms from infringement by the government or by citizen-groups. If a mob shouts down a speaker, they are denying his or her civil liberties. If the government forbids an unpopular group from expressing their views, that too is a violation of their civil liberties.

The second kind of freedom consists of **civil rights**. These include all the rights of democratic citizenship including voting, equal treatment before the law, an equal share of public benefits, and equal access to public facilities. When African Americans were excluded from voting and from jury duty, and denied access to park benches in the South, they were being denied their civil rights.

In the next two exercises, you will examine public opinion about civil liberties and civil rights.

CIVIL LIBERTIES: FREE SPEECH

*Congress shall make no law respecting an establish-
ment of religion, or prohibiting the free exercise thereof;
or abridging the freedom of speech, or of the press; or
the right of the people peaceably to assemble, and to
petition the Government for a redress of grievances.*

FIRST AMENDMENT TO
THE CONSTITUTION,
RATIFIED IN 1791

Tasks: Mapping, Univariate, Cross-Tabulation
Data Files: NATIONS, GSS

The Bill of Rights was written and adopted because there was widespread public concern that, because these civil liberties were not specifically guaranteed by the Constitution, future governments might fail to uphold them. Many amendments making up the Bill of Rights are concerned with keeping the government from committing abuses such as failing to hold a speedy trial or forcing people to testify against themselves in court. But the five freedoms mentioned in the First Amendment (shown above) concern freedom of expression. The first-mentioned freedom in the First Amendment concerns the establishment of religion and the free exercise of religion. Sometimes the religious freedom clauses (known as the Establishment Clause and the Free Exercise Clause) are referred to as the "First Freedom" because they were listed first. James Madison, the "Father of the Constitution," was certainly very concerned with religious freedom. He and Jefferson fought a series of battles in Virginia to protect religious liberty and to prevent the state from favoring one religion over another. Throughout history, many of the battles concerning freedom of expression have been fought over issues of religious liberty.

The other four freedoms in the First Amendment are concerned primarily with enabling people to influence and change the government. The Constitution itself provides the means by which it can be amended. But, without the freedom to speak, write, assemble, or petition, the people would lack the political means to amend the Constitution, influence officials, affect public policy, or successfully vote "the rascals" out of office. Of course, the rights of free speech and a free press extend far beyond direct applications to politics, but these remain the most basic aspects of freedom.

➤ *Data File:* **NATIONS**
➤ *Task:* **Mapping**
➤ *Variable 1:* **6) PETITION?**
➤ *View:* **Map**

PETITION? – Percent Who Have Signed a Political Petition (WVS)

This map shows how people in many nations responded when asked whether they had ever signed a political petition.

Data File: **NATIONS**
Task: **Mapping**
Variable 1: **6) PETITION?**
➤ *View:* **List: Rank**

RANK	CASE NAME	VALUE
1	Canada	77
2	Great Britain	75
3	Sweden	72
4	United States	71
5	Latvia	65
6	Switzerland	63
7	Japan	62
8	Norway	61
9	Germany	60
10	Lithuania	58

More than 7 out of 10 people in Canada, Great Britain, Sweden, and the United States have used their freedom to petition their government. But in many countries few have signed petitions: 14 percent in Turkey and Poland and only 5 percent in Nigeria. Keep in mind that nations with high levels of political freedom are very overrepresented among these nations—public opinion polling is itself an aspect of political expression and therefore is discouraged or controlled in some nations (which is one reason this question was not asked in the Chinese survey).

CIVIL LIBERTIES: UPHOLDING THE RIGHTS OF FREE SPEECH FOR OTHERS

Regardless of what constitutions say about civil liberties, however, a major factor always is the extent to which the citizens are committed to maintaining these rights. Thus, for example, if enough Americans became disgusted with free speech, they would have the right to repeal the First Amendment and substitute laws limiting free speech. Moreover, in actual practice the extent to which people do have free speech depends to some extent on the degree to which other Americans respect that right. "Freedom of speech" is not really a freedom unless people feel free to use it. If a person holds unpopular opinions, other people might resist allowing that person to present his or her views—or they might retaliate against the person for presenting unpopular views. So, let's explore public commitment to free speech.

> *Data File:* **GSS**
> *Task:* **Univariate**
> *Primary Variable:* **36) ATHEIST SP**
> *View:* **Pie**

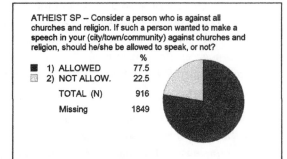

ATHEIST SP -- Consider a person who is against all churches and religion. If such a person wanted to make a speech in your (city/town/community) against churches and religion, should he/she be allowed to speak, or not?

		%
■	1) ALLOWED	77.5
▨	2) NOT ALLOW.	22.5
	TOTAL (N)	916
	Missing	1849

The 2002 General Social Surveys asks: "Consider a person who is against all churches and religion. If such a person wanted to make a speech in your (city/town/community) against churches and religion, should he/she be allowed to speak, or not?"

Here we see that 77.5 percent of those polled would allow an atheist to make a speech. The GSS has been asking Americans this question since 1972, when about 67 percent said the speech should be allowed. But the history of this question goes back to a famous survey by Samuel Stouffer in 1954 during the "McCarthy era" when only 37 percent would allow the speech.[1]

The other information conveyed in the pie chart above is that variation exists among Americans on whether to allow the speeches of atheists. Are you curious about what may explain this variation? We might be able to find out why one-quarter of Americans oppose speeches by atheists while three-quarters would allow such speech if we compare people's answers to this survey question to some other traits of these individuals.

One place to start is with education. Education exposes people to a wider set of viewpoints. Also, as people obtain more education they learn that a core democratic value is to tolerate the speeches of others, even those with which one may disagree. Thus, we might propose that one of the causes of how tolerant people are toward the speeches of atheists may be their level of education. Recalling the terminology from Exercise 2, people's level of education will be the independent variable (or cause) while people's opinions on speeches by atheists will be the dependent variable (or the effect). Because we want to know whether different levels of education cause different levels of tolerance, we will set up our table with education as the column variable and opinions on atheists' speeches as the row variable, and we will request that percentages be calculated within each column of the table.

Data File: **GSS**
> *Task:* **Cross-tabulation**
> *Row Variable:* **36) ATHEIST SP**
> *Column Variable:* **3) EDUCATION**
> *View:* **Table**
> *Display:* **Column%**

ATHEIST SP by EDUCATION
Cramer's V: 0.315**

		EDUCATION					
		NOT HS GRD	HS GRD	SOME COLL	COLL GRAD	Missing	TOTAL
ATHEIST SP	ALLOWED	68	214	218	207	3	707
		48.6%	77.3%	82.0%	90.0%		77.4%
	NOT ALLOW.	72	63	48	23	0	206
		51.4%	22.7%	18.0%	10.0%		22.6%
	Missing	254	587	556	443	9	1849
	TOTAL	140	277	266	230	12	913
		100.0%	100.0%	100.0%	100.0%		

---

[1] Samuel Stouffer, *Communism, Conformity, and Civil Liberties* (New York: Doubleday, 1955).

In this table, we see that 48.6 percent of those without a high school diploma approve of atheists giving speeches, 77.3 percent of those with a high school diploma approve, 82.0 percent of those with some college approve, while 90.0 percent of those with a college degree approve. The differences in these percentages suggest that education has a strong influence on people's approval of speeches by atheists. In fact, college graduates are twice as likely as those without a high school diploma to approve of atheists giving speeches.

Another way to confirm the strength of this relationship is to look at Cramer's V which equals 0.315**. First, the two asterisks confirm that the relationship is statistically significant. The relationship found in this sample is strong enough to exceed that which could happen by chance given normal sampling error. Since the coefficient has two asterisks attached to it, we are 99 percent confident that if we interviewed the entire U.S. population, we would once again find that people with higher education levels would be more supportive of atheists giving speeches. Also notice that the magnitude of Cramer's V (0.315) exceeds .25, which in Exercise 2 we suggested was the cut-off for a strong relationship when analyzing survey data. Our investigation tells us that education is a strong causal factor in explaining the variation in Americans' opinions on tolerating the speeches of atheists.

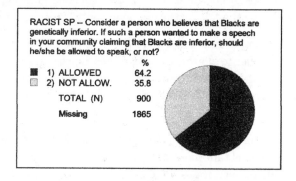

Data File:	**GSS**
➤ Task:	**Univariate**
➤ Primary Variable:	**37) RACIST SP**
➤ View:	**Pie**

RACIST SP -- Consider a person who believes that Blacks are genetically inferior. If such a person wanted to make a speech in your community claiming that Blacks are inferior, should he/she be allowed to speak, or not?

		%
■	1) ALLOWED	64.2
▦	2) NOT ALLOW.	35.8
	TOTAL (N)	900
	Missing	1865

Overall, Americans are less willing to give free speech to "a person who believes that Blacks are genetically inferior," but here too the majority is in favor of allowing the person to speak. Will education also help to explain the variation in answers to this survey question?

Data File:	**GSS**
➤ Task:	**Cross-tabulation**
➤ Row Variable:	**37) RACIST SP**
➤ Column Variable:	**3) EDUCATION**
➤ View:	**Table**
➤ Display:	**Column %**

RACIST SP   by   EDUCATION
Cramer's V: 0.187**

		EDUCATION					
		NOT HS GRD	HS GRD	SOME COLL	COLL GRAD	Missing	TOTAL
RACIST SP	ALLOWED	63	171	172	170	2	576
		46.3%	62.6%	65.6%	75.2%		64.2%
	NOT ALLOW.	73	102	90	56	1	321
		53.7%	37.4%	34.4%	24.8%		35.8%
	Missing	258	591	560	447	9	1865
	TOTAL	136	273	262	226	12	897
		100.0%	100.0%	100.0%	100.0%		

Once again those with higher levels of education are more willing to allow speeches by others, here speeches by racists, even though almost all Americans would disapprove of the message of these racists. The table shows that while 46.3 percent of those with less than a high school diploma would not allow racists to give a speech, while 75.2 percent of those with a college diploma would allow the speech. Note that the difference between the least educated and the most educated is not as large as in the previous table measuring approval of speeches by atheists. The value of Cramer's V for the table investigating racists' speech also is smaller, 0.187**. This relationship is still statistically significant, so we know that the relationship would exist if we asked these questions of the entire U.S. population. The magnitude of the relationship, however, is smaller. This time it fits in our categorization of a moderate relationship, with Cramer's V falling between .10 and .25. Thus, we can conclude that education has a moderate ability to explain toleration of racists' speeches, but other factors probably come into play as well.

Let's look at a third test of support for free speech.

Data File: **GSS**
➤ Task: **Univariate**
➤ Primary Variable: **38) COMMUN.SP**
➤ View: **Pie**

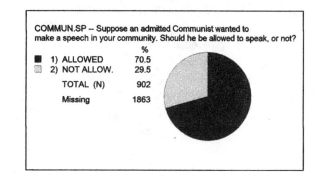

Overall, the number of Americans willing to give free speech to "an admitted Communist" is about halfway between those allowing speeches by racists and those allowing speeches by atheists.

Data File: **GSS**
➤ Task: **Cross-tabulation**
➤ Row Variable: **38) COMMUN.SP**
➤ Column Variable: **3) EDUCATION**
➤ View: **Table**
➤ Display: **Column %**

COMMUN.SP   by   EDUCATION
Cramer's V: 0.308**

		EDUCATION					
		NOT HS GRD	HS GRD	SOME COLL	COLL GRAD	Missing	TOTAL
COMMUN.SP	ALLOWED	54	184	198	199	1	635
		41.9%	66.4%	75.0%	86.9%		70.6%
	NOT ALLOW.	75	93	66	30	2	264
		58.1%	33.6%	25.0%	13.1%		29.4%
	Missing	265	587	558	444	9	1863
	TOTAL	129	277	264	229	12	899
		100.0%	100.0%	100.0%	100.0%		

Once again we see a statistically significant and strong relationship between education and allowing others to give speeches. In the case of Communists giving speeches, Americans with the most education are twice as likely to approve as those with the least education. The value of Cramer's V at 0.308** falls in our strong category, and the relationship is statistically signficant.

The consistency of these findings reflects the fact that each of these three questions really measures the same thing: support for free speech. When political scientists use multiple measures of something, they often combine the results into a single measure called an attitude index or scale.

An **attitude index** measures an attitude on the basis of answers to several questions believed to be measures of the same general attitude. The logic involved is the same logic teachers use when they construct an examination. For example, when teachers give a test made up of true/false or multiple-choice questions, they don't just ask one or two questions. They ask many. They do so because they know that even the best-prepared students can miss any given question and that the worst students could get any particular answer right. So, teachers give tests asking a lot of questions in order to get a more accurate measure of what students have learned.

Just as individual scores on a test are calculated on the basis of the number of correct (or incorrect) answers, attitude indexes "add up" values assigned to some set of questions. In this instance we have three questions measuring support for free speech. Suppose we give each respondent a point for every question to which he or she answered "not allowed" and no points for "allowed" answers. Thus, people who would extend freedom of speech in all three instances would score 0 and those who would deny free speech in all three instances would score 3. To simplify the index slightly, we will combine people with scores of 1 and 2 to make a single category (moderate support for free speech) so that there will be only three rather than four categories.

Data File: **GSS**
➤ *Task:* **Univariate**
➤ *Primary Variable:* **39) FR.SPEECH**
➤ *View:* **Pie**

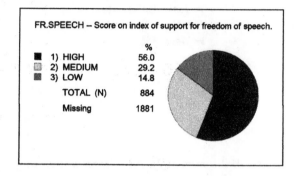

FR.SPEECH -- Score on index of support for freedom of speech.

		%
■	1) HIGH	56.0
▨	2) MEDIUM	29.2
▦	3) LOW	14.8
	TOTAL (N)	884
	Missing	1881

All things considered, Americans have considerable respect for freedom of speech—more than half (56.0 percent) would extend free speech in all three instances. On the other hand, these results suggest that almost half of the American citizenry would deny freedom of speech to some people. Let's examine the results by education again.

Data File: **GSS**
➤ *Task:* **Cross-tabulation**
➤ *Row Variable:* **39) FR.SPEECH**
➤ *Column Variable:* **3) EDUCATION**
➤ *View:* **Table**
➤ *Display:* **Column %**

FR.SPEECH by EDUCATION
Cramer's V: 0.204**

		EDUCATION					
		NOT HS GRD	HS GRD	SOME COLL	COLL GRAD	Missing	TOTAL
FR.SPEECH	HIGH	38	139	159	159	0	495
		30.4%	51.5%	60.9%	70.7%		56.2%
	MEDIUM	46	86	69	54	3	255
		36.8%	31.9%	26.4%	24.0%		28.9%
	LOW	41	45	33	12	0	131
		32.8%	16.7%	12.6%	5.3%		14.9%
	Missing	269	594	561	448	9	1881
	TOTAL	125	270	261	225	12	881
		100.0%	100.0%	100.0%	100.0%		

We see a statistically significant and moderately sized relationship between education and our index measure of free speech, which we should expect given the pattens in the three previous tables.

➤ *Data File:* **NATIONS**
➤ *Task:* **Mapping**
➤ *Variable 1:* **19) CIVIL LIBS**
➤ *View:* **Map**

CIVIL LIBS -- Index of Civil Liberties, Higher = Greater Liberty (FITW, 1997)

Using the same logic as used to construct the index of support for free speech, each year an American organization known as Freedom House scores every nation (including the tiny ones) on an index of civil liberties. Those nations that sustain the maximum amount of civil liberties are scored 7, and the scores go as low as 1 for nations in which people do not have civil liberties.

Data File: **NATIONS**
Task: **Mapping**
Variable 1: **19) CIVIL LIBS**
➤ *View:* **List: Rank**

RANK	CASE NAME	VALUE
1	Finland	7
1	Luxembourg	7
1	Canada	7
1	Malta	7
1	Belize	7
1	Barbados	7
1	Denmark	7
1	Ireland	7
1	Portugal	7
1	Switzerland	7

Here we see that a number of nations including the United States and Canada were scored 7 in civil liberties. At the bottom of the ranking, we find that 18 countries were scored 1.

Data File: **NATIONS**
Task: **Mapping**
Variable 1: **19) CIVIL LIBS**
➤ *Variable 2:* **6) PETITION?**
➤ *Views:* **Map**

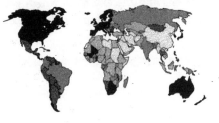

CIVIL LIBS -- Index of Civil Liberties, Higher = Greater Liberty (FITW, 1997)

r = 0.569**

PETITION? -- Percent Who Have Signed a Political Petition (WVS)

As would be expected, there is a very high correlation (r = 0.569**) between scores on the civil liberties index and the percentage in each nation who said they had signed a petition.

Sometimes it is argued that allowing freedom of expression to the people of a country allows them to express their frustrations and that this will prevent pressure from building up that might lead to rebellion. Let's cross-tabulate the civil liberties index by the percentage in nations that agreed their society must be changed radically by revolutionary action.

Data File: **NATIONS**
Task: **Mapping**
Variable 1: **19) CIVIL LIBS**
➤ Variable 2: **9) REVOLUTION**
➤ Views: **Map**

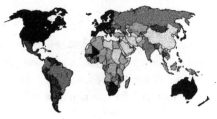

CIVIL LIBS – Index of Civil Liberties, Higher = Greater Liberty (FITW, 1997)

r = –0.392**

REVOLUTION -- Percent Who Agree That Their Society Must Be Changed Radically "By Revolutionary Action" (WVS)

We see that there is a statistically significant negative relationship (r = –0.392**) between civil liberties in nations and the extent to which people in those nations say that a revolution is needed. This supports the idea that having civil liberties reduces pressure for a rebellion.

Your turn.

EXERCISE

4

REVIEW QUESTIONS

Based on the first part of this exercise, answer True or False to the following items:

1. Civil liberties include such things as the right to assemble and to petition the government.   T   F

2. Most Americans would deny free speech to an atheist.   T   F

3. In the United States, no educational differences exist in support of racist speech.   T   F

4. The basic freedoms of expression are contained in the First Amendment to the U.S. Constitution.   T   F

5. People in nations that have more civil liberties are more likely to think that a revolution is needed in their nation.   T   F

6. One can create an attitude index by combining answers from several survey questions measuring the same general attitude.   T   F

EXPLORIT QUESTIONS

EXPLORING THE CAUSES OF CIVIL LIBERTIES ACROSS NATIONS

We've found that nations differ in the extent to which civil liberties are supported. Let's see which characteristics of nations may have an effect on this variable. Perhaps the level of democracy?

> ➤ *Data File:* **NATIONS**
> ➤ *Task:* **Mapping**
> ➤ *Variable 1:* **19) CIVIL LIBS**
> ➤ *Variable 2:* **18) DEMOCRACY**
> ➤ *Views:* **Map**

7. What is the value of r for these comparison maps?   r = _____

8. Is it statistically significant?   Yes   No

9. Which statement best summarizes the relationship between these variables? (Circle the number of the most appropriate answer.)

    a. The more democratic the country, the better its civil liberties rating.

    b. The less democratic the country, the better its civil liberties rating.

    c. Democracy and civil liberties appear to be unrelated.

Let's examine the effect of education on support of civil liberties. In the NATIONS data file, we will use the estimated education level that citizens of a country are expected to achieve as a measure of education.

>   *Data File:*   **NATIONS**
> ➤ *Task:*   **Scatterplot**
> ➤ *Variable 1:*   **19) CIVIL LIBS**
> ➤ *Variable 2:*   **40) EDUC EXPTD**
> ➤ *View:*   **Reg. Line**

10. Write in the Pearson correlation (r) for this relationship.   r = _____

11. Is the relationship statistically significant?   Yes   No

Answer True or False to the following items:

12. There is no relationship between the education level of the populace and the rating on civil liberties.   T   F

13. Countries with higher education levels tend to score higher on the civil liberties index.   T   F

14. These results suggest that there may be a causal relationship between education and civil liberties.   T   F

EXPLORING FURTHER SUPPORT FOR FREE SPEECH IN THE UNITED STATES

In the first section of this exercise we saw that education was a moderate to strong predictor of whether individuals would allow atheists, racists, and Communists to give speeches. We also saw that we could combine the answers to survey questions about these three groups into an index of political speech. Let's see if we can uncover other reasons for the variations in support of free speech. First, let's explore the effects of age.

> ➤ *Data File:*   **GSS**
> ➤ *Task:*   **Cross-tabulation**
> ➤ *Row Variable:*   **39) FR.SPEECH**
> ➤ *Column Variable:*   **9) AGE**
> ➤ *View:*   **Table**
> ➤ *Display:*   **Column%**

15. What is the value of V for this table?   V = _____

16. What is the best interpretation for this V?

    a. The value of V indicates a statistically significant and strong relationship (V is over .25).

    b. The value of V indicates a statistically significant and moderate relationship (V is between .10 and .25).

    c. The value of V indicates a statistically significant and weak relationship (V is less than .10).

    d. Because the value of V is statistically insignificant (i.e., no asterisks attached), there is no relationship.

17. Older Americans are less supportive of free speech than are younger Americans.   T   F

Let's check whether people who work for the government are more supportive of free speech than other Americans.

> Data File: **GSS**
> Task: **Cross-tabulation**
> Row Variable: **39) FR.SPEECH**
> ➤ Column Variable: **19) WORK GOVT**
>   ➤ View: **Table**
>   ➤ Display: **Column%**

18. What is the value of V for this table?   V = _____

19. What is the best interpretation for this V?

    a. The value of V indicates a statistically significant and strong relationship (V is over .25).

    b. The value of V indicates a statistically significant and moderate relationship (V is between .10 and .25).

    c. The value of V indicates a statistically significant and weak relationship (V is less than .10).

    d. Because the value of V is statistically insignificant (i.e., no asterisks attached), there is no relationship.

20. People who work for the government are more supportive of free speech than those who do not work for the government.   T   F

Finally, let's find out if those who vote are more supportive of free speech than those who do not vote.

> Data File: **GSS**
> Task: **Cross-tabulation**
> Row Variable: **39) FR.SPEECH**
> ➤ Column Variable: **24) VOTED 00**
>   ➤ View: **Table**
>   ➤ Display: **Column%**

Exercise 4: Civil Liberties: Free Speech   75

21. What is the value of V for this table?   V = _____

22. What is the best interpretation for this V?

    a. The value of V indicates a statistically significant and strong relationship (V is over .25).

    b. The value of V indicates a statistically significant and moderate relationship (V is between .10 and .25).

    c. The value of V indicates a statistically significant and weak relationship (V is less than .10).

    d. Because the value of V is statistically insignificant (i.e., no asterisks attached), there is no relationship.

23. People who vote are more supportive of free speech than those who do not vote.   T   F

24. Consider the four potential explanations of support for free speech (including the discussion of the effects of education in the first portion of this exercise). Which of these four factors has the strongest influence on support for free speech?

    a. education

    b. age

    c. government worker

    d. voted in last election

FREEDOM OF RELGION

In 1962, the Supreme Court ruled that school prayer violated the establishment clause of the First Amendment. This Supreme Court ban on school prayer was controversial at the time. Let's see how many Americans support or disapprove of this Supreme Court ruling today.

    Data File: **GSS**
    ➤ *Task:* **Univariate**
➤ *Primary Variable:* **45) SCH.PRAY**
    ➤ *View:* **Pie**

25. Most Americans support the Supreme Court ruling and do not want prayer in schools.   T   F

Let's see how a person's level of education influences his or her opinion on school prayer.

    Data File: **GSS**
    ➤ *Task:* **Cross-tabulation**
  ➤ *Row Variable:* **45) SCH.PRAY**
➤ *Column Variable:* **3) EDUCATION**
    ➤ *View:* **Table**
    ➤ *Display:* **Column%**

26. What is the value of V for this table?   V = _____

27. What is the best interpretation for this V?

    a. The value of V indicates a statistically significant and strong relationship (V is over .25).

    b. The value of V indicates a statistically significant and moderate relationship
    (V is between .10 and .25).

    c. The value of V indicates a statistically significant and weak relationship
    (V is less than .10).

    d. Because the value of V is statistically insignificant (i.e., no asterisks attached)
    there is no relationship.

28. Those with a college degree are more likely to support the ban on school
    prayer than those with less education.   T   F

Since the Supreme Court ruling occurred in the 1960s, we might expect older citizens who grew up during an era when school prayer was common to be less supportive than younger Americans of the ban on school prayer.

          Data File: **GSS**
              Task: **Cross-tabulation**
    Row Variable: **45) SCH.PRAY**
➤ *Column Variable:* **9) AGE**
         ➤ *View:* **Table**
      ➤ *Display:* **Column%**

29. What is the value of V for this table?   V = _____

30. What is the best interpretation for this V?

    a. The value of V indicates a statistically significant and strong relationship (V is over .25).

    b. The value of V indicates a statistically significant and moderate relationship
    (V is between .10 and .25).

    c. The value of V indicates a statistically significant and weak relationship
    (V is less than .10).

    d. Because the value of V is statistically insignificant (i.e., no asterisks attached),
    there is no relationship.

31. Older Americans are less supportive of the ban on school prayer than
    are younger Americans.   T   F

Do you think that a man or a woman would be more likely to support the ban on school prayer, or do you think that it won't matter? Let's see.

> *Data File:* **GSS**
> *Task:* **Cross-tabulation**
> *Row Variable:* **45) SCH.PRAY**
> ➤ *Column Variable:* **6) SEX**
>   ➤ *View:* **Table**
>   ➤ *Display:* **Column%**

32. What is the value of V for this table?   V = _____

33. What is the best interpretation for this V?

    a. The value of V indicates a statistically significant and strong relationship (V is over .25).

    b. The value of V indicates a statistically significant and moderate relationship (V is between .10 and .25).

    c. The value of V indicates a statistically significant and weak relationship (V is less than .10).

    d. Because the value of V is statistically insignificant (i.e., no asterisks attached), there is no relationship.

34. Women are less supportive of the ban on school prayer than are men.   T   F

How religious a person is will probably affect his or her opinions about school prayer.

> *Data File:* **GSS**
> *Task:* **Cross-tabulation**
> *Row Variable:* **45) SCH.PRAY**
> ➤ *Column Variable:* **15) RELPERSN**
>   ➤ *View:* **Table**
>   ➤ *Display:* **Column%**

35. What is the value of V for this table?   V = _____

36. What is the best interpretation for this V?

    a. The value of V indicates a statistically significant and strong relationship (V is over .25).

    b. The value of V indicates a statistically significant and moderate relationship (V is between .10 and .25).

    c. The value of V indicates a statistically significant and weak relationship (V is less than .10).

    d. Because the value of V is statistically insignificant (i.e., no asterisks attached), there is no relationship.

37. People who say they are strongly religious are less likely to support the ban
on school prayer than those who say they are not religious.   T   F

38. Which of the four factors that we have examined has the strongest influence on people's
attitudes toward school prayer?

    a. education

    b. age

    c. sex

    d. religiosity

Finally, let's consider whether people's attitudes on free speech might overlap with their attitudes on
religious freedom. In this example, we are not saying that one attitude causes the other. Rather, we
are more interested in whether the two might be related, as they both are aspects of civil liberties.

                Data File: **GSS**
                    Task: **Cross-tabulation**
        Row Variable: **45) SCH.PRAY**
➤ *Column Variable:* **39) FR.SPEECH**
            ➤ *View:* **Table**
       ➤ *Display:* **Column %**

39. What is the value of Cramer's V for this table?   V = _____

40. Is V statistically significant?   Yes   No

41. Which of the following statements most accurately summarizes the relationship between
support for school prayer and support for freedom of speech?

    a. Those who support freedom of speech are more likely to oppose school prayer.

    b. Those who support freedom of speech are more likely to support school prayer.

    c. There is no relationship between support for freedom of speech and support for
school prayer.

WHAT HAVE WE LEARNED?

I.   How tolerant are Americans toward the speeches of groups that they might dislike, such as atheists, racists, or Communists? What factors make an American more or less likely to support the speech of such groups?

II.   In 1962, the Supreme Court ruled that school prayer violated the establishment clause of the First Amendment. Does the American public accept this ruling today? Which Americans are more or less likely to support the ban on school prayer?

III.   The level of civil liberties varies across the nations of the world. Which types of nations are more likely to have high levels of civil liberties? In countries with high levels of civil liberties, what is the opinion of the citizens toward petitioning and revolution?

WHAT ELSE CAN BE EXPLORED?

1. In the HISTORY file is 28) CIVLIB INX, which traces over time the answers to the same free speech index that we explored in this exercise. Are Americans becoming more or less support-ive of free speech over time? Are there trends in other factors that might explain changes in the level of support for free speech?

2. One controversial form of speech is pornography. Obscene material is not protected by the First Amendment, but not all sexually explicit material is deemed obscene. The GSS question 66) PORN.LAW? can be used to explore Americans' attitudes on this subject.

3. Many of the civil liberties listed in the Bill of Rights protect the rights of those accused of or convicted of crimes. One of these protections is against "cruel and unusual punishments." Some people view the death penalty as violating this standard, but others disagree. People's attitudes toward the death penalty can be investigated using the GSS question 40) EXECUTE?.

CIVIL RIGHTS: EQUALITY

We hold these truths to be self-evident: That all men are created equal; that they are endowed by their Creator with certain unalienable rights; that among these are life, liberty, and the pursuit of happiness. . . .

THE DECLARATION OF
INDEPENDENCE,
JULY 4, 1776

Tasks: Mapping, Univariate, Cross-Tabulation, Historical Trends, Scatterplot, Auto-Analyzer
Data Files: NATIONS, GSS, STATES, HISTORY, NES

These shining phrases announced the intention of the American colonists to cast off British rule and assert their "unalienable rights." Unfortunately, as the authors frankly stated, equality did not entirely apply to women ("all men"), and, as they failed to mention, these rights applied not at all to the hundreds of thousands of slaves—many slave-owners were among those who signed the Declaration. Nor did they apply to those inhabitants of America who already were here when Europeans arrived to "discover" the New World.

The struggle to include "all" within the boundaries of equality has gone on since the founding of the nation, and, although civil rights are far more extensive and secure than they were even a few years ago, the politics of "inclusion" and "exclusion" remain a central feature of our time. At a literalist level, one might have thought that the matter of equality would have been solved by the Fourteenth Amendment which, among other things, defines citizenship as "all persons born or naturalized in the United States, and subject to the jurisdiction thereof" and prohibits the states from denying any citizen within their jurisdiction the equal protection of the laws. This, of course, was not sufficient. For example, it took the Nineteenth Amendment to give women even the right to vote. The quest for equality has resulted in a variety of civil rights movements as African Americans, women, ethnic and racial minorities, sexual minorities, and others have sought equal treatment.

Nevertheless, Americans too often mistakenly regard our conflicts over civil rights as unique. In fact, conflicts based on racial, ethnic, and cultural prejudices probably are as old as the human race and exist to some degree in all societies.

➤ *Data File:* **NATIONS**
➤ *Task:* **Mapping**
➤ *Variable 1:* **11) ANTI-RACE**
➤ *View:* **Map**

ANTI-RACE – Percent Who Would Not Want Members of Another Race As Neighbors (WVS)

Here we see the percentage of people in each of 41 nations who indicated that they would not want to have "people of a different race as neighbors."

Data File: **NATIONS**
Task: **Mapping**
Variable 1: **11) ANTI-RACE**
➤ *View:* **List: Rank**

RANK	CASE NAME	VALUE
1	South Korea	58
2	India	44
3	Slovenia	40
4	Bulgaria	39
5	Turkey	34
5	Nigeria	34
5	Slovak Republic	34
8	Czech Republic	28
8	Romania	28
10	Finland	25

The majority of South Koreans don't want people of a different race as neighbors, nor would 44 percent of the populace in India and 40 percent in Slovenia. In contrast, only 10 percent of Americans feel this way and only 5 percent of Canadians.

Data File: **NATIONS**
Task: **Mapping**
Variable 1: **11) ANTI-RACE**
➤ *Variable 2:* **12) ANTI-FORGN**
➤ *Views:* **List: Rank**

RANK	CASE NAME	VALUE
1	South Korea	58
2	India	44
3	Slovenia	40
4	Bulgaria	39
5	Turkey	34

RANK	CASE NAME	VALUE
1	South Korea	53
2	India	48
3	Slovenia	40
4	Czech Republic	34
4	Bulgaria	34

Select the [List: Rank] option on both the upper and lower maps.

The upper box of rankings contains information on Variable 1; the lower box of rankings contains information on the comparison variable.

South Koreans (53 percent) are also least receptive to having "foreigners" as neighbors, and again India (48 percent) is second. Only 10 percent of Americans object to foreigners as neighbors, and people in Switzerland and Argentina are least likely to object.

There is a huge correlation (0.899**) between not wanting neighbors who are of another race and not wanting neighbors who are foreigners. This reveals that prejudice and discrimination tend to be unidimensional phenomena—people tend to reject or accept everyone or no one. Let's pursue this idea.

Data File:	**NATIONS**
Task:	**Mapping**
Variable 1:	**11) ANTI-RACE**
➤ Variable 2:	**13) ANTI-JEW**
➤ Views:	**List: Rank**

RANK	CASE NAME	VALUE
1	South Korea	58
2	India	44
3	Slovenia	40
4	Bulgaria	39
5	Turkey	34

RANK	CASE NAME	VALUE
1	India	86
2	Turkey	59
3	Slovenia	37
4	Nigeria	34
5	Bulgaria	30

If you are continuing from the previous example, return to the variable selection screen, then select 13) ANTI-JEW as the new Variable 2.

The lower table shows the percentages in each nation who don't want Jews in their neighborhood. Indians (86 percent) overwhelmingly take this view as do the majority of Turks (59 percent). About a third of Slovenians, Nigerians, and Bulgarians don't want Jews in their neighborhood. Few Canadians (6 percent) or Americans (5 percent) take this view. But here too the correlation with objecting to persons of another race is very high (0.790**), giving further confirmation to the unidimensional nature of prejudice and the willingness to deny civil rights.

Data File:	**NATIONS**
Task:	**Mapping**
Variable 1:	**11) ANTI-RACE**
➤ Variable 2:	**14) ANTI-GAY**
➤ Views:	**List: Rank**

RANK	CASE NAME	VALUE
1	South Korea	58
2	India	44
3	Slovenia	40
4	Bulgaria	39
5	Turkey	34

RANK	CASE NAME	VALUE
1	Turkey	92
2	India	91
3	Lithuania	87
4	Russia	82
5	Belarus	79

Finally, we see very strong objections in many nations to having homosexual neighbors: 92 percent in Turkey, 91 percent in India, 82 percent in Russia, 73 percent in Nigeria, 69 percent in Japan, 38 percent in the United States, 30 percent in Canada—amazingly, South Koreans, who are most opposed to living near foreigners or members of another race, are not opposed to homosexual neighbors (4 percent). The overlap between these two attitudes, while statistically significant, is not a strong, with r = 0.316*.

Of course, no one objects to having women living in the neighborhood, so that can't be used as a measure of civil rights for women. But the following is a measure of gender equality.

Data File: **NATIONS**
Task: **Mapping**
Variable 1: **11) ANTI-RACE**
➤ Variable 2: **15) %FEM LEGIS**
➤ Views: **List: Rank**

RANK	CASE NAME	VALUE
1	South Korea	58
2	India	44
3	Slovenia	40
4	Bulgaria	39
5	Turkey	34

RANK	CASE NAME	VALUE
1	Sweden	40.4
2	Norway	36.4
3	Finland	33.5
4	Denmark	33.0
5	New Zealand	29.2

This variable shows the percentage of seats in national parliaments that are held by women. Sweden (40.4 percent) is highest, the United States is relatively low with 11.2 percent, whereas in Kuwait and the United Arab Emirates none of the seats are held by women. This variable also is significantly correlated with objecting to having neighbors of another race. In this instance, of course, the correlation is negative (r = -0.450**). Nations where racial prejudice is higher tend to have a lower percentage of females in the legislature.

That the battery of questions about prejudice shown above asked about willingness to have people who are different from them as neighbors reveals a universal aspect of civil rights which is based on an inherent contradiction concerning freedom: that one person's freedom can be another person's fetters. In this case, the freedom of one racial group to live in their own neighborhood curtails the freedom of others to live where they want.

Of course, for generations Americans had the freedom to exclude others from their neighborhoods, clubs, schools, buses, playgrounds, teams, beaches, hotels, theaters, restaurants, and similar settings. The most severe restrictions were imposed by whites on blacks and other nonwhites, but considerable limits also were imposed on Jews, Catholics, and various ethnic groups.

A major consequence of the civil rights movement during the 1950s and 1960s was to curtail this freedom in exchange for the freedom of others to freely associate. That is, equality was used as the standard against which to balance individual freedoms, and efforts by a group to be separated from others (to maintain *segregation*) were outlawed in many aspects of social life, including real estate.

Part II: Freedom: Civil Liberties and Civil Rights

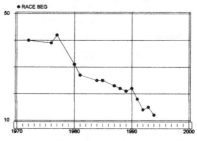

Percent who agree that whites have a right to keep African Americans out of their neighborhoods

During the 1940s, an overwhelming majority of Americans favored separate neighborhoods for African Americans. In 1972, four out of ten Americans thought that it was acceptable for whites to exclude African Americans from their neighborhoods. By 1994, this had dropped to one in ten.

AFFIRMATIVE ACTION

Civil rights advocates in the 1970s and 1980s pushed for the creation of affirmative action programs designed to compensate for past discrimination against minority groups. During this period, government, colleges and universities, businesses, and other groups adopted affirmative action programs to encourage the advancement of members of minority groups.

These programs have also encountered the basic contradiction: Enhancing the rights of one group may restrict the rights of another group. In 1978, the Supreme Court ruled on *Regents of the University of California v. Bakke,* one of the first cases questioning the constitutionality of such programs. Mr. Bakke, a white male, had been denied admission to medical school, while less qualified students had been admitted under a special minority program. The lawyers for Mr. Bakke alleged that the special admissions program was, in effect, reverse discrimination—it excluded Bakke on the basis of his race. The Supreme Court ruled that admission quotas, such as those used by the University of California, violated the Equal Protection Clause of the Fourteenth Amendment. Race and ethnicity, however, could still be part of the admission decision.

In 2003, the Supreme Court again tackled the question of affirmative action programs for universities. In a 5-4 decision, the Court upheld the affirmative action policy of the University of Michigan's law school. The law school policy considered race as one aspect in admission. Justice Sandra Day O'Connor, writing for the majority, noted that "the Equal Protection Clause does not prohibit the Law School's narrowly tailored use of race in admissions decisions to further a compelling interest in obtaining the educational benefits that flow from a diverse student body."[1] On the same day, the Court struck down by a 6-3 vote the University of Michigan's point-based policy for admissions to the undergraduate program. This policy awarded minority students, and various other groups such as athletes and Michigan residents, extra points toward an admissions scale.

These decisions by the Supreme Court reflect the complexity of affirmative action programs, where several values compete. Let's see how this complexity affects public attitudes toward such programs.

---

[1] *Gruttner v. Bollinger,* 539 US 343; the undergraduate decision is *Gratz v. Bollinger,* 539 US 244.

> ➤ *Data File:* **NES**
> ➤ *Task:* **Univariate**
> ➤ *Primary Variable:* **76) GOV BLKHLP**
> ➤ *View:* **Pie**

GOV BLKHLP -- How do you feel? Should the government in Washington see to it that black people get fair treatment in jobs OR is this not the federal government's business?

		%
■	1) GOVT HELP	56.5
▨	2) NO GOVT	43.5
	TOTAL (N)	650
	Missing	562

Here we see that a slim majority of Americans feel that it is a proper role for the federal government to see to it that blacks receive fair treatment in jobs.

> *Data File:* **NES**
> ➤ *Task:* **Cross-tabulation**
> ➤ *Row Variable:* **76) GOV BLKHLP**
> ➤ *Column Variable:* **2) RACE**
> ➤ *View:* **Table**
> ➤ *Display:* **Column %**

GOV BLKHLP by RACE
Cramer's V: 0.337**

		RACE					
		WHITE	BLACK	HISPANIC	ASIAN	Missing	TOTAL
GOV BLKHLP	GOVT HELP	216	94	29	7	21	346
		46.6%	89.5%	74.4%	63.6%		55.9%
	NO GOVT	248	11	10	4	10	273
		53.4%	10.5%	25.6%	36.4%		44.1%
	Missing	412	75	42	17	16	562
	TOTAL	464	105	39	11	47	619
		100.0%	100.0%	100.0%	100.0%		

Blacks are significantly more likely than other Americans to view this as a proper role for the federal government. Almost nine in ten African Americans support this role for the government compared to slightly less than half of whites. What happens to public opinion when the question specifically asks about an affirmative action program to compensate for past discrimination?

> *Data File:* **NES**
> ➤ *Task:* **Univariate**
> ➤ *Primary Variable:* **108) AFFIRM ACT**
> ➤ *View:* **Pie**

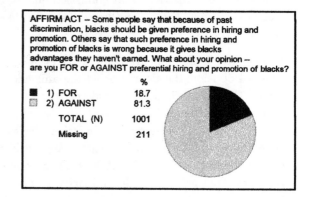

AFFIRM ACT -- Some people say that because of past discrimination, blacks should be given preference in hiring and promotion. Others say that such preference in hiring and promotion of blacks is wrong because it gives blacks advantages they haven't earned. What about your opinion -- are you FOR or AGAINST preferential hiring and promotion of blacks?

		%
■	1) FOR	18.7
▨	2) AGAINST	81.3
	TOTAL (N)	1001
	Missing	211

Here we see that eight out of ten Americans reject preferences in hiring and promotions to compensate for past discrimination.

Data File: **NES**
➤ Task: **Cross-tabulation**
➤ Row Variable: **108) AFFIRM ACT**
➤ Column Variable: **2) RACE**
➤ View: **Table**
➤ Display: **Column %**

AFFIRM ACT   by   RACE
Cramer's V: 0.361**

		RACE					
		WHITE	BLACK	HISPANIC	ASIAN	Missing	TOTAL
A F F I R M A C T	**FOR**	92	71	10	4	10	177
		12.3%	53.0%	16.4%	21.1%		18.4%
	AGAINST	655	63	51	15	30	784
		87.7%	47.0%	83.6%	78.9%		81.6%
	Missing	129	46	20	9	7	211
	TOTAL	747	134	61	19	47	961
		100.0%	100.0%	100.0%	100.0%		

Race is still significantly related to opinions on this issue, but the distribution of opinion within each group is different from the first question. A majority of African Americans approve of affirmative action programs to compensate for past discrimination, while nearly 90 percent of whites disapprove.

Just as the Supreme Court continues to struggle with the proper remedy for a history of racial discrimination in the United States, the American public also makes distinctions between different types of government action.

Your turn.

NAME:

COURSE:

DATE:

REVIEW QUESTIONS

Based on the first part of this exercise, answer True or False to the following items:

1. If a country has a high percentage of its citizens not wanting to live next to someone from a different race, that country's citizens also are likely not to want to live next to a foreigner. T F

2. Countries that exhibit intolerance toward those of other races also tend to exhibit intolerance toward Jews. T F

3. Nations where racial prejudice is higher tend to have a lower percentage of women in their legislatures. T F

4. Public opinion on civil rights varies by what aspect of the issue is contained in the survey question. T F

5. In the past 30 years, there has been a large change in attitudes toward racially segregated housing. T F

EXPLORIT QUESTIONS

CIVIL RIGHTS ATTITUDES IN OTHER COUNTRIES

Let's see if there is any connection between extent of civil liberties in nations and the attitudes of the populace to other groups.

➤ *Data File:* **NATIONS**
➤ *Task:* **Scatterplot**
➤ *Dependent Variable:* **11) ANTI-RACE**
➤ *Independent Variable:* **19) CIVIL LIBS**
➤ *View:* **Reg. Line**

The civil liberties scale is scored from 1 to 7, where countries that receive a score of 1 have a low level of civil liberties (e.g., freedom of speech) and countries that receive a score of 7 have a very high level of civil liberties. A high score on the anti-race variable shows that a large percentage of a country's citizens would not want someone from a different race as a neighbor.

6. The best interpretation of the Pearson's r coefficient of -0.331* is

    a. Because the coefficient is negative, there is no relationship between the level of civil liberties in a country and the public's attitudes toward other races.

    b. Because the coefficient has only one asterisk attached to it, there is no relationship between the level of civil liberties in a country and the public's attitudes toward other races.

    c. A moderate and statistically significant relationship exists. As the level of civil liberties increases, a larger proportion of the public would not want to have people from a different race as neighbors.

    d. A moderate and statistically significant relationship exists. As the level of civil liberties increases, a smaller proportion of the public would not want to have people from a different race as neighbors.

In Exercise 4, we found that the educational level of the population was strongly related to the degree of civil liberties in the country. Let's see if education has any effect on attitudes toward civil rights.

> Data File: **NATIONS**
> Task: **Scatterplot**
> Dependent Variable: **11) ANTI-RACE**
> ➤ Independent Variable: **40) EDUC EXPTD**
> ➤ View: **Reg. Line**

7. Which of the following statements best describes the relationship in the scatterplot?

    a. As the level of education of the populace increases, the level of anti-race attitudes significantly decreases.

    b. As the level of education of the populace increases, the level of anti-race attitudes decreases, but the effect is not significant.

> Data File: **NATIONS**
> Task: **Scatterplot**
> ➤ Dependent Variable: **13) ANTI-JEW**
> ➤ Independent Variable: **40) EDUC EXPTD**
> ➤ View: **Reg. Line**

8. Which of the following statements best describes this relationship?

    a. The higher the level of education, the lower the level of anti-Jewish attitudes, often referred to as anti-Semitism.

    b. The lower the level of education, the lower the level of anti-Semitism.

    c. The relationship between the level of education of the population and the level of anti-Semitism is not statistically significant.

Data File: **NATIONS**
Task: **Scatterplot**
➤ Dependent Variable: **14) ANTI-GAY**
➤ Independent Variable: **40) EDUC EXPTD**
➤ View: **Reg. Line**

9. Which of the following statements best describes this relationship?

   a. Nations that have higher levels of education are less anti-gay. The relationship is strong and statistically significant.

   b. Nations that have higher levels of education are less anti-gay. The relationship is weak but statistically significant.

   c. There is no relationship between educational levels and anti-gay attitudes in a country, because the value of Pearson's r is negative.

AMERICANS' VIEWS ON WOMEN IN POLITICS

In the United States, women won the right to vote in 1920, but that did not automatically assure women of equal rights in all fields. Paternalistic attitudes kept women from serving on juries in some states, from holding certain types of jobs, and from having equal access to credit. Only gradually were these restrictions removed.

What are Americans' views today on an equal role for women in politics?

➤ Data File: **GSS**
➤ Task: **Univariate**
➤ Primary Variable: **59) MEN BETTER**
➤ View: **Pie**

10. What percent of Americans agree that "most men are better suited emotionally for politics than most women"?   _____ %

Let's see whether men and women have different attitudes about the role of women in politics.

Data File: **GSS**
➤ Task: **Cross-tabulation**
➤ Row Variable: **59) MEN BETTER**
➤ Column Variable: **6) SEX**
➤ View: **Table**
➤ Display: **Column %**

11. Women are less likely to agree that men are better qualified to be in politics.   T   F

Using MEN BETTER to indicate attitudes about the role of women in politics, let's use AUTO-ANALYZER to see how such attitudes are related to the demographic characteristics of people.

> Data File: **GSS**
> ➤ Task: **Auto-Analyzer**
> ➤ Variable: **59) MEN BETTER**
> ➤ View: **Religion**

12. Those reporting no religion are the least likely to think that men are better suited emotionally for politics.   T   F

> ➤ View: **Region**

13. Westerners are the most likely to think that men are better suited emotionally for politics.   T   F

> ➤ View: **Age**

14. Those 40 to 49 are the most likely to think that men are better suited emotionally for politics.   T   F

> ➤ View: **Education**

15. The higher the education, the less likely the individual is to think that men are better suited emotionally for politics.   T   F

> ➤ View: **Party**

16. Democrats are the mostly likely to think men are better suited emotionally for politics.   T   F

> ➤ View: **Race**

17. Whites are more likely than African Americans to think that men are better suited emotionally for politics.   T   F

In Exercise 4 we examined civil *liberties* attitudes, and now we are examining civil *rights* attitudes in this exercise. How are civil liberties attitudes related to civil rights attitudes? Let's continue using MEN BETTER as a measurement of civil rights attitudes (specifically, attitudes toward equality for women in politics) and see how it is related to a civil liberties measure, support for freedom of speech as indicated by the FR.SPEECH variable.

> Data File: **GSS**
> ➤ Task: **Cross-tabulation**
> ➤ Row Variable: **59) MEN BETTER**
> ➤ Column Variable: **39) FR.SPEECH**
> ➤ View: **Table**
> ➤ Display: **Column %**

18. On the basis of these results, which of the following is the most appropriate conclusion concerning the relationship between civil liberties attitudes and civil rights attitudes?

    a. People who support civil liberties the most are also likely to support civil rights the most.

    b. People who support civil liberties the most are the least likely to support civil rights.

    c. There is no connection between civil liberties attitudes and civil rights attitudes.

Now let's look at the trend in electing women to public office. To do so, we will look at the average percentage of seats in the state legislatures that have been held by women.

➤ *Data File:* **HISTORY**
    ➤ *Task:* **Historical Trends**
➤ *Variables:* **98) WM ST LEG**

19. Which of the following statements best summarizes this graph?

    a. Today, women are equally as likely as men to be a member of a state legislature.

    b. Today, almost one-quarter of state legislative seats are held by women.

    c. The number of women in state legislatures increased significantly between the 2000 and 2004 elections.

Which of the U.S. states has the highest percentage of women in its legislature, and which state has the lowest percentage?

➤ *Data File:* **STATES**
    ➤ *Task:* **Mapping**
➤ *Variable 1:* **65) WMEN LEG**
    ➤ *View:* **List: Rank**

20. Which state has the highest percentage of women in its legislature?   _____

21. What percent of seats are held by women in this state's legislature?   _____ %

22. Which state has the lowest percentage of women in its legislature?   _____

23. What percent of seats are held by women in this state's legislature?   _____ %

Let's see if we can uncover any patterns in the number of women in state legislatures. We'll begin by looking at a measure of public opinion in the state. In this case, it is the percent of a state's population that is conservatives.

Data File: **STATES**
Task: **Mapping**
Variable 1: **65) WOMEN LEG**
➤ Variable 2: **48) CONSER**
➤ View: **Map**

24. States with a more conservative population tend to have a smaller percentage
of state legislators who are women.   T   F

Let's see how the education level of states is related to the percentage of state legislators who are women.

Data File: **STATES**
Task: **Mapping**
Variable 1: **65) WOMEN LEG**
➤ Variable 2: **31) %COLLEGE**
➤ View: **Map**

25. States with a higher percentage of college graduates tend to have a higher
percentage of state legislators who are women.   T   F

Does the wealth of a state's residents matter?

Data File: **STATES**
Task: **Mapping**
Variable 1: **65) WOMEN LEG**
➤ Variable 2: **20) FAMILY$**
➤ View: **Map**

26. States with a higher median family income tend to have a higher percentage
of state legislators who are women.   T   F

Does it matter whether a state's citizens live mainly in urban areas?

Data File: **STATES**
Task: **Mapping**
Variable 1: **65) WOMEN LEG**
➤ Variable 2: **14) URBAN00**
➤ View: **Map**

27. States with more urban residents tend to have a higher percentage of state
legislators who are women.   T   F

28. Women hold a larger percentage of the seats in the legislatures of states with the following characteristics:

   a. highly educated, more urban, and wealthier residents.

   b. highly educated, wealthier, and less conservative residents.

   c. highly educated, more urban, wealthier, and less conservative residents.

GAY MARRIAGE

One of the hotly debated issues of the 2004 election was the issue of gay marriage. Eleven states had propositions on their ballots which would ban gay marriages. These propositions were approved in all eleven states. Many Americans feel that marriage should be defined only as a union between a man and a woman. Other Americans view gay marriage as an extension of civil rights.

Americans are increasingly accepting of the rights of gays and lesbians. Three-quarters feel the government should protect homosexuals against job discrimination, and about the same percentage feel gays should be allowed to serve in the military. Yet, extending gay rights to include marriage often comes into conflict with Americans' beliefs about the institution of marriage.

> ➤ *Data File:* **NES**
> ➤ *Task:* **Univariate**
> ➤ *Primary Variable:* **56) GAY MARR**
> ➤ *View:* **Pie**

29. What percent of Americans approve of gay marriage?   _____ %

> *Data File:* **NES**
> ➤ *Task:* **Cross-tabulation**
> ➤ *Row Variable:* **56) GAY MARR**
> ➤ *Column Variable:* **1) SEX**
> ➤ *View:* **Table**
> ➤ *Display:* **Column %**

   Remember, if Cramer's V is not statistically significant, you must report no difference between the groups.

30. Women are more likely than men to approve of gay marriage.   T   F

> *Data File:* **NES**
> *Task:* **Cross-tabulation**
> *Row Variable:* **56) GAY MARR**
> ➤ *Column Variable:* **4) EDUCATION**
> ➤ *View:* **Table**
> ➤ *Display:* **Column %**

31. The higher the level of one's education, the more likely a person is to approve of gay marriage.   T   F

       Data File: **NES**
       Task: **Cross-tabulation**
       Row Variable: **56) GAY MARR**
➤ *Column Variable:* **7) AGE**
       ➤ *View:* **Table**
       ➤ *Display:* **Column %**

32. Younger people are more likely than older people to approve of gay marriage.   T   F

       Data File: **NES**
       Task: **Cross-tabulation**
       Row Variable: **56) GAY MARR**
➤ *Column Variable:* **15) RELIG IMP**
       ➤ *View:* **Table**
       ➤ *Display:* **Column %**

33. The importance of religion in one's life has no effect on a person's views on gay marriage.   T   F

       Data File: **NES**
       Task: **Cross-tabulation**
       Row Variable: **56) GAY MARR**
➤ *Column Variable:* **5) PARTY**
       ➤ *View:* **Table**
       ➤ *Display:* **Column %**

34. Republicans are less likely than either Democrats or independents to support gay marriage.   T   F

<u>WHAT HAVE WE LEARNED?</u>

I.   Ensuring equality to all is a struggle facing the entire world, not just the United States. Does it appear that prejudice is unidimensional? That is, if the citizens of a country are unwilling to be neighbors with one group, are they also unwilling to be neighbors with a second group? What are some of the characteristics of countries that tend to be less prejudicial toward a wide variety of religious, racial, and gender groups?

II. What are Americans' opinions on women in politics? Which Americans are less likely and which Americans are more likely to view men as better qualified than woman for politics? Which American states tend to have a greater proportion of women serving in their legislatures?

III. Gay marriage was a controversial topic in the 2004 election. Which Americans support and which oppose gay marriage? Do you think attitudes on this issue will change over the next 10 years? Why or why not?

WORKSHEET

EXERCISE 5

WHAT ELSE CAN BE EXPLORED?

1. In the opening section of this exercise, we looked at attitudes on whether the government should ensure that blacks receive equal treatment in employment and support for preferential hiring to compensate for past discrimination. Only one potential cause for these attitudes was explored–that of race. What other characteristics of individuals might be linked to these two attitudes?

2. The NES survey contains additional questions on gay rights. One question explores whether the government should protect gays against job discrimination, one asks about gays serving in the military, and the third measures attitudes toward adoption by gay or lesbian couples. One investigation strategy would be to take one of these issues (i.e., using it as a single dependent variable) and look for a number of potential causes of this attitude (i.e., using several independent variables). A second investigation strategy would be to see how one independent variable (e.g., religion or education) links up with these three questions on gay rights as well as with the issue of gay marriage (i.e., having four dependent variables).

3. Are Americans' attitudes on civil rights issues concerning African Americans, women, and homosexuals interrelated? Do people hold a single attitude on civil rights that they apply to all groups, or do people have different attitudes about different groups of Americans? Some tentative conclusions could be drawn by exploring the overlap between survey questions asking about the different groups of Americans.

Part III

GOVERNMENT AND THE INDIVIDUAL

Exercise 6   **Public Opinion and Political Socialization**

Exercise 7   **The Media**

Exercise 8   **Political Participation**

Exercise 9   **Political Parties**

Exercise 10   **Elections**

Exercise 11   **Interest Groups and PACs**

The basis of political freedom is simple to identify and very difficult to maintain: We the People. But who are the people? Are they everyone? Or only everyone who cares? Or are they only those who try to influence political decisions? What is consent? Do elections provide an adequate measure of it? Or should elected officials simply vote according to the polls? If not, how should they represent us? How shall governments distinguish between the abiding interests of the people and our momentary enthusiasms? As we shall see, there are no clear or final answers to these questions. But only as we constantly apply them to our political realities, can we sustain a free society.

PUBLIC OPINION AND POLITICAL SOCIALIZATION

About things on which the public thinks long it commonly attains to think right.

SAMUEL JOHNSON, 1778

Tasks: Univariate, Cross-Tabulation, Mapping
Data Files: GSS, STATES

The opinion poll (or survey) has become an essential part of our political life offering constant reflections of the opinions, interests, anxieties, and antagonisms of the American public. Yet, not so many years ago there were no polls and no one could really know how the public felt about anything. The first reliable pre-election polls of voters were conducted in 1936 by George Gallup, founder of the Gallup Poll, and by his rival Elmo Roper, founder of the Roper Poll. Then, as now, the polls often revealed surprises—if it were easy to gauge public opinion, no one would pay the large sums needed to conduct a trustworthy survey.

In Exercise 3 you learned that public opinion polls work because they are based on *random samples* of sufficient size. Using correct sampling procedures, however, is only one component to a successful survey. Constructing unbiased and understandable questions about complex political issues is a difficult task. Survey questions have to allow individuals to reveal their true opinions. The survey question cannot coax respondents to give one answer over another. If it does, then it is a biased question. Survey questions also cannot be confusing. This is a difficult task for a large national sample, where respondents will vary in their levels of education, their ages, the regions of the country they live in, and so on. Each of these factors could contribute to a misunderstanding of a survey question. However, reputable survey firms have been working for years to develop unbiased and understandable questions.

ASKING QUESTIONS ABOUT COMPLEX ATTITUDES

Many political issues are quite complex. Listening to some discussions on abortion could lead one to view Americans as sharply divided between those who are pro-life (opposing abortion in all cases) and those who are pro-choice (favoring abortion in all cases). In fact, many Americans fall between these two camps—they approve of abortion in some circumstances but not others. Thus, the GSS asks several questions in its surveys to ascertain people's opinions on abortion. Let's look at three of them.

➤ *Data File:* **GSS**
➤ *Task:* **Univariate**
➤ *Primary Variable:* **61) ABORT.HLTH**
➤ *View:* **Pie**

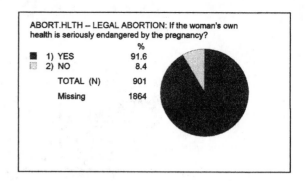

Someone might look at these results and report that nearly all Americans (91.6 percent) favor allowing abortions to be legal. Clearly, it is true that about 9 Americans out of 10 favor allowing abortions when a woman's own health is seriously endangered by the pregnancy. (Notice that the question was not asked of all respondents; thus, data are missing on the attitudes of 1,864 persons. This does not weaken our confidence in the results because random techniques were used not only to select the total sample but also to decide which members of the sample were asked this question.)

However, before we rush to report the huge public support for abortion, notice that the question is not about abortion in general, but about abortions for a very specific reason. Perhaps Americans line up rather differently when the reason for an abortion is less compelling than to save the woman's life?

Data File: **GSS**
Task: **Univariate**
➤ *Primary Variable:* **60) ABORT.WANT**
➤ *View:* **Pie**

ABORT.WANT -- LEGAL ABORTION: If she is married and does not want any more children?

		%
■	1) YES	44.8
▨	2) NO	55.2
	TOTAL (N)	893
	Missing	1872

Based on these results alone, someone might report that most Americans (55.2 percent) oppose abortion. Here, again, abortion opinions are linked to a very specific circumstance, a married woman who does not want any more children. So, what do Americans think about abortion in general?

Data File: **GSS**
Task: **Univariate**
➤ *Primary Variable:* **62) ABORT ANY**
➤ *View:* **Pie**

ABORT ANY -- LEGAL ABORTION: If the woman wants it for any reason?

		%
■	1) YES	43.0
▨	2) NO	57.0
	TOTAL (N)	900
	Missing	1865

When asked whether abortions ought to be legal "if the woman wants it for any reason," most Americans (57.0 percent) disapprove.

So, in response to the question "Do Americans favor or oppose abortion?" the most accurate answer is "It depends."

Let's look at another example where the question wording affects the responses given. The GSS survey includes a series of questions asking people whether they think spending on certain government programs is too little, just right, or too much. When the GSS asks people about spending on welfare, the following results occur.

<table>
<tr><td align="right">Data File:</td><td>**GSS**</td></tr>
<tr><td align="right">Task:</td><td>**Univariate**</td></tr>
<tr><td align="right">➤ Primary Variable:</td><td>**30) WELFARE $**</td></tr>
<tr><td align="right">➤ View:</td><td>**Bar Freq.**</td></tr>
</table>

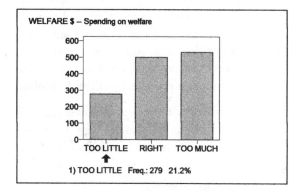

This bar chart shows the number of respondents in each category. When asked about spending on welfare, the largest number of people chose the "too much" category. The category chosen by the most respondents is called the modal category. By moving the cursor and clicking anywhere on the "too much" category, the MicroCase software will tell you the exact number of respondents in this category and the percentage of respondents. You will see that 40.6 percent felt too much money was being spent on welfare. Results like these have stimulated many accusations that Americans lack compassion, that they don't care what happens to poor people.

<table>
<tr><td align="right">Data File:</td><td>**GSS**</td></tr>
<tr><td align="right">Task:</td><td>**Univariate**</td></tr>
<tr><td align="right">➤ Primary Variable:</td><td>**33) POOR $**</td></tr>
<tr><td align="right">➤ View:</td><td>**Bar Freq.**</td></tr>
</table>

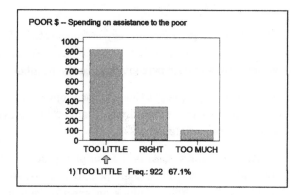

But if that's so, what are we to make of this result? When asked about spending on assistance to the poor rather than spending on welfare ... the modal category shifts. When asked about spending on the poor, the largest number of respondents chooses the "too little" category. How might you explain these answers which show that 40.6 percent of Americans think that too much money is spent on welfare but 67.1 percent think too little is being spent on assisting the poor? Obviously, to Americans, questions about "the poor" and people on "welfare" are interpreted differently. Pollsters concerned with obtaining an accurate reflection of public opinion need to keep in mind the subtle, and sometimes confusing, distinctions Americans might make between similar terms.

POLITICAL IDEOLOGIES: WHO ARE THE LIBERALS, WHO ARE THE CONSERVATIVES?

Suppose that rather than asking why people give such different answers to these two questions, we asked a far more basic question: *How do people come to hold any of the opinions and beliefs that they do?*

There are, of course, many answers to that question because many factors influence our opinions. However, there is a very general and basic difference between people in the way they assess political issues. Some people form their political opinions issue by issue, and surveys reveal very little consistency among their opinions. That is, some people take a very liberal position on one issue, a very conservative position on another, and a moderate position on a third. However, when we identify liberal and conservative positions on issues, we are assuming that there exist consistent sets of political opinions. Such sets are called **political ideologies**.

Unlike people who form their opinions issue by issue, others have acquired and developed a general frame of reference, an ideology, against which to judge specific issues as they arise. In American politics the labels "liberal," "moderate," and "conservative" identify the major ideologies.

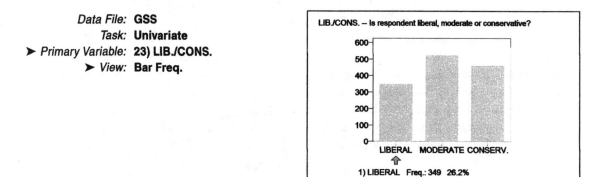

Data File: **GSS**
Task: **Univariate**
➤ Primary Variable: **23) LIB./CONS.**
➤ View: **Bar Freq.**

The modal category for ideology is "moderate." When you move the cursor over to this bar and click, MicroCase will tell you that 39.2 percent of Americans view themselves as moderates. The number of conservatives at 34.6 percent exceeds the number of liberals at 26.2 percent.

But where do people get their political opinions, especially their political ideologies? The answer is, of course, that we learn them from others and from experience. And this learning process often is referred to as political socialization.

Political socialization is the complex process by which individuals become aware of politics, learn political facts, and form their political views. Although political socialization helps to explain how people acquire their opinions on *specific* issues, it is especially useful for examining how people acquire a general perspective or political ideology. Political scientists take a special interest in political socialization, paying particular attention to **agents of socialization**, the primary sources of political socialization.

Part III: Government and the Individual

Our political socialization begins early as our families are the initial agents of our socialization. Considerable research shows that people tend to resemble their parents in terms of their political ideologies and interest. This is especially true of party preferences. Democrats tend to raise Democrats, while the children of Republicans tend to grow up as Republicans.

But, although childhood influences may be an important source of political socialization, they are soon reinforced or countermanded by other primary agents of socialization: school, church, work, region, and community. In addition to these, our political outlooks are greatly shaped by our life experiences. How might socialization explain who is a liberal versus who a conservative? In the following examples, ideology will be the dependent variable, and so it will be listed as the row variable. The potential causes of ideology will be the independent variables and will be listed as the column variables. To judge the effect of these independent variables on ideology, we will compare percentages based on the column variables. Let's begin with one's level of education.

Data File:	**GSS**
➤ Task:	**Cross-tabulation**
➤ Row Variable:	**23) LIB./CONS.**
➤ Column Variable:	**3) EDUCATION**
➤ View:	**Table**
➤ Display:	**Column %**

LIB./CONS. by EDUCATION
Cramer's V: 0.106**

		EDUCATION					
		NOT HS GRD	HS GRD	SOME COLL	COLL GRAD	Missing	TOTAL
LIB./CONS.	LIBERAL	40	98	96	115	0	349
		21.3%	23.2%	25.3%	34.1%		26.3%
	MODERATE	84	182	161	92	3	519
		44.7%	43.0%	42.4%	27.3%		39.1%
	CONSERV.	64	143	123	130	0	460
		34.0%	33.8%	32.4%	38.6%		34.6%
	Missing	206	441	442	336	9	1434
	TOTAL	188	423	380	337	12	1328
		100.0%	100.0%	100.0%	100.0%		

Cramer's V for this table tells us that education and ideology are moderately related to one another in a statistically significant fashion. However, the patterns shown in the percentages are a bit complex. Regardless of one's own educational level, the percent of conservatives is about the same–varying only from 32.4 percent to 38.6 percent. College graduates, however, are less likely than others to be moderates. One-third of college graduates are liberal, more than in any other educational category. A college education may crystallize one's ideology–some become more firmly conservative and some become more firmly liberal with fewer opting for the middle-of-the road position.

We often hear that the South is a conservative region of the country and that the Northeast is liberal. Let's see if these generalities are reflected in the ideologies of individuals living in those areas.

Data File:	**GSS**
Task:	**Cross-tabulation**
Row Variable:	**23) LIB./CONS.**
➤ Column Variable:	**20) REGION**
➤ View:	**Table**
➤ Display:	**Column %**

LIB./CONS. by REGION
Cramer's V: 0.106**

		REGION				
		EAST	MIDWEST	SOUTH	WEST	TOTAL
LIB./CONS.	LIBERAL	86	86	96	81	349
		30.2%	25.4%	21.2%	31.8%	26.2%
	MODERATE	122	148	161	91	522
		42.8%	43.7%	35.6%	35.7%	39.2%
	CONSERV.	77	105	195	83	460
		27.0%	31.0%	43.1%	32.5%	34.6%
	Missing	308	345	505	276	1434
	TOTAL	285	339	452	255	1331
		100.0%	100.0%	100.0%	100.0%	

Southerners are the least apt to identify themselves as liberals, and Westerners and Easterners are the most likely. Southerners are the most likely to say they are conservatives. Here, too, although the differences are statistically significant, they are modest.

An important agent of political socialization is the church.

	Data File:	**GSS**
	Task:	**Cross-tabulation**
	Row Variable:	**23) LIB./CONS.**
➤	Column Variable:	**14) RELIGION**
	➤ View:	**Table**
	➤ Display:	**Column %**

LIB./CONS.   by   RELIGION
Cramer's V: 0.168**

		RELIGION						
		MAINL.PROT	EVNGL.PROT	CATHOLIC	JEWISH	NONE	Missing	TOTAL
L I B . / C O N S .	LIBERAL	58	56	95	12	77	51	298
		24.1%	15.9%	28.1%	50.0%	42.5%		26.2%
	MODERATE	84	150	145	5	64	74	448
		34.9%	42.6%	42.9%	20.8%	35.4%		39.4%
	CONSERV.	99	146	98	7	40	70	390
		41.1%	41.5%	29.0%	29.2%	22.1%		34.3%
	Missing	281	393	335	24	198	203	1434
	TOTAL	241	352	338	24	181	398	1136
		100.0%	100.0%	100.0%	100.0%	100.0%		

Here we see that members of mainline Protestant denominations (Methodists or Episcopalians, for example) are most likely to view themselves as conservatives, but one-third adopt the moderate label and another quarter view themselves as liberals. Evangelical Protestants (Baptists or Assemblies of God, for example) are most apt to identify themselves as either moderates or conservatives, and very few see themselves as liberals. Catholics are most likely to view themselves as moderates, with the remainder evenly split between liberals and conservatives. The two most distinctive religious groups are Jews and those with no religion. Members of these two groups are most likely to view themselves as liberals.

A person's gender is also an important element of socialization. Let's see if this has any effect on political views.

	Data File:	**GSS**
	Task:	**Cross-tabulation**
	Row Variable:	**23) LIB./CONS.**
➤	Column Variable:	**6) SEX**
	➤ View:	**Table**
	➤ Display:	**Column %**

LIB./CONS.   by   SEX
Cramer's V: 0.008

		SEX		
		MALE	FEMALE	TOTAL
L I B . / C O N S .	LIBERAL	166	183	349
		26.4%	26.1%	26.2%
	MODERATE	244	278	522
		38.8%	39.6%	39.2%
	CONSERV.	219	241	460
		34.8%	34.3%	34.6%
	Missing	599	835	1434
	TOTAL	629	702	1331
		100.0%	100.0%	

A respondent's gender has no effect on whether they are liberal, moderate, or conservative. In fact, the percentages are almost identical. Perhaps, the more important distinction is one's martial status.

	Data File:	**GSS**
	Task:	**Cross-tabulation**
	Row Variable:	**23) LIB./CON.**
➤	Column Variable:	**1) MARITAL**
	➤ View:	**Table**
	➤ Display:	**Column %**

LIB./CONS.   by   MARITAL
Cramer's V: 0.102**

		MARITAL				
		MARRIED	WIDOWED	DIV./SEP.	NEV.MARR	TOTAL
L I B . / C O N S .	LIBERAL	139	21	70	119	349
		23.4%	17.2%	26.9%	33.6%	26.2%
	MODERATE	227	46	114	135	522
		38.2%	37.7%	43.8%	38.1%	39.2%
	CONSERV.	229	55	76	100	460
		38.5%	45.1%	29.2%	28.2%	34.6%
	Missing	674	125	281	354	1434
	TOTAL	595	122	260	354	1331
		100.0%	100.0%	100.0%	100.0%	

Martial status does matter. People who are currently married tend to be moderates or conservatives. Widows and widowers are most likely to be conservatives. Individuals who are divorced or separated tend to be moderates. Those who have never married fall in the moderate or liberal categories.

Finally, let's investigate whether age is related to ideology.

Data File: **GSS**
Task: **Cross-tabulation**
Row Variable: **23) LIB./CONS.**
➤ Column Variable: **9) AGE**
➤ View: **Table**
➤ Display: **Column %**

LIB./CONS. by AGE
Cramer's V: 0.101**

		AGE						
		UNDER 30	30 TO 39	40 TO 49	50 TO 64	65 & OVER	Missing	TOTAL
LIB./CONS.	LIBERAL	86	70	68	77	47	1	348
		34.4%	25.8%	25.9%	26.0%	19.3%		26.3%
	MODERATE	96	120	105	99	97	5	517
		38.4%	44.3%	39.9%	33.4%	39.8%		39.0%
	CONSERV.	68	81	90	120	100	1	459
		27.2%	29.9%	34.2%	40.5%	41.0%		34.7%
	Missing	280	319	282	303	243	7	1434
	TOTAL	250	271	263	296	244	14	1324
		100.0%	100.0%	100.0%	100.0%	100.0%		

The older the individual, the less likely he or she is to be liberal and the more likely to be conservative. This suggests that these political attitudes may change as a person gets older. This would be an aging effect. However, these data are not adequate to establish that a change in opinion occurs with aging. It also is possible that today's elderly were more conservative in their youth and have remained conservative throughout their lifetimes. This would be a generational effect. In order to distinguish between an aging effect and a generational effect, we would need to follow the *same respondents* over their lifetimes. A cross-sectional survey, like the General Social Survey, can tell us only that older people differ from younger people.

Your turn.

EXERCISE

6

REVIEW QUESTIONS

Based on the first part of this exercise, answer True or False to the following items:

1. Most Americans think abortions should be legally available to a woman who wants one for any reason.   T   F

2. There are more liberals than conservatives in the United States.   T   F

3. Most Americans oppose helping the poor.   T   F

4. Jews are more likely to be liberals than either Catholics or Protestants.   T   F

5. The West is the region with the highest percentage of conservatives.   T   F

EXPLORIT QUESTIONS

THE INFLUENCE OF IDEOLOGY ON PUBLIC OPINION

In the opening section of this exercise, we explored who was likely to be a liberal and who was likely to be a conservative. We were looking for causes of one's ideology. Thus, ideology was our dependent variable and factors such as age, religion, and marriage were the independent variables.

In this section of the exercise, we want to explore how ideology might influence attitudes on political issues, such as school prayer. In this case, ideology now is viewed as a potential cause of these attitudes, so ideology becomes the independent variable and will be listed as the column variable. Attitudes on the issues are the dependent variables and will be the row variables. Because we want to know whether liberals and conservatives hold different positions on these issues, we will ask for column percents.

Remember, in order for a real difference to exist between the opinions of liberals and conservatives, Cramer's V has to be statistically significant (i.e., at least one asterisks attached to it). If the relationship is not statistically significant, you must conclude that there are no differences between liberals and conservatives on the issue.

Let's begin with a look at school prayer in the GSS file.

    45) SCH.PRAY

The United States Supreme Court has ruled that no state or local government may require the reading of the Lord's Prayer or Bible verses in public schools. What are your views on this?

➤ *Data File:* **GSS**
  ➤ *Task:* **Cross-tabulation**
➤ *Row Variable:* **45) SCH.PRAY**
➤ *Column Variable:* **23) LIB./CONS.**
  ➤ *View:* **Table**
  ➤ *Display:* **Column %**

6. What percent of liberals oppose school prayer?   _____%

7. What percent of conservatives oppose school prayer?   _____%

8. What is the value of V for this table?   V = _____

9. Is V statistically significant?   Yes   No

10. Liberals are more likely than conservatives to oppose school prayer.   T   F

41) GUN LAW?

Would you favor or oppose a law which would require a person to obtain a police permit before he or she could buy a gun?

Data File: **GSS**
Task: **Cross-tabulation**
➤ *Row Variable:* **41) GUN LAW?**
➤ *Column Variable:* **23) LIB./CONS.**
  ➤ *View:* **Table**
  ➤ *Display:* **Column %**

11. What percent of liberals favor requiring a permit to buy a gun?   _____%

12. What percent of conservatives favor requiring a permit
    to buy a gun?   _____%

13. What is the value of V for this table?   V = _____

14. Is V statistically significant?   Yes   No

35) TAXES?

Do you consider the amount of federal income tax which you have to pay as too high, about right, or too low?

Data File: **GSS**
Task: **Cross-tabulation**
➤ *Row Variable:* **35) TAXES?**
➤ *Column Variable:* **23) LIB./CONS.**
  ➤ *View:* **Table**
  ➤ *Display:* **Column %**

15. What percent of liberals feel their taxes are too high? _____%

16. What percent of conservatives feel their taxes are too high? _____%

17. What is the value of V for this table? V = _____

18. Is V statistically significant? Yes   No

19. Conservatives are more likely than liberals to feel their taxes are too high. T   F

49) BIG BIZ?

How much confidence do you have in major companies?

> Data File: **GSS**
> Task: **Cross-tabulation**
> ➤ Row Variable: **49) BIG BIZ?**
> ➤ Column Variable: **23) LIB./CONS.**
> ➤ View: **Table**
> ➤ Display: **Column %**

20. What percent of liberals have a great deal of confidence in major companies? _____%

21. What percent of conservatives have a great deal of confidence in
major companies? _____%

22. What is the value of V for this table? V = _____

23. Is V statistically significant? Yes   No

24. Conservatives are more likely than liberals to have a great deal of
confidence in major companies. T   F

58) MILITARY?

How much confidence do you have in the military?

> Data File: **GSS**
> Task: **Cross-tabulation**
> ➤ Row Variable: **58) MILITARY?**
> ➤ Column Variable: **23) LIB./CONS.**
> ➤ View: **Table**
> ➤ Display: **Column %**

25. What percent of liberals have a great deal of confidence in the military? _____%

26. What percent of conservatives have a great deal of confidence in the military? _____%

27. What is the value of V for this table? V = _____

28. Is V statistically significant? Yes   No

29. Conservatives are more likely than liberals to have a great deal of confidence in the military.

T   F

40) EXECUTE?

Do you favor or oppose the death penalty for persons convicted of murder?

> Data File: **GSS**
>   Task: **Cross-tabulation**
> ➤ Row Variable: **40) EXECUTE?**
> ➤ Column Variable: **23) LIB./CONS.**
>   ➤ View: **Table**
>   ➤ Display: **Column %**

30. What percent of liberals favor the death penalty?   _____%

31. What percent of conservatives favor the death penalty?   _____%

32. What is the value of V for this table?   V = _____

33. Is V statistically significant?   Yes   No

34. Conservatives are more likely than liberals to favor the death penalty.   T   F

Notice that on some issues, even when ideology appears to play a role, the majority of each ideological group make the *same* response.

We saw that people's ideology influences their opinions on the death penalty. Another factor that could influence people's opinions on the death penalty is whether or not the state in which they live has a death penalty law. In recent decades, around a dozen states have not had capital punishment laws, while the majority of states have such laws. The presence of a law can produce a legitimation effect, whereby the public is more likely to adopt the position incorporated in the law. Thus, we would expect the public in states without death penalty laws to have a lower level of approval for capital punishment while Americans living in states with death penalty laws should express more approval.

It is often difficult to test the influence of state laws on public opinion, because we rarely find public opinion polls with samples of each of the 50 states. The National Election Studies, however, in the early 1990s took such a poll. The average approval level of the death penalty in each state is listed in the STATES file, along with the existence of a capital punishment law in the prior year.

> ➤ Data File: **STATES**
> ➤ Task: **Mapping**
> ➤ Variable 1: **54) DTH OPIN**
> ➤ Variable 2: **136) DTH LAW**
>   ➤ View: **Map**
>   ➤ Display: **Legend**

35. What is the Pearson's r between public approval of the death penalty
    and state laws on capital punishment?   r = _____

36. Do these figures support the **legitimation effect** whereby we would expect
    higher levels of approval of capital punishment in states with death penalty
    laws than in states without such a law?   Yes   No

37. Most other countries across the world do not have death penalty laws.
    Based on the results above, would you expect lower levels of approval for
    capital punishment in countries without death penalty laws?   Yes   No

WHAT HAVE WE LEARNED?

I.   Who is most likely to be a conservative? Who is most likely to be a moderate? Who is most likely to be a liberal? Look back at the results from this exercise to describe your typical conservative, moderate, and liberal.

II. Do liberals and conservatives hold different opinions on the issues? On which issues do statistically significant differences exist between the viewpoints of liberals versus conservatives? On which issues is there no difference?

III. Sometimes, even when a statistically significant difference exists between liberals and conservatives, both groups fall on the same side of the issue. On which of the issues explored is there a statistically significant difference between liberals and conservatives, yet both groups tend to favor the same position?

<u>WHAT ELSE CAN BE EXPLORED?</u>

1.   Both the GSS and NES files contain survey questions on a variety of political issues. One of these issues could be the dependent variable, while several independent variables could be tested for their ability to explain people's positions on this issue. The independent variables could be demographic variables (e.g., sex, race, education, income) or broad-based attitudes (e.g., ideology, partisanship).

2.   A second research strategy would be to see how one independent variable is related to a number of dependent variables. For example, the gender gap could be explored by seeing which issues reveal differences between men's and women's attitudes.

3.   Public opinion in other countries can be investigated with the NATIONS file. One variable, 10) LEFT/RIGHT, gives a higher value when a country has more left (liberal) citizens and a lower value when a country has more right (conservative) citizens. Are there any other factors about these countries that can be matched up with this indicator of public opinion?

THE MEDIA

Where the press is free and every[one] able to read, all is safe.

THOMAS JEFFERSON, 1816

Tasks: Mapping, Univariate, Cross-Tabulation, Historical Trends
Data Files: NATIONS, NES, GSS, HISTORY

Few Americans have ever attended a political gathering, met a candidate for national office, or observed a session of an elected body—neither Congress nor their local city council. For most Americans, politics is a media event, and in that sense they resemble the old-time cowboy comedian Will Rogers who liked to claim "All I know is what I read in the papers."

For generations, newspapers were one of the most important mass media—newsmagazines are far more recent. *Time* was founded in 1923 but did not gain much circulation during its first few years of operation, and *Newsweek* did not appear until several years later. The many magazines of political opinion, such as *National Review, Nation, New Republic,* and *American Spectator,* are much more recent and have only small circulations—*National Review* is the largest but has a total circulation of less than 200,000. By the 1930s, radio competed with the print media to bring the news, to offer live broadcasts of political conventions, and to report returns on election nights. Following World War II, television soon became the dominant medium—the first political conventions were televised in 1948, and that also was the first time a computer (weighing many tons) was used on election night.

Today, Americans gain their knowledge and impressions of politics from both the print and electronic media. The same is true in most of the world.

> ➤ *Data File:* **NATIONS**
> ➤ *Task:* **Mapping**
> ➤ *Variable 1:* **30) NEWSPAPERS**
> ➤ *View:* **List: Rank**

RANK	CASE NAME	VALUE
1	Norway	607
2	Japan	576
3	Croatia	575
4	Iceland	515
5	Sweden	483
6	Finland	473
7	Austria	472
8	Switzerland	409
9	South Korea	404
10	Kuwait	401

Newspaper readership differs a lot among these nations. In Norway, 607 newspapers are circulated daily for every 1,000 persons. By comparison, newspaper readership is rather low in the United States, about one paper for every four persons. However, newspaper circulation once was much higher in the United States.

> ➤ *Data File:* **HISTORY**
> ➤ *Task:* **Historical Trends**
> ➤ *Variables:* **25) NEWS/100**

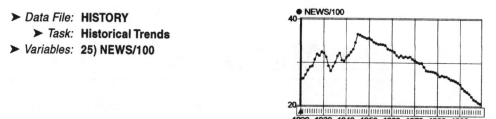

Newspaper circulation per 100 population in U.S.

One reason newspaper readership has declined in the United States, and probably in some other nations as well, is the prevalence of television.

> ➤ *Data File:* **NATIONS**
> ➤ *Task:* **Mapping**
> ➤ *Variable 1:* **31) TELEVISION**
> ➤ *View:* **List: Rank**

RANK	CASE NAME	VALUE
1	United States	81.73
2	Malta	73.91
3	Canada	68.26
4	Japan	68.00
5	Oman	66.78
6	France	58.89
7	Germany	55.75
8	Denmark	53.59
9	New Zealand	51.93
10	Finland	51.12

The United States leads the world in the number of television sets per 100 persons, with 81.73. Next is Malta, followed by Canada, Japan, and Oman. In contrast, there are few television sets in Nigeria (4.24) and India (4.04).

> ➤ *Data File:* **HISTORY**
> ➤ *Task:* **Historical Trends**
> ➤ *Variables:* **26) TV/100 HH**

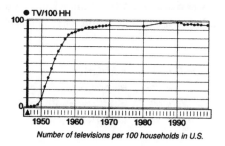

Number of televisions per 100 households in U.S.

The spread of television sets in the United States was amazingly rapid. In 1949 hardly anyone had a set, whereas in 1959 almost everyone did. The 1952 presidential campaign was the first to use television advertisements. While the technological aspects of these early television ads were simpler than what we see today, the content of the ads was similar. In one format the opposing candidate was criticized for "flip flopping" on the issues, while in another design the sponsoring candidate was praised by a variety of "typical" Americans.

Of course, many people with TV sets don't watch television news.

> *Data File:* **NES**
> *Task:* **Univariate**
> *Primary Variable:* **19) TV NEWS?**
> *View:* **Pie**

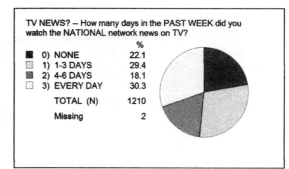

TV NEWS? -- How many days in the PAST WEEK did you watch the NATIONAL network news on TV?

		%
■	0) NONE	22.1
▨	1) 1-3 DAYS	29.4
▨	2) 4-6 DAYS	18.1
☐	3) EVERY DAY	30.3
	TOTAL (N)	1210
	Missing	2

One in three Americans say they watch TV news every day.

Data File: **NES**
Task: **Univariate**
> *Primary Variable:* **20) READ PAPER**
> *View:* **Pie**

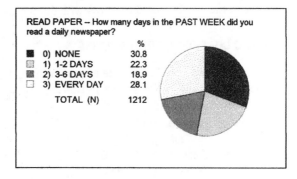

READ PAPER -- How many days in the PAST WEEK did you read a daily newspaper?

		%
■	0) NONE	30.8
▨	1) 1-2 DAYS	22.3
▨	2) 3-6 DAYS	18.9
☐	3) EVERY DAY	28.1
	TOTAL (N)	1212

About the same number say they read a newspaper every day.

Data File: **NES**
Task: **Univariate**
> *Primary Variable:* **113) NEWS TYPE**
> *View:* **Pie**

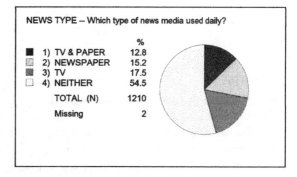

NEWS TYPE -- Which type of news media used daily?

		%
■	1) TV & PAPER	12.8
▨	2) NEWSPAPER	15.2
▨	3) TV	17.5
☐	4) NEITHER	54.5
	TOTAL (N)	1210
	Missing	2

Here the questions about watching TV news and reading newspapers have been combined to produce four basic types of persons. The first consists of those who read newspapers and watch TV news every day. They make up about 13 percent of the adult population. The second type only reads the newspapers daily, watching TV news less often. They are about 15 percent of Americans. The third type watches TV news daily but reads the paper less often. Finally, the fourth type consists of those who do not watch TV news or read a newspaper daily—about half of the public.

Does it matter if a person both watches the TV news and reads the newspaper in terms of being informed about politics?

<table>
<tr><td>Data File:</td><td>NES</td></tr>
<tr><td>➤ Task:</td><td>Cross-tabulation</td></tr>
<tr><td>➤ Row Variable:</td><td>111) KNOW</td></tr>
<tr><td>➤ Column Variable:</td><td>113) NEWS TYPE</td></tr>
<tr><td>➤ View:</td><td>Table</td></tr>
<tr><td>➤ Display:</td><td>Column %</td></tr>
</table>

KNOW by NEWS TYPE
Cramer's V: 0.239**

	NEWS TYPE					
	TV & PAPER	NEWSPAPER	TV	NEITHER	Missing	TOTAL
0-1 CORREC	17	39	64	241	1	361
	12.2%	23.8%	34.0%	42.1%		33.9%
2 CORRECT	37	46	75	215	0	373
	26.6%	28.0%	39.9%	37.5%		35.1%
3-4 CORREC	85	79	49	117	1	330
	61.2%	48.2%	26.1%	20.4%		31.0%
Missing	16	20	24	86	0	146
TOTAL	139	164	188	573	2	1064
	100.0%	100.0%	100.0%	100.0%		

Yes! Nearly two-thirds of those who both read newspapers and watch TV news on a daily basis correctly identified at least three of the four political officials. Almost half of those who read a daily newspaper correctly identified as many political officials. However, those who watched TV news were only slightly better informed than those who did not use one of these media sources on a daily basis.

PUBLIC CONFIDENCE IN THE PRESS

But what about credibility? The effects of the news media depend, at least in part, on how much confidence readers and viewers place in them.

<table>
<tr><td>➤ Data File:</td><td>NATIONS</td></tr>
<tr><td>➤ Task:</td><td>Mapping</td></tr>
<tr><td>➤ Variable 1:</td><td>22) PRESS?</td></tr>
<tr><td>➤ View:</td><td>List: Rank</td></tr>
</table>

RANK	CASE NAME	VALUE
1	Nigeria	75
2	Estonia	73
3	Lithuania	67
4	South Korea	66
5	India	63
6	Latvia	60
7	South Africa	59
8	United States	56
8	China	56
10	Brazil	55

People in each nation were asked how much confidence they had in the press. Here we see the percentage who said they had at least some confidence in the press as compared with little or no confidence. Three of four people in Nigeria said they had at least some confidence in the press. The United States and China are tied, with 56 percent saying they had some confidence. Keeping in mind that this is the most generous estimate of confidence in the press, it would appear that large numbers of people simply don't trust what they read in the papers, hear on the radio, or see on TV. In Great Britain only 14 percent say they have some confidence in the press as do 18 percent in Austria.

<table>
<tr><td>➤ Data File:</td><td>HISTORY</td></tr>
<tr><td>➤ Task:</td><td>Historical Trends</td></tr>
<tr><td>➤ Variables:</td><td>37) CONF.PRESS</td></tr>
</table>

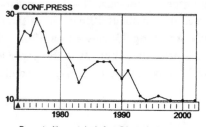

Percent with great deal of confidence in the press (survey data)

Confidence in the press has been declining in the United States.

> *Data File:* **GSS**
> *Task:* **Cross-tabulation**
> *Row Variable:* **54) PRESS?**
> *Column Variable:* **23) LIB./CONS.**
> *View:* **Table**
> *Display:* **Column %**

PRESS? by LIB./CONS.
Cramer's V: 0.116**

		LIB./CONS.				
		LIBERAL	MODERATE	CONSERV.	Missing	TOTAL
P R E S S ?	GREAT DEAL	35	31	21	5	87
		15.1%	8.9%	7.1%		9.9%
	ONLY SOME	120	174	121	10	415
		51.7%	49.9%	41.0%		47.4%
	HARDLY ANY	77	144	153	8	374
		33.2%	41.3%	51.9%		42.7%
	Missing	117	173	165	1411	1866
	TOTAL	232	349	295	1434	876
		100.0%	100.0%	100.0%		

Conservatives are more likely than liberals to have hardly any confidence in the press.

THE INTERNET: THE NEWEST MEDIUM

The three traditional news media sources over the past 50 years have been newspapers, TV, and radio. The Internet has now joined these traditional news sources. Many newspapers and television outlets have expanded to include Internet sites. Candidates, interest groups, and the political parties now use the Internet to bring their messages directly to the public.

> *Data File:* **GSS**
> *Task:* **Cross-tabulation**
> *Row Variable:* **101) CHAT POL**
> *Column Variable:* **9) AGE**
> *View:* **Table**
> *Display:* **Column %**

CHAT POL by AGE
Cramer's V: 0.176**

		AGE						
		UNDER 30	30 TO 39	40 TO 49	50 TO 64	65 & OVER	Missing	TOTAL
C H A T P O L	YES	71	45	38	27	2	2	183
		29.7%	16.5%	16.2%	14.4%	3.9%		18.6%
	NO	168	228	197	160	49	2	802
		70.3%	83.5%	83.8%	85.6%	96.1%		81.4%
	Missing	291	317	310	412	436	10	1776
	TOTAL	239	273	235	187	51	14	985
		100.0%	100.0%	100.0%	100.0%	100.0%		

Less than 20 percent of Americans use the Internet to join a chat room discussion on politics. Younger Americans are more likely to use this new technology than older Americans.

Now you will have a chance to find out more about the audience for different types of media and what impact the media have on political opinions.

Your turn.

WORKSHEET

NAME:

COURSE:

DATE:

EXERCISE

7

Workbook exercises and software are copyrighted. Copying is prohibited by law.

REVIEW QUESTIONS

Based on the first part of this exercise, answer True or False to the following items:

1. Because it can provide live video, TV is more effective than newspapers in
   communicating political information.   T   F

2. Newspaper circulation is increasing, primarily because Americans are becoming
   more educated.   T   F

3. A majority of Americans watch TV news every day.   T   F

4. Confidence in the press has been declining in the United States.   T   F

5. The British have less confidence in the press than do Americans.   T   F

EXPLORIT QUESTIONS

WHO USES THE MEDIA?

For the media to have any impact, someone must read, or listen to, or watch the medium. Let's see
how education and age influence what and how much people read or watch.

> ➤ *Data File:* **NES**
> ➤ *Task:* **Cross-tabulation**
> ➤ *Row Variable:* **20) READ PAPER**
> ➤ *Column Variable:* **4) EDUCATION**
> ➤ *View:* **Table**
> ➤ *Display:* **Column %**

When answering these questions, first check the statistical significance of the relationship.

6. Which educational level is most likely to read the newspaper every day?
   a. No high school degree
   b. High school graduate
   c. Some college
   d. College graduate
   e. There is no difference among the different groups.

Data File: **NES**
Task: **Cross-tabulation**
➤ *Row Variable:* **19) TV NEWS?**
➤ *Column Variable:* **4) EDUCATION**
➤ *View:* **Table**
➤ *Display:* **Column %**

7. Which educational level is most likely to watch television news every day?

    a. No high school degree

    b. High school graduate

    c. Some college

    d. College graduate

    e. There is no difference among the different groups.

Data File: **NES**
Task: **Cross-tabulation**
➤ *Row Variable:* **20) READ PAPER**
➤ *Column Variable:* **7) AGE**
➤ *View:* **Table**
➤ *Display:* **Column %**

8. Which age group is most likely to read a newspaper every day?

    a. Under 30

    b. 30 to 39

    c. 40 to 49

    d. 50 to 64

    e. 65 and over

    f. There is no difference among the groups.

Data File: **NES**
Task: **Cross-tabulation**
➤ *Row Variable:* **19) TV NEWS?**
➤ *Column Variable:* **7) AGE**
➤ *View:* **Table**
➤ *Display:* **Column %**

9. Which age group is most likely to watch TV news every day?

    a. Under 30

    b. 30 to 39

    c. 40 to 49

    d. 50 to 64

    e. 65 and over

    f. There is no difference among the groups.

10. In summary:

    a. Both education and age influence whether someone watches both TV news and reads a newspaper on a daily basis.

    b. Education influences whether someone watches both TV news and reads a newspaper on a daily basis, while age only influences whether someone reads a newspaper on a daily basis.

    c. Age influences whether someone watches both TV news and reads a newspaper on a daily basis, while education only influences whether someone reads a newspaper on a daily basis.

    d. Neither age nor education influence whether someone uses these two media sources on a daily basis.

EFFECTS OF MEDIA USAGE

Earlier we saw that frequentl media usage increased the knowledge of four officeholders. Another piece of political knowledge is which party controls Congress. Respondents to the NES survey were asked which party controlled the U.S. House of Representatives before the 2004 elections and which party controlled the U.S. Senate. About 40 percent of the NES respondents knew that the Republicans controlled both houses of Congress, 20 percent correctly identified the Republicans as controlling one of the two houses, and 37 percent did not know which party controlled either chamber. Let's first look at the effects of reading the newspaper on awareness of which party controls Congress.

> *Data File:* **NES**
> *Task:* **Cross-tabulation**
> ➤ *Row Variable:* **112) CONG KNOW**
> ➤ *Column Variable:* **20) READ PAPER**
> ➤ *View:* **Table**
> ➤ *Display:* **Column %**

11. Those who read a newspaper every day are the most likely to know that Republicans controlled both houses of Congress.   T   F

In general, newspapers provide more in-depth coverage of political news than television news. Reading the newspaper also forces one to pay attention, while people often casually watch television news while doing other tasks. Therefore, one might suspect that in many cases watching television news does not increase one's level of political information beyond what a person already learned from reading the newspaper. To test this possibility, we will look at the effects of watching television news on knowing which party was the majority in Congress while controlling for the individual's habit of reading the newspaper.

Data File: **NES**
Task: **Cross-tabulation**
Row Variable: **112) CONG KNOW**
➤ Column Variable: **19) TV NEWS?**
➤ Control Variable: **20) READ PAPER**
➤ View: **Table**
➤ Display: **Column %**

The use of 20) READ PAPER as the control variable will produce four tables. Use the arrow keys in the bottom left-hand corner of the screen to move among the four tables.

12. Looking at the first table labeled READ PAPER: NONE, what is the value of Cramer's V for this table?   V = _____

13. For those who do not read a newspaper, watching television news increases their awareness of which party controls Congress.   T   F

14. Looking at the second table labeled READ PAPER: 1–2 DAYS, what is the value of Cramer's V for this table?   V = _____

15. For those who read a newspaper one to two days a week, watching television news increases their awareness of which party controls Congress.   T   F

16. Looking at the third table labeled READ PAPER: 3–6 DAYS, what is the value of Cramer's V for this table?   V = _____

17. For those who read a newspaper three to six days a week, watching television news increases their awareness of which party controls Congress.   T   F

18. Looking at the fourth table labeled READ PAPER: EVERY DAY, what is the value of Cramer's V for this table?   V = _____

19. For those who read a newspaper every day, watching television news increases their awareness of which party controls Congress.   T   F

20. Watching television news helps to increase the level of political knowledge about Congress for those who infrequently read the newspaper, but watching television news does not increase the knowledge of those who read a newspaper at least three times a week.   T   F

Before proceeding to the next question, be sure to erase 20) READ PAPER as the control variable. One easy way to do this is to click on [Clear All] on the cross-tabulation menu screen.

Some critics of media coverage of government contend that the media present only the negative side of the story, such as when a government program is not working. If these critics are correct, then people who frequently watch TV news and read newspapers should be less trusting of the government than other Americans. Other pundits might contend that people who are very distrustful of the government would not bother watching TV news or reading the newspaper, since these Americans would be less interested in news about a government they distrusted. Finally, a third group of scholars might speculate that since most Americans tend to distrust the government, media usage would have little to no influence on any individual's evaluation of the government. Let's see which of these three possible explanations might be correct.

> *Data File:* **NES**
> *Task:* **Cross-tabulation**
> ➤ *Row Variable:* **101) TRUST GOV**
> ➤ *Column Variable:* **113) NEWS TYPE**
> ➤ *View:* **Table**
> ➤ *Display:* **Column %**

21. Which of the three contending explanations is best supported by the survey data?

    a. Those who watch TV news and read the newspaper every day are less trusting of the government.

    b. Those who neither watch TV news nor read the newspaper every day are less trusting of the government.

    c. Media usage has little to no influence on political trust.

PUBLIC CONFIDENCE IN THE PRESS

In the opening section of this exercise, we saw that conservatives are less trusting of the press than are liberals. Who else is likely to express a low level of trust in the media?

> ➤ *Data File:* **GSS**
> ➤ *Task:* **Cross-tabulation**
> ➤ *Row Variable:* **54) PRESS?**
> ➤ *Column Variable:* **3) EDUCATION**
> ➤ *View:* **Table**

22. Which educational group is most likely to have hardly any confidence in the press?

    a. Not high school graduate

    b. High school graduate

    c. Some college

    d. College graduate

    e. There is no difference between the educational groups.

       Data File: **GSS**
          Task: **Cross-tabulation**
   Row Variable: **54) PRESS?**
➤ *Column Variable:* **9) AGE**
       ➤ *View:* **Table**

23. Which age group is most likely to have hardly any confidence in the press?
    a.   Under 30
    b.   30 to 39
    c.   40 to 49
    d.   50 to 64
    e.   65 and over
    f.   There is no difference between the age groups.

       Data File: **GSS**
          Task: **Cross-tabulation**
   Row Variable: **54) PRESS?**
➤ *Column Variable:* **6) SEX**
       ➤ *View:* **Table**

24. Women are more likely than men to express hardly any confidence in the press.   T   F

       Data File: **GSS**
          Task: **Cross-tabulation**
   Row Variable: **54) PRESS?**
➤ *Column Variable:* **71) NEWSPAPER?**
       ➤ *View:* **Table**

25. The less often one reads the newspaper the more likely one is to express
hardly any confidence in the press.   T   F

<u>WHAT HAVE WE LEARNED?</u>

I.   How frequently do Americans watch the national news on television? Who is more likely to watch television news, and how does this affect their knowledge about politics?

II.   How frequently do Americans read a newspaper? Who is mostly likely to read the newspaper, and how does this affect their knowledge about politics?

III.   How much confidence does the average American have in the press? How have these evalua-tions changed over time? Which Americans have more confidence and which Americans have less confidence in the press?

<u>WHAT ELSE CAN BE EXPLORED?</u>

1.   The Internet is the newest media. In this exercise we saw that very few people use Internet chat rooms to discuss political issues. How many Americans consult the Internet, in any format, for information on elections? The GSS survey question, 102) WEB POL, asks this more general question on Internet usage. Which Americans are more likely to use the Internet to obtain political information?

2.   The past couple of decades saw a proliferation of "talk radio" programs, where the listening audience can call in and express their opinions on air. The NES survey question, 85) TALK RADIO, can be used to explore which Americans are more likely to listen to talk radio programs.

3.   What is the relationship between using the mass media and engaging in interpersonal communications about politics? About three-quarters of the NES survey respondents report talking about politics with their friends and family, 84) POL DISC. Do people who frequently read the newspaper, watch television news, listen to talk radio, or consult the Internet for political news engage in more political conversations than other Americans?

POLITICAL PARTICIPATION

Politics ought to be the part-time profession of every citizen ...

DWIGHT D. EISENHOWER, 1954

Tasks: Mapping, Univariate, Cross-Tabulation, Historical Trends, Auto-Analyzer
Data Files: NATIONS, NES, STATES, HISTORY

Political participation refers to the actions by ordinary citizens in pursuit of their political goals. The usual modes of participation are conventional—they are legal and regarded as appropriate. For example, voting, signing petitions, or campaigning on behalf of candidates or issues are conventional modes of political participation (at least they are in democratic nations). Sometimes, however, groups utilize unconventional means in pursuit of their goals. These are unusual modes of participation, often outside the law and in defiance of the government or social conventions—these include protests, demonstrations, even rebellions. Keep in mind too, as noted above, that what are conventional means of political participation in some nations, such as free elections, are unavailable in others. However, while many people (usually the overwhelming majority) do not engage in unconventional political participation, many also fail to utilize conventional modes of participation. For example, many people don't bother to vote.

POLITICAL PARTICIPATION PATTERNS AROUND THE WORLD

Let's begin with measures of unconventional participation.

➤ *Data File:* **NATIONS**
➤ *Task:* **Mapping**
➤ *Variable 1:* **8) SIT-INS**
➤ *View:* **List: Rank**

RANK	CASE NAME	VALUE
1	South Korea	10.7
2	Italy	9.7
3	France	7.9
4	Mexico	5.2
5	Belgium	4.3
6	Chile	4.2
7	Poland	3.8
8	Canada	3.0
9	Spain	2.9
10	Argentina	2.7

Few people in any of these nations have "occupied buildings or factories" as an act of direct political action. South Koreans are highest (10.7 percent), closely followed by the Italians (9.7 percent) and the French (7.9 percent). Two percent of Americans, Brazilians, and the Irish have done so. Only one person out of a thousand has taken part in a "sit-in" in Hungary.

RANK	CASE NAME	VALUE
1	Slovak Republic	78.0
2	Czech Republic	77.3
3	Finland	74.9
4	Mexico	73.0
5	Latvia	71.7
6	Belarus	71.0
7	Lithuania	68.8
8	South Korea	66.6
9	Russia	61.6
10	Netherlands	60.7

In contrast, large numbers in most countries think it sometimes is justified to fight with the police—about three-fourths of those in the Slovak, the Czech Republic, Finland, and Mexico hold this view of illegal political expression. About half of Americans also think it sometimes is justified to battle the cops, as do Italians, Poles, Canadians, and the French. Small minorities expressed this opinion in Denmark, Romania, and Brazil.

Data File: **NATIONS**
Task: **Mapping**
➤ Variable 1: **5) PERSUASION**
➤ View: **List: Rank**

RANK	CASE NAME	VALUE
1	Denmark	34.0
2	Lithuania	32.6
3	Romania	31.6
4	Hungary	30.2
5	Belarus	27.5
6	Bulgaria	26.9
7	Nigeria	26.1
8	Argentina	24.2
9	Chile	23.5
10	Estonia	23.2

Turning to more conventional modes of participation, here we see the percentage in each nation who often try to persuade others to accept their political views. In no nation is this something that most people do often. Denmark is highest with 34 percent, only 16.9 percent of Americans said they did this often, and fewer than one in ten did so in Great Britain, France, India, Japan, and Finland.

Data File: **NATIONS**
Task: **Mapping**
➤ Variable 1: **38) % VOTED**
➤ View: **List: Rank**

RANK	CASE NAME	VALUE
1	Malta	98.0
2	Uruguay	96.1
3	Indonesia	92.8
4	Cambodia	88.8
5	Angola	88.3
6	Iceland	87.8
7	Italy	87.3
8	Somalia	87.1
9	Western Samoa	86.3
10	South Africa	85.5

Here we see the percentage of the population who voted in the most recent national election (although the percentages are quite stable from one election to the next). In many nations, more than 80 percent vote (98 percent in Malta). Voter turnout is about 50 percent in the United States. In the close and heated election of 2000, voter turnout was approximately 51 percent in the United States.

POLITICAL PARTICIPATION IN THE UNITED STATES

Much mention is made in the press about low voter turnouts in the United States, but the reasons are rather obvious. For one thing, because of the frequency of state and local elections, Americans are asked to vote far more often than are people in most nations; even so, the American voter usually faces a much longer and far more complex ballot than do most voters—far more American offices are elective, and in many nations there are no bond issues or initiatives on the ballot. A second reason is registration. Americans must register themselves to vote whereas in many other nations the government sees to it that everyone is registered. A third reason is that some nations—including Australia and Belgium—have compulsory voting laws. Citizens who fail to vote must pay a fine or are subject to a special tax. Finally, many critics believe that American voters lack motivation to vote because their choices are limited to two parties.

➤ *Data File:* **NES**
➤ *Task:* **Univariate**
➤ *Primary Variable:* **64) BUTTON**
➤ *View:* **Pie**

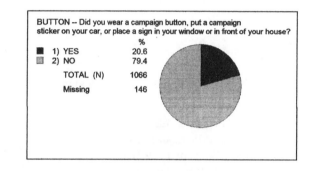

BUTTON -- Did you wear a campaign button, put a campaign sticker on your car, or place a sign in your window or in front of your house?

		%
■	1) YES	20.6
▦	2) NO	79.4
	TOTAL (N)	1066
	Missing	146

Until recently, campaign buttons, bumper stickers, and yard signs were widely used forms of American political expression. As election day neared, a substantial number of people wore buttons in support of candidates (especially presidential candidates) and automobile bumpers offered an instant education in partisan politics. But in the past several years, bumper stickers and campaign buttons are much less common. In fact, only 20 percent reported wearing a button, displaying a bumper sticker, or putting a sign in their window or yard.

Data File: **NES**
Task: **Univariate**
➤ *Primary Variable:* **65) CONTRIBUTE**
➤ *View:* **Pie**

CONTRIBUTE -- During an election year people are often asked to make a contribution to support campaigns. Did you give money to an INDIVIDUAL CANDIDATE running for public office?

		%
■	1) YES	9.6
▦	2) NO	90.4
	TOTAL (N)	1066
	Missing	146

One American in 10 reported that he or she had made a campaign contribution to a candidate for political office during the previous year.

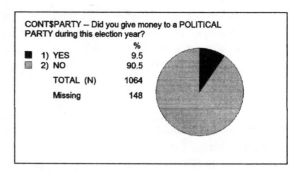

Data File: **NES**
Task: **Univariate**
➤ Primary Variable: **66) CONT$PARTY**
➤ View: **Pie**

The same number of Americans had given money to a political party. How, then, does the average American participate in politics?

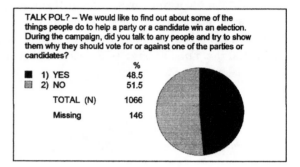

Data File: **NES**
Task: **Univariate**
➤ Primary Variable: **63) TALK POL?**
➤ View: **Pie**

Nearly half try to influence the political views of others in informal conversations.

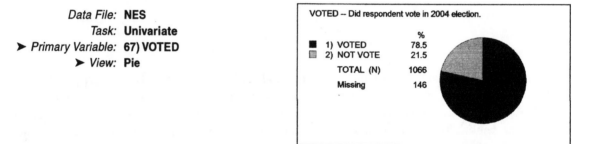

Data File: **NES**
Task: **Univariate**
➤ Primary Variable: **67) VOTED**
➤ View: **Pie**

The most common and conventional form of political participation in the United States is voting. Here we see the percentage who said they voted, based on the National Election Study, conducted in 2004. The NES found that 78.5 percent claimed to have voted in the 2004 election, but in fact, only 55.5 percent voted.

There are three reasons for the overestimate. One is that some people who meant to vote and often vote, but who didn't vote this time, said they did. But an equally important reason for the overestimate is that all survey studies more accurately represent some kinds of people than others, whereas population voting statistics are based on the entire population. That is, not everyone is easily found by survey interviewers, nor is everyone willing to be interviewed. Consider the problems of finding or of gaining interviews with migrant workers, the homeless, or people in illegal occupations such as prostitution or drug dealing. In addition, institutional populations such as those in jails, prisons, college dorms, convents, or the armed forces are not included in national survey samples. The same people who are hard for pollsters to locate and to interview also are those who are least apt to vote. Finally, many people don't like to admit that they skipped an election.

Still, even poll results show that a large number of Americans don't vote, even in presidential elections. Worse yet, the proportion voting in the 20th century has never approached the level recorded in the election of 1900. Keep in mind, however, that the 20th century saw major expansions in the types and numbers of people who were eligible to vote, and this no doubt affected the percentages of the eligible voters who actually voted. In 1900, in general, only males who were age 21 and above could vote. The 19th Amendment (1920) doubled this eligibility by giving women the right to vote. But women were not in the habit of voting, and so look at what happened to the voting participation curve in 1920 and 1924—it dropped drastically. It was not until the 1928 election that voting participation began to rise again. The 26th Amendment (1971) reduced the voting age to 18 nationally—the requirement had been 21 in all but a couple of states. The drop in voting participation in the 1972 election can be attributed partly to the fact that a new age group had been added to the eligible electorate and that this age group was not in the habit of voting. Turnout rose in the 2004 election due to a close presidential race and various efforts to mobilize voters.

➤ *Data File:* **HISTORY**
➤ *Task:* **Historical Trends**
➤ *Variable:* **12) VOTER PART**

Percent of those eligible who voted for president

VOTER TURNOUT IN THE 50 STATES

Turnout rates are not equal across all 50 states.

➤ *Data File:* **STATES**
➤ *Task:* **Mapping**
➤ *Variable 1:* **234) VOTED'04**
➤ *View:* **List: Rank**

RANK	CASE NAME	VALUE
1	Minnesota	73.3
2	Maine	71.6
2	Wisconsin	71.6
4	New Hampshire	68.2
5	Oregon	67.0
6	South Dakota	66.9
6	Alaska	66.9
8	Iowa	66.3
8	Ohio	64.8
10	Vermont	64.2

Minnesota had the highest percentage of voter turnout in the 2004 presidential election, with 73.3 percent. Maine (71.6 percent) and Wisconsin (71.6 percent) were next highest. Hawaii had the lowest percentage of voter turnout (44.5 percent).

Data File: **STATES**
Task: **Mapping**
Variable 1: **234) VOTED'04**
➤ Variable 2: **5) THE SOUTH**
➤ Views: **Map**

VOTED'04 -- 2004: Percent of Voting Age Population Who Voted in Presidential Election (SOS & Census)

r = -0.382**

THE SOUTH -- Circulation of Southern Accents Magazine Per 100,000 (ABC)

Here we see that southern states had lower voter turnouts in the 2004 election, as indicated by the significant, negative correlation: –0.382**.

Data File: **STATES**
Task: **Mapping**
Variable 1: **234) VOTED'04**
➤ Variable 2: **3) SUNBELT**
➤ Views: **Map**

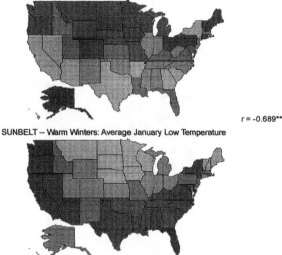

VOTED'04 -- 2004: Percent of Voting Age Population Who Voted in Presidential Election (SOS & Census)

r = -0.689**

SUNBELT -- Warm Winters: Average January Low Temperature

In fact, however, low turnouts are typical in the Sunbelt, which includes states in much of the South as well as some of the West. The correlation is stronger than with the South alone: –0.689**.

Voting turnout might also be affected by the demographic characteristics of states such as the degree of urbanism, education level, and income level.

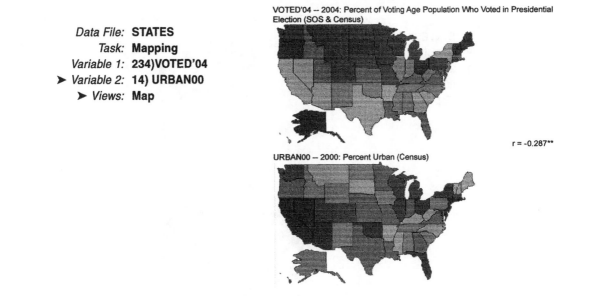

Data File: **STATES**
Task: **Mapping**
Variable 1: **234)VOTED'04**
➤ Variable 2: **14) URBAN00**
➤ Views: **Map**

VOTED'04 -- 2004: Percent of Voting Age Population Who Voted in Presidential Election (SOS & Census)

r = -0.287**

URBAN00 -- 2000: Percent Urban (Census)

Here we see that there is a small relationship (r = –0.287*) between urbanism and voter turnout. Since the coefficient is negative, it indicates turnout is higher in rural states.

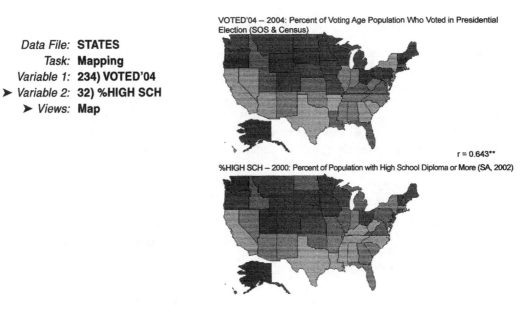

Data File: **STATES**
Task: **Mapping**
Variable 1: **234) VOTED'04**
➤ Variable 2: **32) %HIGH SCH**
➤ Views: **Map**

VOTED'04 -- 2004: Percent of Voting Age Population Who Voted in Presidential Election (SOS & Census)

r = 0.643**

%HIGH SCH -- 2000: Percent of Population with High School Diploma or More (SA, 2002)

Here we see that voter turnout is positively related to the percentage of the state's population that has a high school degree. The correlation coefficient r is 0.643** and it is statistically significant.

VOTED'04 – 2004: Percent of Voting Age Population Who Voted in Presidential Election (SOS & Census)

r = 0.169**

FAMILY$ – 2000: Median Family Income (2000 Inflation-Adjusted Dollars) (Census)

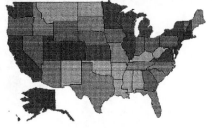

Voter turnout is not, however, related to the per capita income of states. The correlation coefficient **r** is only 0.169 and it is not statistically significant.

WHICH AMERICANS VOTE?

Now let's turn to survey data to examine who is most likely to vote. Remember, however, that some of the people in surveys who say they voted did not actually vote. Nevertheless, these self-reports are sufficiently accurate to serve as a basis for analyzing who votes.

In general terms, we might expect that voting participation among citizens would vary according to demographic characteristics (e.g., education, age, income), political knowledge, and attitudes toward the workings of the political system (e.g., political trust). Let's begin with a demographic variable, education.

➤ Data File: **NES**
➤ Task: **Cross-tabulation**
➤ Row Variable: **67) VOTED**
➤ Column Variable: **4) EDUCATION**
➤ View: **Table**
➤ Display: **Column %**

VOTED by EDUCATION
Cramer's V: 0.281**

		EDUCATION				
		NO HS DEGR	HS GRAD	SOME COLLE	COLL GRAD	TOTAL
V O T E D	**VOTED**	50	218	272	297	837
		52.1%	71.2%	79.8%	92.0%	78.5%
	NOT VOTE	46	88	69	26	229
		47.9%	28.8%	20.2%	8.0%	21.5%
	Missing	15	49	43	39	146
	TOTAL	96	306	341	323	1066
		100.0%	100.0%	100.0%	100.0%	

When we examined the relationship between voter turnout and the education level of states, we found that states with higher percentages of high school graduates had higher rates of voter turnout. Here the survey results confirm the link between education level and voting participation: The higher the education level of people, the more likely they are to vote. Note that 92.0 percent of those with a college degree said they had voted—which is almost twice as high as the voting turnout among those who didn't finish high school.

Data File:	**NES**
Task:	**Cross-tabulation**
Row Variable:	**67) VOTED**
➤ Column Variable:	**9) REGION**
➤ View:	**Table**
➤ Display:	**Column %**

VOTED by REGION
Cramer's V: 0.100*

		REGION				
		EAST	MIDWEST	SOUTH	WEST	TOTAL
V O T E D	VOTED	146	230	269	192	837
		79.3%	81.3%	73.1%	83.1%	78.5%
	NOT VOTE	38	53	99	39	229
		20.7%	18.7%	26.9%	16.9%	21.5%
	Missing	34	31	49	32	146
	TOTAL	184	283	368	231	1066
		100.0%	100.0%	100.0%	100.0%	

These findings show that Southerners and Easterners are less likely to have voted.

Data File:	**NES**
Task:	**Cross-tabulation**
Row Variable:	**67) VOTED**
➤ Column Variable:	**60) INTEREST?**
➤ View:	**Table**
➤ Display:	**Column %**

VOTED by INTEREST?
Cramer's V: 0.380**

		INTEREST?				
		VERY	SOMEWHAT	NOT MUCH	Missing	TOTAL
V O T E D	VOTED	504	297	36	0	837
		90.3%	72.3%	37.1%		78.5%
	NOT VOTE	54	114	61	0	229
		9.7%	27.7%	62.9%		21.5%
	Missing	0	0	0	146	146
	TOTAL	558	411	97	146	1066
		100.0%	100.0%	100.0%		

Not surprisingly, people expressing more interest in the campaign were more apt to have voted.

Data File:	**NES**
Task:	**Cross-tabulation**
Row Variable:	**67) VOTED**
➤ Column Variable:	**111) KNOW**
➤ View:	**Table**
➤ Display:	**Column %**

VOTED by KNOW
Cramer's V: 0.281**

		KNOW				
		0-1 CORREC	2 CORRECT	3-4 CORREC	Missing	TOTAL
V O T E D	VOTED	229	306	302	0	837
		63.3%	82.0%	91.2%		78.5%
	NOT VOTE	133	67	29	0	229
		36.7%	18.0%	8.8%		21.5%
	Missing	0	0	0	146	146
	TOTAL	382	373	331	146	1066
		100.0%	100.0%	100.0%		

And the more informed they were, the more apt people also were to have voted.

Data File:	**NES**
Task:	**Cross-tabulation**
Row Variable:	**67) VOTED**
➤ Column Variable:	**106) GOVT ATTN**
➤ View:	**Table**
➤ Display:	**Column %**

VOTED by GOVT ATTN
Cramer's V: 0.034

		GOVT ATTN				
		GOOD DEAL	SOME	NOT MUCH	Missing	TOTAL
V O T E D	VOTED	130	531	173	3	834
		80.2%	79.4%	76.2%		78.8%
	NOT VOTE	32	138	54	5	224
		19.8%	20.6%	23.8%		21.2%
	Missing	0	0	0	146	146
	TOTAL	162	669	227	154	1058
		100.0%	100.0%	100.0%		

Here we see, somewhat unexpectedly, that voting participation is the same for those who feel that the government pays attention to what the public wants as it is for those who feel the government does not.

Do patterns of voting make a difference in terms of policy? If certain types of people are less likely to vote, we might expect that their impact on public policy would be reduced. So far in this analysis we have been trying to find explanations for why some people vote and others do not. Thus, whether someone voted was the dependent variable (which we placed as the row variable) and the potential causes of participation were the independent variables (which were the column variables). The column percentages told us if those with higher education were more likely to vote than those with lower levels of education.

Now, we want to know if voters are different from nonvoters in their opinions. In order to compare these attitudes, we need to know what percent of voters hold a specific opinion versus what percent of nonvoters hold the same opinion. To obtain these percentages, we will use whether someone voted as the column variable, and their opinions on an issue as the row variable, and ask for column percentages. Let's examine differences between voters and nonvoters on the issue of abortion.

Data File:	**NES**
Task:	**Cross-tabulation**
➤ Row Variable:	**79) ABORTION**
➤ Column Variable:	**67) VOTED**
➤ View:	**Table**
➤ Display:	**Column %**

ABORTION by VOTED
Cramer's V: 0.097**

ABORTION	VOTED	NOT VOTE	Missing	TOTAL
NOT PERMIT	96	43	0	139
	11.7%	19.1%		13.3%
LIMITED	408	111	0	517
	49.4%	49.3%		49.4%
NO RESTRIC	320	71	0	391
	38.9%	31.6%		37.3%
Missing	15	4	146	165
TOTAL	822	225	146	1047
	100.0%	100.0%		

Here there is a policy difference between voters and nonvoters: Voters are somewhat more likely to allow abortions than nonvoters are.

Your turn.

EXERCISE

8

REVIEW QUESTIONS

Based on the first part of this exercise, answer True or False to the following items:

1. Because of the increase in the average level of education, Americans are
   more likely to vote now than they were early in the 20th century.   T   F

2. Because presidential elections are held in November when the weather has
   gotten cold, voter turnouts are higher in the Sunbelt states.   T   F

3. Turnout is higher in states with a better educated population.   T   F

4. Turnout is higher in states where the median family income is higher.   T   F

5. People who are more interested and informed about politics are more likely to vote.   T   F

6. There are no differences in the political views of voters and nonvoters. T   F

EXPLORIT QUESTIONS

WHO VOTES?

Let's see what demographic characteristics affect how likely an individual is to vote.

> ➤ Data File: **NES**
>   ➤ Task: **Auto-Analyzer**
> ➤ Variable: **67) VOTED**
>   ➤ View: **Univariate**

Look first at the statistical significance of the patterns before answering the following questions.

>   ➤ View: **Sex**

7. Men are more likely than women to vote.   T   F

>   ➤ View: **Race**

8.   Race has no effect on who votes.   T   F

     ➤ *View:* **Party**

9.   Independents are less likely to vote than Republicans.   T   F

     ➤ *View:* **Religion**

10.   Catholics are the most likely to vote and Jews are the least likely.   T   F

     ➤ *View:* **Marital**

11.   Married people are more likely to vote than those who have never been married.   T   F

     ➤ *View:* **Income**

12.   People with higher levels of income are less likely to vote than those with lower levels of income.   T   F

Let's look at the age differences in political participation, political interest, and political knowledge.

> *Data File:* **NES**
> ➤ *Task:* **Cross-tabulation**
> ➤ *Row Variable:* **67) VOTED**
> ➤ *Column Variable:* **7) AGE**
> ➤ *View:* **Table**
> ➤ *Display:* **Column %**

13.   Which age group is most likely to have reported voting?
     a.   Under 30
     b.   30 to 39
     c.   40 to 49
     d.   50 to 64
     e.   65 and over
     f.   All age groups vote at the same rate.

> *Data File:* **NES**
> *Task:* **Cross-tabulation**
> ➤ *Row Variable:* **60) INTEREST?**
> ➤ *Column Variable:* **7) AGE**
> ➤ *View:* **Table**
> ➤ *Display:* **Column %**

14. Which age group is most likely to be very interested in politics?
   a.   Under 30
   b.   30 to 39
   c.   40 to 49
   d.   50 to 64
   e.   65 and over
   f.   All age groups are equally interested in politics.

   Data File: **NES**
   Task: **Cross-tabulation**
   ➤ *Row Variable:* **111) KNOW**
   ➤ *Column Variable:* **7) AGE**
   ➤ *View:* **Table**
   ➤ *Display:* **Column %**

15. Which age group is most likely to correctly identify three or four of the political officials?
   a.   Under 30
   b.   30 to 39
   c.   40 to 49
   d.   50 to 64
   e.   65 and over
   f.   All age groups are equally likely to correctly identify three or four of the political officials.

   Data File: **NES**
   Task: **Cross-tabulation**
   ➤ *Row Variable:* **66) CONT$PARTY**
   ➤ *Column Variable:* **7) AGE**
   ➤ *View:* **Table**
   ➤ *Display:* **Column %**

16. Which age group is most likely to have contributed money to a political party?
   a.   Under 30
   b.   30 to 39
   c.   40 to 49
   d.   50 to 64
   e.   65 and over
   f.   All age groups are equally as likely to have contributed money.

17. Based on these results concerning age, which of the following statements is most accurate? (Circle one.)

    a.   Overall, younger people have higher political interest, political knowledge, and political participation than older people do.

    b.   Overall, older people have higher political interest, political knowledge, and political participation than younger people do.

    c.   Older people have higher political participation, but younger people have higher political interest and political knowledge.

    d.   Older people have higher political interest and political knowledge, but younger people have higher political participation.

Let's examine relationships between voting participation and some political attitudes.

Data File:	**NES**
Task:	**Cross-tabulation**
➤ Row Variable:	**67) VOTED**
➤ Column Variable:	**90) PRTY_DIFFS**
➤ View:	**Table**
➤ Display:	**Column %**

18. On the basis of these results, who is more likely to vote?

    a.   Those who think that there are important differences between what the Democrats and the Republicans stand for

    b.   Those who think that there are not important differences between what the Democrats and the Republicans stand for

Data File:	**NES**
Task:	**Cross-tabulation**
Row Variable:	**67) VOTED**
➤ Column Variable:	**107) ELECT ATTN**
➤ View:	**Table**
➤ Display:	**Column %**

19. On the basis of these results, which of the following statements is most accurate? (Circle one.)

    a.   The more that people feel that elections make the government pay attention, the more likely they are to vote.

    b.   The more that people feel that elections make the government pay attention, the less likely they are to vote.

    c.   There is no pattern here; voting participation is not related to how people view elections.

> *Data File:* **NES**
> *Task:* **Cross-tabulation**
> *Row Variable:* **67) VOTED**
> ➤ *Column Variable:* **103) GOVT WASTE**
> ➤ *View:* **Table**
> ➤ *Display:* **Column %**

20. On the basis of these results, which of the following statements is most accurate? (Circle one.)

    a.   People who feel that the government is wasteful are more likely to vote.

    b.   People who feel that the government is wasteful are less likely to vote.

    c.   There is no relationship between voting participation and perception of governmental wastefulness.

OPINION DIFFERENCES BETWEEN VOTERS AND NONVOTERS

Next we will examine differences between voters and nonvoters in terms of political issue stands. Remember, this requires us to change the survey question asking if someone voted from the row variable to the column variable.

> *Data File:* **NES**
> *Task:* **Cross-tabulation**
> ➤ *Row Variable:* **53) GUN CNTRL**
> ➤ *Column Variable:* **67) VOTED**
> ➤ *View:* **Table**
> ➤ *Display:* **Column %**

21. On the basis of these results, which of the following statements is most accurate? (Circle one.)

    a.   There is no difference between voters and nonvoters in terms of attitudes toward gun control.

    b.   Voters favor tougher gun-control laws more than nonvoters do.

    c.   Nonvoters favor tougher gun-control laws more than voters do.

> *Data File:* **NES**
> *Task:* **Cross-tabulation**
> ➤ *Row Variable:* **46) GOVJOBS**
> ➤ *Column Variable:* **67) VOTED**
> ➤ *View:* **Table**
> ➤ *Display:* **Column %**

22. On the basis of these results, which of the following statements is most accurate? (Circle one.)

    a.   There is no difference between voters and nonvoters in terms of attitudes toward the government guaranteeing a standard of living for people.

    b.   Voters favor a guaranteed standard of living more than nonvoters do.

    c.   Nonvoters favor a guaranteed standard of living more than voters do.

Data File: **NES**
Task: **Cross-tabulation**
➤ Row Variable: **78) IMMIGRANTS**
➤ Column Variable: **67) VOTED**
➤ View: **Table**
➤ Display: **Column %**

23. On the basis of these results, which of the following statements is most accurate? (Circle one.)

    a. There is no difference between voters and nonvoters in terms of attitudes toward immigration.

    b. Voters favor a decrease in immigration more than nonvoters do.

    c. Nonvoters favor a decrease in immigration more than voters do.

24. Overall, on the basis of the preceding analysis of policy differences between voters and non-voters, which of the following statements is most accurate? (Circle one.)

    a. Voters and nonvoters are virtually identical in terms of their policy preferences.

    b. There are some policy differences between voters and nonvoters, but these differences are not extremely high.

    c. Voters and nonvoters are extremely different from one another in terms of their policy preferences.

WHAT HAVE WE LEARNED?

I. Turnout varies across the 50 states from a high of 71.6 percent in Minnesota to a low of 44.5 percent in Hawaii. What factors explain why turnout is higher in one state than another? Are the factors that explain turnout levels across the states similar to or different from the factors that explain why specific individuals do or do not vote?

II. What factors influence whether someone votes or not? Discuss both the influences of demographic traits (e.g., age, education) and attitudes (e.g., political interest).

III. Turnout in the United States is lower than in most other democracies across the world. Low turnout could distort government policies if voters held vastly different policy preferences than nonvoters. What is the evidence on the similarity or dissimilarity in issue positions of voters versus nonvoters? How will this affect the representation of public opinion in public policy in the United States?

WHAT ELSE CAN BE EXPLORED?

1.   Some social scientists are concerned not only that participation in politics is low in the United States, but also that participation in voluntary organizations has dwindled. The NES survey contains two questions on such activity, 96) CIV INVOLV and 97) VOLUNTR. How likely are Americans to report belonging to an organization or volunteering their time? Which Americans are more likely to be engaged in such activities?

2.   In this exercise, age was shown to be a major factor in influencing participation. Younger Americans are less likely to vote than older Americans. Yet, are there differences within the youngest generation of Americans that would explain why some are more likely to vote than others? You can subset the NES survey to include only those respondents from the youngest generation. On the cross-tabulation menu screen, enter 7) AGE as the subset variable. When the next screen appears, click to include "Under 30." This will greatly reduce the sample size to under 300 cases, which will make it more difficult for relationships to be confirmed as statistically significant (i.e., as existing in the population as well as the sample). However, moderate to strong patterns in the sample of survey respondents under 30 also will likely be statistically significant. Do the factors that explain (or do not explain) participation by young Americans differ from those for the American population as a whole?

3.   An increasing number of Americans are taking advantage of changes in state election laws that allow them to vote early. These Americans either send in an absentee ballot or go to a specific location where they can vote prior to election day. Are early voters different from voters who cast their ballot on election day? The NES question, 68) EARLY VOTE, distinguishes between those who voted early and those who voted on election day. One could explore a variety of individual traits as potential independent variables, while using early voting as the dependent variable.

POLITICAL PARTIES

No free Country has ever been without parties,
which are a natural offspring of Freedom.
JAMES MADISON, 1787

Tasks: Mapping, Univariate, Cross-Tabulation, Scatterplot, Historical Trends
Data Files: NATIONS, NES, HISTORY

Political parties can be defined as organizations that sponsor candidates for political office and attempt (to a greater or lesser degree) to coordinate the actions of their elected members. Within this definition of party are three distinct groups of people, each with its important contribution.

First are the people who hold elective or appointive office or who run for office as candidates of the party. These can be identified as the *party-in-government*.

Second are the staff members and political activists who constitute the formal *party organization*. Included here are several million Americans who belong to political parties in the same way that people belong to other organizations: They contribute money, they attend meetings, and they may perform various duties such as passing out campaign literature or helping to turn out voters on election day.

Third, a party also includes all those members of the public who regard themselves as supporters of the party, and these people often are referred to as the *party-in-the-electorate*.

➤ *Data File:* **NATIONS**
➤ *Task:* **Mapping**
➤ *Variable 1:* **36) # PARTIES**
➤ *View:* **Map**

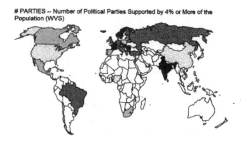

PARTIES -- Number of Political Parties Supported by 4% or More of the Population (WVS)

Nations differ a lot in their number of political parties. Some nations allow only one party and thus provide citizens with no political choices—one-party states are undemocratic and limit many freedoms people take for granted in democracies. In some nations there are two primary parties and any additional parties are too small to have any influence. But many nations have more than two major parties.

<table>
<tr><td>Data File: NATIONS</td></tr>
<tr><td>Task: Mapping</td></tr>
<tr><td>Variable 1: 36) # PARTIES</td></tr>
<tr><td>➤ View: List: Rank</td></tr>
</table>

RANK	CASE NAME	VALUE
1	Slovenia	9
2	Belgium	8
3	Norway	7
3	France	7
3	Romania	7
6	India	6
6	Denmark	6
6	Hungary	6
6	Sweden	6
10	Brazil	5

Here we see that Slovenia has nine significant parties, defined as those able to attract at least 4 percent of the electorate (there are many additional smaller parties in Slovenia and elsewhere). Belgium has eight significant parties, while France, Norway, and Romania have seven each. At the bottom of the list, Ireland, Poland, and Japan have three parties, the United States and Nigeria have only two, and China allows only one.

Data File: NATIONS
Task: Mapping
Variable 1: 36) # PARTIES
➤ <i>Variable 2:</i> 37) %BIG PARTY
➤ <i>Views:</i> Map

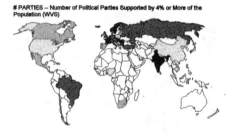

PARTIES -- Number of Political Parties Supported by 4% or More of the Population (WVS)

r = –0.467**

%BIG PARTY -- Percent of Support for the Largest Party (WVS)

This map shows the strength of the leading party. In each nation interviewers asked, "If there were a general election tomorrow, which party would you vote for?" Because some voters in each nation said they were undecided, only in Ireland did 50 percent support the same party. In Chile, 46 percent supported the same party, as did 45 percent of Americans. But in Slovenia and Belgium, the most popular party drew support from only 18 percent of the public and in Switzerland only 16 percent. Clearly, then, where there are many parties, each tends to be small, as is indicated by the negative correlation of –0.467**.

Nations not only differ in how many parties they have, they also differ in how easy it is to join a party. For example, in many nations (including Canada and Great Britain), parties are very tightly controlled national organizations and only candidates selected by the central party committees can run for office under the party label.

By comparison, American political parties are extremely easy to join. Even at the party-in-government level, people often run in and win party primaries without prior party participation and even in opposition to candidates backed by the party organization. For example, Dwight David Eisenhower successfully gained the Republican nomination for president in 1952, defeating Senator Robert A. Taft in primaries and in the convention, without any prior connections to the Republican Party. In fact, he had never even voted before (at that time, many military officers did not vote on the grounds that their allegiance was to the nation, not to any party). As for becoming an official member of the Republican or Democratic parties, it is pretty much a case of just showing up and joining. Even so, few Americans are actual party members (recall how few give money to a party). For most people, political parties are labels attached to candidates and political positions, and their own party "membership" is really only a preference or self-identification.

> ➤ *Data File:* **NES**
> ➤ *Task:* **Univariate**
> ➤ *Primary Variable:* **5) PARTY**
> ➤ *View:* **Pie**

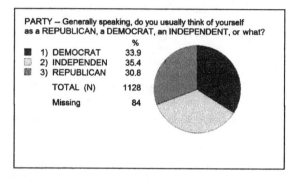

Most Americans are partisans, either Democrats or Republicans, but one in three Americans calls themselves a political independent. Those naming a third party fall below 1 percent.

Partisanship influences a number of other attitudes and activities. Partisanship has a strong effect on the candidates that people support.

> *Data File:* **NES**
> ➤ *Task:* **Cross-tabulation**
> ➤ *Row Variable:* **69) PRESVOTE**
> ➤ *Column Variable:* **5) PARTY**
> ➤ *View:* **Table**
> ➤ *Display:* **Column %**

PRESVOTE   by   PARTY
Cramer's V: 0.726**

| | PARTY | | | | |
	DEMOCRAT	INDEPENDEN	REPUBLICAN	Missing	TOTAL
KERRY	240	128	16	15	384
	90.9%	57.1%	5.5%		49.4%
BUSH	24	96	273	19	393
	9.1%	42.9%	94.5%		50.6%
Missing	118	175	58	50	401
TOTAL	264	224	289	84	777
	100.0%	100.0%	100.0%		

This table clearly shows the strong influence partisanship had on voters' choices in the 2004 presidential election. Ninety-one percent of Democrats voted for John Kerry, while 95 percent of Republicans voted for George W. Bush. Independent voters split their ballots with a slight edge to Kerry. Ralph Nader and various third-party candidates each received less than 1 percent of the vote in the 2004 presidential election. One reason that minor party candidates have such a difficult time in gaining votes is that two-thirds of Americans are either Democrats or Republicans and tend to vote for their own party's candidate. Even independent voters are more likely to support one of the major party candidates rather than voting for a minor party candidate.

While partisanship clearly is linked to voters' choices in presidential elections, partisanship is not always as strongly linked to other political attitudes. Let's examine the relationship between partisanship and political ideology.

Data File: **NES**
Task: **Cross-tabulation**
➤ Row Variable: **16) IDEOLOGY**
➤ Column Variable: **5) PARTY**
➤ View: **Table**
➤ Display: **Column %**

IDEOLOGY by PARTY
Cramer's V: 0.406**

| | | PARTY | | | | |
		DEMOCRAT	INDEPENDEN	REPUBLICAN	Missing	TOTAL
IDEOLOGY	LIBERAL	139	77	14	11	230
		51.3%	26.5%	4.6%		26.5%
	MODERATE	88	128	59	22	275
		32.5%	44.0%	19.3%		31.7%
	CONSERV	44	86	233	19	363
		16.2%	29.6%	76.1%		41.8%
	Missing	111	108	41	32	292
	TOTAL	271	291	306	84	868
		100.0%	100.0%	100.0%		

Republicans show the greatest consistency in their ideology. Nearly three out of four Republicans call themselves conservatives. The Democratic party is much more diverse in terms of ideology. Democrats are split between liberals and moderates. Furthermore, one in six Democrats considers themselves to be conservative.

The Democratic and Republican party organizations rely on individual American citizens to contribute money to support their activities. In the exercise on political participation, we saw that only 6 percent of Americans contribute money to a political party. Are partisans more willing to contribute money than independents?

Data File: **NES**
Task: **Cross-tabulation**
➤ Row Variable: **66) CONT$PARTY**
➤ Column Variable: **5) PARTY**
➤ View: **Table**
➤ Display: **Column %**

CONT$PARTY by PARTY
Cramer's V: 0.161**

| | | PARTY | | | | |
		DEMOCRAT	INDEPENDEN	REPUBLICAN	Missing	TOTAL
CONT$PARTY	YES	30	16	52	3	98
		9.1%	4.6%	16.3%		9.8%
	NO	298	332	267	66	897
		90.9%	95.4%	83.7%		90.2%
	Missing	54	51	28	15	148
	TOTAL	328	348	319	84	995
		100.0%	100.0%	100.0%		

Republicans are slightly more likely to contribute money to a political party than either Democrats or independents. Yet, only one in six Republicans contributes money to the party. Contributing to the political parties is a very infrequent task for all U.S. citizens.

Your turn.

WORKSHEET

NAME:

COURSE:

DATE:

EXERCISE

9

Workbook exercises and software are copyrighted. Copying is prohibited by law.

REVIEW QUESTIONS

Based on the first part of this exercise, answer True or False to the following items:

1. Most democratic nations have at least three major political parties.   T   F

2. Three-fourths of Democrats say they are liberals.   T   F

3. Nearly one-half of the American electorate considers themselves to be political independents.   T   F

4. In the 2004 presidential election, at least three-fourths of partisans supported their own party's presidential candidate.   T   F

5. Republicans are more likely than Democrats to have contributed money to a political party.   T   F

EXPLORIT QUESTIONS

PARTY IN GOVERNMENT

In the opening section of this exercise, we noted that American political parties are often discussed in terms of three components: the party in government, the party in the electorate, and the party organization. Beginning with the party-in-government component, one can note that two major parties, the Democrats and the Republicans, have dominated the government over the past century. All other parties are referred to as third parties or minor parties. How many third-party candidates have been a part of the government? Let's investigate by looking at the percentage of seats in the U.S. House and Senate controlled by members of a third party or by political independents.

> ➤ Data File: **HISTORY**
> ➤ Task: **Historical Trends**
> ➤ Variables: **68) HSE-OTH**
>   **69) SEN-OTH**

Answer True or False to the following items:

6. The percentage of third-party members in the U.S. House often exceeds 20 percent. (*Hint:* Look at the scale on the left-hand side of the graph. The numbers listed are the percentages of seats held by third parties.)   T   F

Exercise 9: Political Parties   155

7. The percentage of third-party members in the U.S. House and Senate has increased substantially in recent years.   T   F

Now let's compare the percentage of seats held by the Democratic versus the Republican party in the U.S. House. The party that has the most seats is referred to as the majority party. The majority party leader becomes the Speaker of the House, and the majority party controls the chairs of all of the congressional committees. The majority party has considerable influence over the decisions made by Congress.

> Data File: **HISTORY**
>> Task: **Historical Trends**
> ➤ Variables: **16) %DEM HOUSE**
>> **70) %REP HOUSE**

Answer True or False to the following items:

8. The Democratic Party was the majority party in the U.S. House from the middle of the 1950s to the middle of the 1990s.   T   F

9. Throughout the 20th century, the Democratic Party was more likely to be the majority party in the House than was the Republican Party.   T   F

Recently, the two political parties have been characterized as becoming more polarized at the elite level–with the Democrats being more consistently liberal and Republicans being more consistently conservative. Let's see if this pattern is confirmed by the voting records of the members of each party in the U.S. House of Representatives. Political scientists Keith Poole and Howard Rosenthal created a method to summarize the voting records of every member of Congress over the entire history of Congress. If the two parties in Congress are becoming more polarized, the voting record of the average Republican in Congress should be moving away from the voting record of the average Democrat in Congress. Let's take a look at the evidence.

> Data File: **HISTORY**
>> Task: **Historical Trends**
> ➤ Variables: **109) C DEM IDEO**
>> **110) C REP IDEO**

10. The two parties in Congress were most polarized in the early 20th century, before 1930.   T   F

11. The two parties in Congress have become more polarized since about 1980 compared to the parties' positions in the mid-20th century (1940–1970).   T   F

PARTY IN THE ELECTORATE

Now let's look at the party in the electorate. Earlier we saw that partisans were more likely than independents to contribute money to political parties. Are partisans more likely than independents to participate in other types of political activities?

> ➤ *Data File:* **NES**
> ➤ *Task:* **Cross-tabulation**
> ➤ *Row Variable:* **67) VOTED**
> ➤ *Column Variable:* **5) PARTY**
> ➤ *View:* **Table**
> ➤ *Display:* **Column %**

12. Democrats and Republicans are about equally likely to vote, but independents
    are considerably less likely to vote.   T   F

> ➤ *Row Variable:* **60) INTEREST?**
> ➤ *Column Variable:* **5) PARTY**
> ➤ *View:* **Table**
> ➤ *Display:* **Column %**

13. Those who claim a party preference are generally less interested in politics
    than are independents.   T   F

> ➤ *Row Variable:* **111) KNOW**
> ➤ *Column Variable:* **5) PARTY**
> ➤ *View:* **Table**
> ➤ *Display:* **Column %**

14. Democrats and independents are about equally as well informed about politics, but
    Republicans are the most informed.   T   F

In Exercise 8, low voter turnouts in the United States were attributed, at least in part, to the limited
choices posed by the two-party system. Let's look at other nations to see if there is any support for
this idea.

> ➤ *Data File:* **NATIONS**
> ➤ *Task:* **Scatterplot**
> ➤ *Dependent Variable:* **38) % VOTED**
> ➤ *Independent Variable:* **36) # PARTIES**
> ➤ *View:* **Reg. Line**

Answer True or False to the following items:

15. The greater the number of political parties in a nation, the higher the percentage
    voting.   T   F

16. This scatterplot supports the idea that the limited choice of parties in the
    United States may be depressing the voter turnout rate.   T   F

Let's see who's most likely to be a Democrat and who's most likely to be a Republican.

> *Data File:* **NES**
>   *Task:* **Cross-tabulation**
> *Row Variable:* **5) PARTY**
> *Column Variable:* **1) SEX**
>   *View:* **Table**
>   *Display:* **Column %**

Remember to look to see whether the relationship is statistically significant before answering the following questions.

17. Women are slightly more likely to be Democrats, while men are slightly
    more likely to be independents.   T   F

> *Data File:* **NES**
>   *Task:* **Cross-tabulation**
> *Row Variable:* **5) PARTY**
> *Column Variable:* **2) RACE**
>   *View:* **Table**
>   *Display:* **Column %**

18. African Americans are the most likely to be Democrats.   T   F

> *Data File:* **NES**
>   *Task:* **Cross-tabulation**
> *Row Variable:* **5) PARTY**
> *Column Variable:* **8) RELIGION**
>   *View:* **Table**
>   *Display:* **Column %**

19. Protestant, and Catholics are very similar in their partisanship, while Jews are more likely to be
    Democrats.

> *Data File:* **NES**
>   *Task:* **Cross-tabulation**
> *Row Variable:* **5) PARTY**
> *Column Variable:* **11) UNION**
>   *View:* **Table**
>   *Display:* **Column %**

20. Union members are more likely to be Democrats than people who do
    not belong to unions.   T   F

Data File:	**NES**
Task:	**Cross-tabulation**
Row Variable:	**5) PARTY**
➤ *Column Variable:*	**6) MARITAL**
➤ *View:*	**Table**
➤ *Display:*	**Column %**

21. Those who are married are more likely to be Republicans while those who have never married are more likely to be independents.   T   F

Data File:	**NES**
Task:	**Cross-tabulation**
Row Variable:	**5) PARTY**
➤ *Column Variable:*	**3) INCOME**
➤ *View:*	**Table**
➤ *Display:*	**Column %**

22. The higher the income, the more likely one is a Republican.   T   F

How different are Democrats from Republicans? The parties in Congress have become more polarized in recent years, with Democrats being liberal and Republicans being conservative. Is the party in the electorate polarized as well? To compare Democrats to Republicans, we will make party the column variable and various issues as the row variables.

Data File:	**NES**
Task:	**Cross-tabulation**
➤ *Row Variable:*	**88) GAY MIL**
➤ *Column Variable:*	**5) PARTY**
➤ *View:*	**Table**
➤ *Display:*	**Column %**

23. Based on the value of Cramer's V, the relationship between party and opinions on gays serving in the military is

    a.   nonexistent; the relationship is statistically insignificant.

    b.   weak but statistically significant; Cramer's V is between .00 and .10.

    c.   moderate; Cramer's V is between .10 and .25.

    d.   strong; Cramer's V is over .25.

> *Data File:* **NES**
> *Task:* **Cross-tabulation**
> ➤ *Row Variable:* **45) INSURANCE**
> ➤ *Column Variable:* **5) PARTY**
> ➤ *View:* **Table**
> ➤ *Display:* **Column %**

24. Based on the value of Cramer's V, the relationship between party and opinions on government-provided versus private health insurance is

    a. nonexistent; the relationship is statistically insignificant.

    b. weak but statistically significant; Cramer's V is between .00 and .10.

    c. moderate; Cramer's V is between .10 and .25.

    d. strong; Cramer's V is over .25.

> *Data File:* **NES**
> *Task:* **Cross-tabulation**
> ➤ *Row Variable:* **52) DEATH PEN**
> ➤ *Column Variable:* **5) PARTY**
> ➤ *View:* **Table**
> ➤ *Display:* **Column %**

25. Based on the value of Cramer's V, the relationship between party and opinions on the death penalty is

    a. nonexistent; the relationship is statistically insignificant.

    b. weak but statistically significant; Cramer's V is between .00 and .10.

    c. moderate; Cramer's V is between .10 and .25.

    d. strong; Cramer's V is over .25.

> *Data File:* **NES**
> *Task:* **Cross-tabulation**
> ➤ *Row Variable:* **33) INTL POLCY**
> ➤ *Column Variable:* **5) PARTY**
> ➤ *View:* **Table**
> ➤ *Display:* **Column %**

26. Based on the value of Cramer's V, the relationship between party and opinions on the usefulness of diplomacy versus military force is

    a. nonexistent; the relationship is statistically insignificant.

    b. weak but statistically significant; Cramer's V is between .00 and .10.

    c. moderate; Cramer's V is between .10 and .25.

    d. strong; Cramer's V is over .25.

27. Which of the following statements best summarizes the preceding patterns between partisanship and issue positions. (Circle one.)

    a. The American public is deeply polarized. Democrats and Republicans hold vastly different opinions on all of these issues. The relationships between partisanship and issues are all strong.

    b. The American public is somewhat polarized. Democrats and Republicans often display moderate to strong differences on these issues.

    c. The American public is only mildly polarized. While Democrats and Republicans have different positions on these issues, the relationships are mostly weak.

    d. The American public is not polarized. The relationships between party identification and these issues were neither statistically nor substantively significant.

PARTY ORGANIZATION

Finally, let's examine the financial standing of the two major parties. An important component of the party organization is the ability to raise money. Money is needed to fund the national headquarters, to pay staff, to conduct polling, and to assist the party's candidates. Are the two political parties on an equal financial footing? Let's examine the money raised (in millions of dollars) by the Democratic and Republican parties over recent decades.

    ➤ *Data File:* **HISTORY**
        ➤ *Task:* **Historical Trends**
    ➤ *Variables:* **71) DEM$**
             72) REP$

28. The Republican Party raises more funds than the Democratic Party.   T   F

WHAT HAVE WE LEARNED?

I.   The two-party system greatly influences Congressional politics. Describe the strength of the Democratic and Republican parties over the years in Congress. How important have third parties been in Congress? What have been the voting patterns of the average Democratic versus the average Republican member of the U.S. House in the 20th century?

II.   How distinctive are the two parties in the electorate? Are there groups of Americans who are more likely to view themselves as Republicans and other groups of Americans who view themselves as Democrats? How different are the issue positions of Democrats versus Republicans?

III.   "Because of their keen interest in following politics, independents make their decisions on an issue-by-issue basis and refused to be categorized by party." Do you agree or disagree with this statement based on the analyses in this exercise?

<u>WHAT ELSE CAN BE EXPLORED?</u>

1. The NES survey asked a number of questions about the performance of President Bush and his actions during his first administration. Respondents were asked if they generally approved of Bush's performance as president, 21) BUSH APP; if they approved of the U.S. war in Afghanistan, 38) AFGHAN WAR and in Iraq, 39) IRAQ WAR; and whether they approved or disapproved of Bush's tax cuts, 44) TAXCUT. How strongly does partisanship shape public opinion toward Bush's presidency? Does partisanship matter more for specific elements of Bush's record, or does partisanship have a uniform effect for all the elements?

2. Divided government is when one party controls Congress and the president is from the other party. Advocates of divided government feel that this adds to the division of power in the United States and prevents one party or one branch of government from becoming too powerful. Others, however, point out that the creation of dramatically new public policy often requires the additional coordination that comes when one party controls both the presidency and Congress. What is the preference of the American public for divided versus unified government? The NES survey question, 29) DIV GOVT, asked respondents which one they preferred. What might be some factors that explain why some Americans prefer divided government and others prefer unified government?

3. Does the American public differentiate between the two parties in their policy effectiveness? The NES survey asked respondents if they felt the Democratic or Republican party would be more effective at handling the nation's economy, 34) PRTY ECON; the war on terrorism, 35) PRTY TERRO; and keeping the U.S. out of war, 36) PRTY PEACE. Which party is seen more effective in each of these policy areas? How strongly does an individual's partisanship affect their evaluations of the effectiveness of the two parties in these policy areas?

ELECTIONS

Bad politicians are sent to Washington by good people who don't vote.

WILLIAM E. SIMON, 1985

Tasks: Mapping, Cross-Tabulation
Data Files: STATES, NES

By law, all positions in the House of Representatives and one-third of those in the Senate are filled by an election held on the first Tuesday after the first Monday in November in every even-numbered year. Consequently, all members of the House face reelection every two years and all senators every six. In addition, every second national election is a presidential election as presidents of the United States serve a four-year term (and are limited to two elected terms by the 22nd Amendment, adopted in 1951). Unlike elections for other offices, both national and local, American presidents are elected in a somewhat unusual way.

➤ *Data File:* **STATES**
➤ *Task:* **Mapping**
➤ *Variable 1:* **207) GWBUSH'00**
➤ *Variable 2:* **218) GWBUSH'04**
➤ *View:* **Map**

GWBUSH'00 – 2000: Percent Voting for George W. Bush (Republican) (SOS)

r = 0.0973**

GWBUSH'04 – 2004: Percent Voting for George W. Bush (Republican) (SOS)

These two maps show how people voted for George W. Bush in the 2000 and 2004 presidential elections. Since these are the ballots cast by individual voters, they are referred to as the popular vote. In these maps, the darker the state, the higher percentage of that state's voters who supported Bush. In 2004, Bush received over 62 million votes compared to the 59 million votes cast for his opponent, John Kerry. In percentage terms, Bush won 51 percent of the popular vote while Kerry attracted 48 percent. Also notice that Bush's popular vote in the 50 states in 2004 was very similar to his popular vote in 2000, with Pearson's r showing an almost perfect correlation of 0.973**.

Yet one major difference exists between the 2000 and 2004 presidential elections. In 2000 Bush lost the popular vote to Al Gore, with Gore receiving approximately 500,000 more votes than George W. Bush. However, 105 million votes were cast in the 2000 presidential election, so Gore's margin of victory over Bush in the popular vote was less than 1 percent of the total votes cast. The popular vote in the 2000 presidential election was one of the closest in history. Despite winning the popular vote, Gore lost the presidential election to Bush. Let's see how this happened.

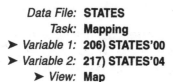

Data File: **STATES**
Task: **Mapping**
➤ Variable 1: **206) STATES'00**
➤ Variable 2: **217) STATES'04**
➤ View: **Map**

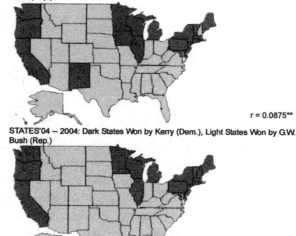

STATES'00 – 2000: Dark States Won by Gore (Dem.), Light States Won by G.W. Bush (Rep.)

r = 0.0875**

STATES'04 – 2004: Dark States Won by Kerry (Dem.), Light States Won by G.W. Bush (Rep.)

In 2000, Gore had the most votes in 20 states plus Washington D.C. George W. Bush won 30 states. Bush garnered 271 electoral college votes from those 30 states. A candidate needs to win a majority of the electoral college votes to become president. Since there are 538 electoral college votes, a candidate needs to win a minimum of 270 electoral college votes to become president. George W. Bush won the presidency with only one more electoral college vote than needed. The 2000 presidential election was indeed an extremely close race.

In 2004, Bush once again won the electoral college vote, but this time by a slightly larger margin. Bush picked up the electoral college vote from two new states in 2004, Iowa and New Mexico, while losing one state (New Hampshire) that he carried in 2000. Thus, in 2004 Bush carried 31 states for 286 electoral college votes, while Kerry carried 19 states to earn 252 electoral college votes.

Electoral votes exist because the Constitution does not provide for the direct election of the president or vice president. Instead, Article II of the Constitution directs that the president and vice president shall be elected by a group known as the **electoral college**:

> Each State shall appoint, in such Manner as the Legislature thereof may direct, a Number of Electors, equal to the whole Number of Senators and Representatives to which the State may be entitled in the Congress; but no Senator or Representative, or Person holding an Office of Trust or Profit under the United States, shall be appointed an Elector.

Once appointed, each state's electors were directed to gather (thereby constituting an electoral college) whereupon each would vote for two persons—at least one of whom could not be a resident of their state—and these votes then were to be forwarded to the president of the Senate (who always is the current vice president). The votes of all electors from all states then were to be opened and counted.

The person receiving a majority of the electoral college votes was elected president. After the president was elected, the person receiving the second most votes was elected vice president. When no person received a majority, or a tie occurred, then the House of Representatives chose the president from the five highest vote getters in the electoral college. The representatives of each state voted as a state delegation and thus had one vote. The person having the majority of the votes was elected president. If there was a tie for vice president, the Senate elected the vice president. Each senator cast a vote, and it required a majority to be elected.

In 1804 the 12th Amendment made several changes in this procedure. Each elector was to cast two separate votes, one for president, the other for vice president. When no person received a majority, or a tie occurred, in the vote for president, then the House of Representatives chose the president from the three highest vote getters in the electoral college. Again, the representatives of each state voted as a state delegation and thus had one vote. The person having the majority of the votes was elected president. When no person received the majority, or a tie occurred, in the vote for vice president, the Senate elected the vice president from the top two vote getters in the electoral college. Each senator cast a vote, and it required a majority to be elected.

Because each state has the number of electors equal to its total membership in Congress, and each state is guaranteed at least one representative and two senators, no state will have fewer than three electors. The 23rd Amendment to the Constitution, which took effect in 1961, gives three electoral college votes to the residents of Washington D.C. Since the nation's capital is not part of any state, prior to that date, residents of Washington D.C. had no say in the selection of the president. The Constitution leaves it to the states *how* the electors shall be selected, and in early days they often were selected by the state legislatures. As time passed, and political parties emerged, people began to campaign to be selected as electors on the basis of their promise to vote for a specific presidential candidate. Eventually, electors were selected by the voters in each state.

Thus, we do not vote directly for the president or vice president. Instead, each party files a slate of electors committed to cast their votes (now called electoral votes) for the party's presidential and vice presidential candidates. When we mark our ballots for a particular person for president, what we really are doing is voting for the appropriate slate of electors. The winning candidate in each state, the one with the most votes whether or not these are more than half of all votes, receives *all* of that state's electoral votes because the winner's slate of electors is elected. Following each election, in December, each elector casts his or her official vote, and these are sent to the U.S. Senate where they are counted under the supervision of the vice president (of the previous administration) and reported to Congress. Once in a while an elector votes for someone other than the candidate he or she was pledged to support. In 2000, one of the electors chosen from Washington D.C. left the ballot blank, reducing Al Gore's electoral college vote from 267 to 266. The elector left the ballot blank to protest the fact that residents of Washington D.C. have no voting members in the U.S. Congress.

Although it takes a majority of electoral votes to be elected, at the state level it's winner-take-all. All of a state's electoral votes go to the candidate receiving the most votes. Maine and Nebraska use winner-take-all at the state level to assign two of their electors and winner-take-all at the congressional district to assign their remaining electors. Sometimes, candidates win a state's electors with less than a majority vote. In fact, a candidate only needs to win more votes than any other candidate on the ballot. This is winning by a **plurality** of the votes cast. Typically in U.S. presidential elections, almost all of the votes are cast for the Democratic or Republican presidential candidate. However, when a significant portion of the vote is cast for a third-party or independent candidate, a presidential candidate may win many of the electoral college votes by plurality victories in the states' popular vote. When this occurs in a number of states, the candidate winning the electoral college may have a plurality of the popular vote but not a majority of the popular vote. Presidents who receive less than half of the total popular vote are sometimes called "minority presidents." President Clinton won less than a majority of the popular vote in the 1992 and 1996 presidential elections due to the number of votes cast for third-party candidate Ross Perot.

Data File: **STATES**
Task: **Mapping**
➤ Variable 1: **238) ELECTOR'00**
➤ View: **List: Rank**

RANK	CASE NAME	VALUE
1	California	55
2	Texas	34
3	New York	31
4	Florida	27
5	Pennsylvania	21
5	Illinois	21
7	Ohio	20
8	Michigan	17
9	New Jersey	15
9	North Carolina	15

Here we see the current distribution of electoral votes by state in 2004. California has 55 electoral votes, or 10 percent of the total. Next come Texas (34), New York (31), Florida (27), Pennsylvania (21), Illinois (21), and Ohio (20). In contrast, seven states have only 3 electoral votes and five have only 4. Put another way, the 12 least populous states have fewer electoral votes (41) among them than does California alone.

Every ten years, following each census, the House of Representatives is **reapportioned** as seats in the House are shifted to growing states. Reapportionment of the House automatically shifts electoral votes too. Consequently, the number of electoral votes shifts in response to shifts in the relative size of state populations.

Electoral college vote totals changed for some states by the 2004 presidential election. Results from the 2000 census show which states gained more citizens and which states lost citizens, or at least not grown as fast. The 2000 census figures were used to reapportion the seats in the House of Representatives and thus adjust the electoral college votes for each state as well.

Data File: **STATES**
Task: **Mapping**
➤ Variable 1: **240) EC GAIN'00**
➤ View: **Map**

EC GAIN'00 -- 1990-2000: Gain (Loss) of Electoral Votes

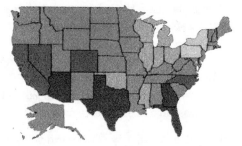

Two states, New York and Pennsylvania, had two fewer electoral college votes in 2004 than they did in the 2000 presidential election. Eight other states, mostly in the Midwest, lost one electoral college vote. On the other hand, four states—Arizona, Florida, Georgia, and Texas—gained two electoral college votes, while four additional states picked up one vote each. Once again the movement of Americans away from the "rust belt" of the Midwest and East to the Sunbelt of the South and West has altered the political clout of the states in presidential elections.

Your turn.

Part III: Government and the Individual

WORKSHEET

NAME:

COURSE:

DATE:

EXERCISE

10

REVIEW QUESTIONS

Based on the first part of this exercise, answer True or False to the following items:

1. Reapportionment is the process of adjusting seats in the House based on population shifts in the United States.   T   F

2. In case of a tie in electoral votes, the Senate selects the president.   T   F

3. No state may have fewer than three electoral votes.   T   F

4. "Minority president" refers to presidents who won because of their overwhelming support by racial and ethnic minority voters.   T   F

5. In 2000, George W. Bush won the electoral college vote while losing the popular vote.   T   F

6. George W. Bush's vote in 2004 came primarily from the same states that he won in the 2000 election.   T   F

EXPLORIT QUESTIONS

THE EFFECTS OF THE ELECTORAL COLLEGE

It takes 270 electoral college votes to win an election. Although each state has at least three electoral college votes, the number of electoral college votes varies across the states.

> ➤ Data File: **STATES**
> ➤ Task: **Mapping**
> ➤ Variable 1: **238) ELECTOR'00**
> ➤ View: **List: Rank**

7. How many states have 20 or more electoral college votes?   _____

8. How many states have 5 or fewer electoral college votes?   _____

Suppose you are the campaign manager for a presidential candidate. One of your tasks is to determine which voters you want to reach in the campaign. Remember, it is a majority vote in the electoral college, rather than a plurality victory in the popular vote, that ultimately determines the winner of the

Exercise 10: Elections

presidency. Thus, a winning campaign strategy requires a plan to garner 270 electoral college votes. One way to investigate candidate strategy is to see which states, candidates visit during the fall campaign. No candidate can visit all 50 states in the crucial campaign months of September and October. Rather, candidates select states which they view as essential to an electoral college victory.

One strategy might be to build on past support. If Bush followed this strategy in 2004, he should have campaigned more frequently in states where he received a higher percentage of the vote in 2000.

> Data File: **STATES**
> Task: **Mapping**
> ➤ Variable 1: **243) BSH-VIS'04**
> ➤ Variable 2: **207) GWBUSH'00**
> ➤ View: **MAP**

9. What is the Pearson's r between number of Bush visits to a state in 2004 and
his support from that state in 2000?   r = _____

Another electoral difference between the states is how close the vote was in the last presidential election. We all remember the close vote and subsequent ballot recounts in Florida in 2000. The Florida vote was essentially a tie, with Bush winning a few hundred votes more than Gore. At the other extreme is a state such as Utah, where Bush led Gore by 41 percentage points. Variable CMPTV'00 measures how close the vote was in the 2000 election, with a score of 1 indicating a 50-50 split in the vote and a score of 0 indicating one candidate received all the votes.

> Data File: **STATES**
> Task: **Mapping**
> Variable 1: **243) BSH-VIS'04**
> ➤ Variable 2: **247) CMPTV'00**
> ➤ View: **MAP**

10. What is the Pearson's r between number of Bush visits to a state and
the competitiveness of a state?   r = _____

11. Based solely on these results, in what types of states would you advise your presidential candidate to spend a great deal of time and money campaigning?

     a.   States where a candidate (or the candidate's party) has done well in the past so as to maximize the total number of popular votes received.

     b.   States which have been the most competitive in the past so as to increase the total number of states won in the electoral college.

In 1992, Ross Perot ran as a third-party candidate for president and won almost 20 percent of the popular vote, yet he received no electoral college votes. Let's see how this happened.

Data File: **STATES**
Task: **Mapping**
➤ Variable 1: **201) %PEROT'92**
➤ View: **List: Rank**

The chart below lists the six states in which Perot received his highest vote totals. Already listed are the vote percentages for Bill Clinton and George H. W. Bush. Enter the percent of vote Perot received in each of these states based on the information in variable 201) PEROT'92.

	Perot	Clinton	Bush
12. Maine	_____%	38.8%	30.4%
13. Alaska	_____%	30.3%	39.5%
14. Utah	_____%	24.7%	43.4%
15. Kansas	_____%	33.7%	38.9%
16. Idaho	_____%	28.4%	42.0%
17. Nevada	_____%	37.4%	34.7%

18. In how many of these states was Perot the plurality winner? _____ (Enter a number from 0 to 6.)

19. Based on these results, in how many of these states would Perot receive electoral college votes? _____ (Enter a number from 0 to 6.)

In 1968, George Wallace ran as a third-party candidate for president and won 14 percent of the popular vote. He won 46 electoral college votes. Let's see how Wallace could win so many electoral college votes when Perot, with a higher percentage of the popular vote, won none.

Data File: **STATES**
Task: **Mapping**
➤ Variable 1: **185) WALLACE'68**
➤ View: **List: Rank**

The chart below lists the six states in which Wallace received his highest vote totals. Already listed are the vote percentages for Richard Nixon and Hubert Humphrey. Enter the percent of vote Wallace received in each of these states based on the information in variable 185) WALLACE'68.

	Wallace	Nixon	Humphrey
20. Alabama	_____%	14.0%	18.8%
21. Mississippi	_____%	13.5%	23.0%
22. Louisiana	_____%	23.5%	28.2%
23. Georgia	_____%	30.4%	26.8%
24. Arkansas	_____%	30.8%	30.4%
25. Tennessee	_____%	37.9%	28.1%

26. In how many of these states was Wallace the plurality winner? _____ (Enter a number from 0 to 6.)

27. Based on these results, in how many of these states would Wallace receive electoral college votes? _____ (Enter a number from 0 to 6.)

28. A third-party candidate, receiving 20 percent of the popular vote nationwide, can win electoral college votes

     a.   by receiving an equal percentage of the popular vote in each state.

     b.   by having support concentrated in a smaller number of states.

     c.   under no circumstances.

INDIVIDUAL-LEVEL VOTING BEHAVIOR

Now let's explore factors that may have led individual voters to decide to support Bush over Kerry, or vice versa. One of the major models used by political scientists to explain voters' choices looks at the influence of partisanship, issues, and candidate evaluations. In Exercise 9, we saw that partisanship had an extremely strong effect on voters' choices in the 2004 presidential election. The value of Cramer's V was 0.726**. How important were issues in shaping voters' decisions? We'll begin with a basic question on the role of the government: Should the government provide more or fewer services?

         ➤ Data File: **NES**
            ➤ Task: **Cross-tabulation**
       ➤ Row Variable: **69) PRESVOTE**
    ➤ Column Variable: **41) GOVT SPEND**
           ➤ View: **Table**
         ➤ Display: **Column %**

29. What is the value of Cramer's V for this table?   V = _____

30. Those who favored more government services were the most likely to
    vote for George Bush.   T   F

> Data File: **NES**
> Task: **Cross-tabulation**
> Row Variable: **69) PRESVOTE**
> ➤ Column Variable: **82) SS REFORM?**
> ➤ View: **Table**
> ➤ Display: **Column**

31. What is the value of Cramer's V for this table?   V = _____

32. Those who favored Social Security reforms that included placing a portion of
    their payroll taxes into personal retirement accounts were the most likely to vote
    for George Bush.   T   F

> Data File: **NES**
> Task: **Cross-tabulation**
> Row Variable: **69) PRESVOTE**
> ➤ Column Variable: **56) GAY MARR**
> ➤ View: **Table**
> ➤ Display: **Column**

33. What is the value of Cramer's V for this table?   V = _____

34. Those opposed to gay marriage were more likely to vote for George Bush than
    were those who favored gay marriage.   T   F

35. Which of the following had the strongest influence on voters' choices in the 2004 presidential
    election?
    a.   partisanship
    b.   level of government services
    c.   Social Security reform
    d.   gay marriage

A second model that political scientists apply to explain voters' choices is one that uses evaluations
of the performance of the incumbent president. Under this model, if a person liked the performance
of the incumbent president, that person would vote to reelect the president. If a person disliked the
performance of the incumbent president, that person would vote "to throw the rascal out." Presidents
are blamed or credited for the performance of the economy during their term in office. Let's see how
these evaluations influenced voters' choices in the 2004 election.

Data File: **NES**
Task: **Cross-tabulation**
Row Variable: **69) PRESVOTE**
➤ Column Variable: **32) ECONOMY**
➤ View: **Table**
➤ Display: **Column**

36. What is the value of Cramer's V for this table?   V = _____

37. Evaluations of the economy had a strong influence on voters' choices: Those
who thought the economy had gotten better voted overwhelmingly for George
Bush and those who thought the economy had gotten worse voted
overwhelmingly for John Kerry.   T   F

A major decision of President Bush in his first term in office was to go to war with Iraq. How did evaluations of this decision influence voters' decisions?

Data File: **NES**
Task: **Cross-tabulation**
Row Variable: **69) PRESVOTE**
➤ Column Variable: **39) IRAQ WAR**
➤ View: **Table**
➤ Display: **Column**

38. What is the value of Cramer's V for this table?   V = _____

39. Evaluations of the Iraq war strongly influenced voters' decisions in the 2004
presidential election.   T   F

40. The evidence from the last two tables _____ the notion that voters use evaluations of the
incumbent president's performance when deciding how to vote in presidential elections.

    a.   strongly supports

    b.   weakly supports

    c.   does not support

WHAT HAVE WE LEARNED?

I.   How does the electoral college shape the conduct and outcome of presidential elections? In your answer, include an explanation of (1) how the electoral college influences candidates' strategies, (2) how the electoral college influences the fate of third-party candidates, and (3) the unusual effect of the electoral college in the 2000 presidential election.

II.   How did the 2000 presidential election shape the outcome of the 2004 presidential election? Did George Bush draw his support from the same states in both elections? How did President Bush's performance in office during his first term influence voters' choices in the 2004 election?

III. How did people's partisanship and views on political issues shape their choice of candidates in the 2004 presidential election? What had a stronger influence, partisanship or issues?

WHAT ELSE CAN BE EXPLORED?

1. Which groups of Americans supported George Bush and which groups of Americans cast their ballots for John Kerry? The AUTO-ANALYZER function in MicroCase can be used to uncover the effects of demographic variables such as race, education, and income. What might explain these patterns in group voting?

2. In this exercise we explored the effects of three issues (level of government services, Social Security reform, and gay marriage). The NES survey contains questions on a variety of other issues. How strongly did some of these other issues affect voters' choices in the 2004 presidential election?

3. In this exercise the analyses focused on the presidential election. Yet, each election year the ballot is filled with other races. The NES survey contains voters' choices for the U.S. House of Representatives and the U.S. Senate: 70) VOTE HOUSE and 71) VOTE SEN. What types of factors might explain whether an individual voter chose the Democratic or Republican candidate in these races? One factor to keep in mind is that in congressional races incumbents generally win. Thus, the variables 58) HSE TYPE and 59) SENTYPE indicate whether a contest had a Democratic or Republican incumbent running. This variable on type of contest could be entered as a control variable on the MicroCase cross-tabulation menu screen.

INTEREST GROUPS AND PACS

> *Politics has got so expensive that it takes lots of money to even get beat with nowadays.*
> WILL ROGERS, 1931

Tasks: Mapping, Univariate, Cross-Tabulation
Data Files: NATIONS, GSS, HOUSE108

Quite often in politics, elected public officials or candidates for political office attack "special interest groups" or "pressure groups," or they suggest that their opponents or critics are in league with such groups. What is the difference between a "special interest group," an "interest group," a "pressure group," and a "group of public-spirited citizens"? The answer a person gives to this question might very well depend on which side of an issue the person favors. People tend to view groups on the other side of an issue in negative terms, referring to them as "special interest groups" or "pressure groups." On the other hand, groups involved in political issues often tend to view themselves as citizens who are looking out for the public interest either directly or indirectly.

Here we will use the term "interest group" in a neutral fashion to refer to any group of people who share some political value and attempt to pursue that value in the political system. This shared political value might be economic (e.g., views on tax decreases, aid to education, minimum wage laws) or noneconomic (e.g., views on abortion, freedom of speech, the rights of defendants in court).

Two basic kinds of interest groups exist: *affinity groups*, which are unorganized publics sharing a particular condition or concern such as elderly people who feel that current Social Security payments are inadequate, and *organized groups* (such as the American Association of Retired Persons), which collect dues and use them to sustain professional staffs to influence both public opinion and public officials. Another example of an affinity group consists of people who share certain views about civil liberties. Not everyone who shares this set of views is part of an organized group, but an example of an organized group dealing with civil liberties is the American Civil Liberties Union.

If you think about affinity groups, you will recognize that most, if not all, Americans belong to an interest group and most of us belong to many. The problem is that we tend to define *our* interest groups as unselfish and in the general interest while opposing *other* people's interest groups as selfish and out to harm the rest of us.

➤ *Data File:* **GSS**
➤ *Task:* **Univariate**
➤ *Primary Variable:* **31) SOC.SEC.$**
➤ *View:* **Pie**

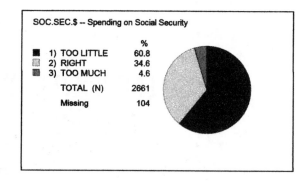

Here we see that over half (60.8 percent) of Americans think we are spending too little on Social Security. There can be little doubt that among those wanting an increase is an interest group that has become a favorite in political campaigning, variously referred to as "our neglected senior citizens" or as the "selfish Social Security lobby," depending on the candidate.

Data File: **GSS**
➤ *Task:* **Cross-tabulation**
➤ *Row Variable:* **31) SOC.SEC.$**
➤ *Column Variable:* **9) AGE**
➤ *View:* **Table**
➤ *Display:* **Column %**

SOC.SEC.$ by   AGE
Cramer's V: 0.113**

| | | AGE | | | | | | |
		UNDER 30	30 TO 39	40 TO 49	50 TO 64	65 & OVER	Missing	TOTAL
SOC.SEC.$	TOO LITTLE	289	374	344	365	240	6	1612
		58.0%	66.1%	65.5%	62.4%	50.3%		60.8%
	RIGHT	174	159	156	198	229	4	916
		34.9%	28.1%	29.7%	33.8%	48.0%		34.6%
	TOO MUCH	35	33	25	22	8	0	123
		7.0%	5.8%	4.8%	3.8%	1.7%		4.6%
	Missing	32	24	20	14	10	4	104
	TOTAL	498	566	525	585	477	14	2651
		100.0%	100.0%	100.0%	100.0%	100.0%		

Everyone knows that people on Social Security are militant about their rights and never think they are getting enough benefits. But in this case, what "everyone" knows, isn't so. People over 65 are least likely to think too little is being spent on Social Security.

Data File: **GSS**
Task: **Cross-tabulation**
➤ *Row Variable:* **41) GUN LAW?**
➤ *Column Variable:* **69) OWN GUN?**
➤ *View:* **Table**
➤ *Display:* **Column %**

GUN LAW?   by   OWN GUN?
Cramer's V: 0.254**

| | | OWN GUN? | | | |
		YES	NO	Missing	TOTAL
GUN LAW?	FAVOR	206	527	4	733
		66.9%	88.0%		80.8%
	OPPOSE	102	72	5	174
		33.1%	12.0%		19.2%
	Missing	2	6	1841	1849
	TOTAL	308	599	1850	907
		100.0%	100.0%		

Something else we all know is that gun owners bitterly oppose all gun-control legislation. But this table shows that isn't so. Here we see that 66.9 percent of gun owners favored a law requiring that a person obtain a police permit before buying a gun. It's not gun owners as an affinity interest group who oppose gun-control laws; rather, it is the organized interest group known as the National Rifle Association that is in opposition to such laws.

These findings let us recognize something very important about interest groups—that organized interest groups may or may not represent the constituency for whom they claim to speak.

Data File: **GSS**
Task: **Cross-tabulation**
Row Variable: **41) GUN LAW?**
➤ Column Variable: **31) SOC.SEC.$**
➤ View: **Table**
➤ Display: **Total %**

GUN LAW? by SOC.SEC.$
Cramer's V: 0.126**

		SOC.SEC.$				
		TOO LITTLE	RIGHT	TOO MUCH	Missing	TOTAL
GUN LAW?	FAVOR	441	250	22	24	713
		49.8%	28.2%	2.5%		80.6%
	OPPOSE	88	69	15	7	172
		9.9%	7.8%	1.7%		19.4%
	Missing	1089	601	86	73	1849
	TOTAL	529	319	37	104	885
		59.8%	36.0%	4.2%		

An extremely important point about memberships in interest groups is that the same person is usually included in a variety of such groups. Thus, a person might side with particular people on one issue and different people on another issue. Here we see that the views of people on Social Security overlap somewhat with their views on gun control (V = 0.126**). This time the instructions asked for the total percent to be listed in each cell of the table. The total percent is the number of respondents in each cell divided by the total number of respondents answering the two questions. Thus, 49.8 percent of the respondents to the 2002 GSS indicated that they wanted both tougher gun-control laws and more spending on Social Security. However, half of the sample had some other combination of answers. On another set of issues we might find that some of those who favor tougher gun-control laws might be on one side of the issue while another portion of those who favor tougher gun-control laws takes a different position on the second issue. People do not consistently line up on the same side of every issue.

This is important for the stability of a political system because it means that there are not just two permanent "sides" in political conflict. The coalitions for or against something can shift with the issue. A person who loses on one issue might win on another issue. This helps to reduce the overall conflict within society.

➤ Data File: **NATIONS**
➤ Task: **Mapping**
➤ Variable 1: **7) INTEREST G**
➤ View: **List: Rank**

RANK	CASE NAME	VALUE
1	Iceland	27
2	Netherlands	24
2	Norway	24
4	Latvia	23
4	United States	23
4	Finland	23
7	South Korea	20
8	Switzerland	18
8	Austria	18
8	Brazil	18

Organized interest groups are not peculiar to American politics. About 1 person in 4 belongs to an organized political interest group in Iceland, the Netherlands, Norway, the United States, Finland, and Latvia. That drops to 1 in 20 persons in Argentina, Spain, and Rumania, and to only 1 in 33 in Japan.

We noted earlier that organized interest groups may or may not accurately reflect the concerns and preferences of those they presume to represent. But, if this is so, why do politicians pay so much attention to organized interest groups? Because they are one of the sources of campaign funds.

INTEREST GROUPS AND CONGRESSIONAL ELECTIONS

A primary fact of life facing every elected official is that the next election is always just around the corner and it costs money to win elections. Since they are up for reelection every two years, many members of the House are never really able to cease campaigning, and perhaps the single most central aspect of campaigning is fund-raising.

➤ *Data File:* **HOUSE108**
➤ *Task:* **Univariate**
➤ *Primary Variable:* **26) CAMPAIGN $**
➤ *View:* **Pie**

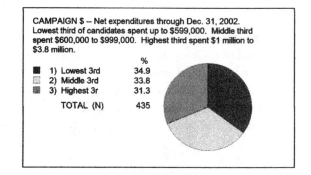

CAMPAIGN $ – Net expenditures through Dec. 31, 2002. Lowest third of candidates spent up to $599,000. Middle third spent $600,000 to $999,000. Highest third spent $1 million to $3.8 million.

		%
■	1) Lowest 3rd	34.9
▒	2) Middle 3rd	33.8
▓	3) Highest 3r	31.3
	TOTAL (N)	435

More than two-thirds of the representatives spent at least $600,000 on their 2002 campaigns. The highest amount ($3.8 million) was spent by Nancy Johnson (R-CT), Representative Tom Osborne (R-NE) spent the least amount of money on his campaign, $81,357, but he had no opponent. Representative Joel Hefley (R-CO) spent the lowest amount ($100,786) for a candidate with an opponent. On average, the typical winning candidate in the 2002 House elections spent $916,000.

Data File: **HOUSE108**
Task: **Univariate**
➤ *Primary Variable:* **32) $ PER VOTE**
➤ *View:* **Pie**

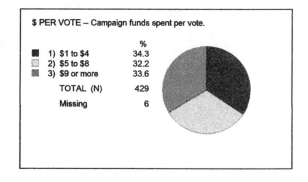

$ PER VOTE – Campaign funds spent per vote.

		%
■	1) $1 to $4	34.3
▒	2) $5 to $8	32.2
▓	3) $9 or more	33.6
	TOTAL (N)	429
	Missing	6

Another way to examine campaign spending is on the basis of the amount spent for each vote the candidate received. Nearly one-third of the representatives spent at least $9 per vote. Now let's see where all of this money comes from.

Data File: **HOUSE108**
Task: **Univariate**
➤ Primary Variable: **29) %PAC CONTR**
➤ View: **Pie**

%PAC CONTR -- PAC contributions as percent of total receipts. Lowest third received 38% or less from PACs, middle third received 39% to 50% from PACs, highest third received 51% to 88% from PACs.

		%
■	1) Lowest 3rd	32.4
▨	2) Middle 3rd	33.1
▨	3) Highest 3r	34.5
	TOTAL (N)	435

Much of the campaign money came from political action committees—PACs. Almost any organization—a corporation, a union, a professional association, a neighborhood club, or even a bowling team—can create its own PAC and then raise funds from member contributions or even by seeking funds from nonmembers. Over a third of the members of the House received more than half of their total funding from PACs. Keep in mind that individual contributors are still the largest source of campaign funds, providing about half of all campaign funds for House races. However, PACs are the second largest source, accounting for about one-third of all campaign funds. PACs also can give larger contributions, up to $5,000 per candidate, and there are a large number of PACs, nearly 4,500.

Data File: **HOUSE108**
Task: **Univariate**
➤ Primary Variable: **31) INDPAC**
➤ View: **Pie**

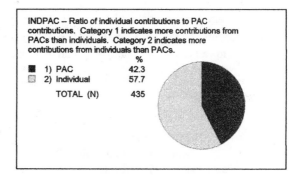

INDPAC -- Ratio of individual contributions to PAC contributions. Category 1 indicates more contributions from PACs than individuals. Category 2 indicates more contributions from individuals than PACs.

		%
■	1) PAC	42.3
▨	2) Individual	57.7
	TOTAL (N)	435

Here we see that 42.3 percent of the members of the 108th House received a larger proportion of their campaign funds from PACs than from individuals. Yet, 57.7 percent received a greater proportion of their campaign money from individuals than from PACs.

INTEREST GROUPS' RATINGS OF CONGRESS

Many interest groups rate members of Congress based on whether they agree or disagree with the members' voting records. The interest group selects bills from each legislative session that the group associates with its cause. The interest group then designates the direction of the vote that supports their cause. Finally, the interest group calculates the percent agreement with these votes for each member of Congress. Interest groups use these ratings to inform their members and the public about the voting records of Congress.

Three interest group ratings are included in the 108th House file. The National Taxpayers Union ranks members of Congress on how their votes affect taxes, government spending, and the national debt. A high score indicates a member of Congress consistently voted to cut taxes and reduce spending, which in turn would decrease the national debt. The League of Conservation Voters ranks members of Congress on environmental issues, with a high score indicating agreement between the League of Conservation Voters' position and that of the representative. Finally, the American Civil Liberties Union (ACLU) ranks members highly for voting records that protect freedom of speech and other civil liberties.

The major distinction between members of the House is their party affiliation. Democrats and Republicans vote quite differently on a host of bills. Let's see how members' party affiliations match up with the rankings by these interest groups.

Data File: **HOUSE108**
➤ Task: **Cross-tabulation**
➤ Row Variable: **45) ACLU RATE**
➤ Column Variable: **11) PARTY**
➤ View: **Table**
➤ Display: **Column**

ACLU RATE   by   PARTY
Cramer's V: 0.914**

		PARTY			
		Democrat	Republican	Missing	TOTAL
ACLU RATE	Low	7	213	0	220
		3.4%	93.0%		50.7%
	Mod. Low	22	13	0	35
		10.7%	5.7%		8.1%
	Mod. High	60	3	0	63
		29.3%	1.3%		14.5%
	High	116	0	1	116
		56.6%	0.0%		26.7%
	TOTAL	205	229	1	434
		100.0%	100.0%		

Party is very strongly related to the rankings given by the American Civil Liberties Union. Among Democrats, 56.6 percent are ranked by the ACLU in the highest category, while 93.0 percent of Republicans fall in the lowest category. Cramer's V is an extremely strong 0.914** and is statistically significant.

One might suspect that members of Congress who are lawyers would rank higher on the ACLU ratings. Let's see.

Data File: **HOUSE108**
Task: **Cross-tabulation**
Row Variable: **45) ACLU RATE**
➤ Column Variable: **10) LAWYER?**
➤ View: **Table**
➤ Display: **Column**

ACLU RATE   by   LAWYER?
Cramer's V: 0.124

		LAWYER?		
		Lawyer	Non-lawyer	TOTAL
ACLU RATE	Low	75	145	220
		45.5%	53.7%	50.6%
	Mod. Low	11	24	35
		6.7%	8.9%	8.0%
	Mod. High	32	31	63
		19.4%	11.5%	14.5%
	High	47	70	117
		28.5%	25.9%	26.9%
	TOTAL	165	270	435
		100.0%	100.0%	

Actually, no relationship exists between a member being a lawyer and his or her ACLU ranking. What matters for voting patterns in Congress is not whether a member is a lawyer or not but whether the member is a Democrat or a Republican.

Do the rankings by the National Taxpayers Union match up with members' party affiliations as strongly as the rankings by the ACLU?

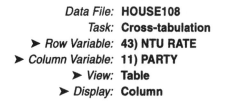

Data File:	**HOUSE108**
Task:	**Cross-tabulation**
➤ Row Variable:	**43) NTU RATE**
➤ Column Variable:	**11) PARTY**
➤ View:	**Table**
➤ Display:	**Column**

NTU RATE   by   PARTY
Cramer's V: 0.961**

NTU RATE		PARTY			
		Democrat	Republican	Missing	TOTAL
	Low	193	0	1	193
		95.1%	0.0%		45.2%
	Mod. Low	9	37	0	46
		4.4%	16.5%		10.8%
	Mod. High	1	142	0	143
		0.5%	63.4%		33.5%
	High	0	45	0	45
		0.0%	20.1%		10.5%
	Missing	2	5	0	7
	TOTAL	203	224	1	427
		100.0%	100.0%		

Yes, they do. Democrats and Republicans disagree about taxes and spending. As a result, Republicans tend to be scored more highly by this group, while Democrats receive lower scores.

Finally, let's consider whether the wealth of a representative's district might influence his or her voting patterns in Congress. Wealthier constituents probably would favor lower taxes, while poorer constituents might favor more government services.

Data File:	**HOUSE108**
Task:	**Cross-tabulation**
Row Variable:	**43) NTU RATE**
➤ Column Variable:	**19) DIST.FAM$**
➤ View:	**Table**
➤ Display:	**Column**

NTU RATE   by   DIST.FAM$
Cramer's V: 0.136**

NTU RATE		DIST.FAM$			
		Low	Medium	High	TOTAL
	Low	80	54	60	194
		56.3%	40.9%	39.0%	45.3%
	Mod. Low	17	16	13	46
		12.0%	12.1%	8.4%	10.7%
	Mod. High	37	47	59	143
		26.1%	35.6%	38.3%	33.4%
	High	8	15	22	45
		5.6%	11.4%	14.3%	10.5%
	Missing	4	2	1	7
	TOTAL	142	132	154	428
		100.0%	100.0%	100.0%	

Representatives from wealthier districts are rated more highly by this interest group, while representatives from poorer districts are more likely to receive lower scores. The strength of the pattern, while statistically significant, is much weaker than found for partisanship. What matters most for how members vote is their party.

Your turn.

REVIEW QUESTIONS

Based on the first part of this exercise, answer True or False to the following items:

1. Most gun owners oppose gun-control legislation.   T   F

2. Only a small minority of Americans belong to an affinity interest group.   T   F

3. Organized interest groups exist in only a few countries.   T   F

4. Congressional elections are expensive. The average campaign expenditure by a winning candidate in the 2002 congressional elections was more than $900,000.   T   F

5. Most members of Congress receive more of their campaign funds from PACs than from individual contributors.   T   F

6. Lawyers rank more highly in the ACLU ratings than do representatives who are not lawyers.   T   F

7. A representative's party is strongly associated with the ratings he or she receives from the ACLU and the National Taxpayers Union.   T   F

EXPLORIT QUESTIONS

EXAMINING AFFINITY GROUPS

As indicated before, older people constitute an affinity group. Older Americans receive health insurance from the government through the Medicare program. Given this, we might expect that the elderly would be more likely than others to agree that health care is a responsibility of the government. However, in the first part of this exercise, we found that contrary to what we might assume, people over 65 were the least likely to think increases in Social Security were needed. Let's now see whether older people were more likely to want the government to help with medical costs.

> ➤ *Data File:* **GSS**
> ➤ *Task:* **Cross-tabulation**
> ➤ *Row Variable:* **77) GOV.MED.**
> ➤ *Column Variable:* **9) AGE**
> ➤ *View:* **Table**
> ➤ *Display:* **Column %**

Make sure to read the variable description for GOV.MED., to check whether Cramer's V is statistically significant, and then answer True or False to the following items.

8. People 65 and older were the ones who most favored government help
    with medical costs.   T   F

9. Generally, those under retirement age (65) favor individuals being responsible for
    their own medical costs.   T   F

African Americans form an affinity group.

Data File:	**GSS**
Task:	**Cross-tabulation**
➤ *Row Variable:*	**27) BLACK$**
➤ *Column Variable:*	**7) RACE**
➤ *View:*	**Table**
➤ *Display:*	**Column %**

10. Most African Americans think too little is being spent on improving the conditions
    of blacks.   T   F

There are various kinds of religious-political groups that constitute both affinity groups (e.g., those who believe in prayer in public schools versus those who don't) and organized groups (the Christian Coalition, People for the American Way, Bread for the World, American Jewish Committee, etc.). Let's see whether views on prayer and Bible reading in the public schools are affected by how religious people consider themselves to be.

Data File:	**GSS**
Task:	**Cross-tabulation**
➤ *Row Variable:*	**45) SCH.PRAY**
➤ *Column Variable:*	**15) RELPERSN**
➤ *View:*	**Table**
➤ *Display:*	**Column %**

11. People who consider themselves to be very religious are the ones who most
    support prayer in public schools.   T   F

12. A majority of those who are not at all religious oppose prayer in public schools.   T   F

PACs AND CAMPAIGN CONTRIBUTIONS

In the opening section of this exercise, we saw that interest groups provide a significant portion of the funds that members of Congress use in their campaigns. Let's see if we can uncover any patterns as to which members of Congress receive a greater proportion of their campaign funds from interest groups.

One might suspect that Republican members of Congress would receive a greater proportion of their campaign funds from PACs. A larger number of PACs are associated with businesses rather than unions, which should favor Republican candidates. The Republican party also is the majority party in Congress and controls more of the agenda. PACs make campaign contributions to ensure access to powerful members of Congress. Therefore, we might expect Republican candidates to receive more PAC money because they are the majority party. On the other hand, the Republican party also can tap into the wealth of its individual supporters. Thus, Republican candidates might receive a large number of contributions from individual Americans such that they offset any advantages among PACs. Let's see what the data show.

> *Data File:* **HOUSE108**
> *Task:* **Cross-tabulation**
> *Row Variable:* **29) %PAC CONTR**
> *Column Variable:* **11) PARTY**
> *View:* **Table**
> *Display:* **Column %**

13. Republicans are more likely than Democrats to receive a high percentage
   of their campaign funds from PACs.   T   F

Members of Congress who run for reelection win more than 90 percent of the time. If PACs are interested in attaining access to representatives, PACs are probably more likely to have contributed money to incumbents rather than new members of Congress. Let's see if that is true.

       Data File: **HOUSE108**
          Task: **Cross-tabulation**
    Row Variable: **29) %PAC CONTR**
> *Column Variable:* **24) INCUMBENT**
>   *View:* **Table**
>   *Display:* **Column %**

14. Incumbent members of Congress are more likely than new members to have
   received a higher percentage of their campaign contributions from PACs.   T   F

Finally, PACs may want to contribute to the members of Congress who have the most power. Representatives who are chairs of the committees and subcommittees have a great deal of influence over which legislation eventually becomes a law. In Congress, all of these chair positions are held by the majority party or, in the case of the 108th Congress, by Republicans. In addition, the Republican party leaders (Speaker of the House, Majority Leader, Whip) also are very powerful representatives that PACs may want to contact. Since only members of the majority party can hold one of these power positions, we will limit our analysis to Republicans by asking MicroCase to subset the data.

To subset the data file, use the cross-tabulation menu screen and insert 11) PARTY in the space under "Subset Variables." A new screen will appear. Click on "Republican" and make sure the "Include Selected Categories" is chosen.

Data File:	**HOUSE108**
Task:	**Cross-tabulation**
Row Variable:	**29) %PAC CONTR**
➤ Column Variable:	**15) POWER**
➤ Subset Variable:	**11) PARTY**
➤ Subset Categories:	**Include: 2) Republican**
➤ View:	**Table**
➤ Display:	**Column %**

15. Republican representatives who hold power positions are more likely than other Republicans to receive a higher percentage of their campaign funds from PACs.   T   F

INTEREST GROUPS AND THE VOTING RECORD OF REPRESENTATIVES

Let's return to the interest group ratings of Congress. This time we will look at the rankings by the League of Conservation Voters. We will begin once again with looking for the pattern of rankings across the two parties.

Before proceeding with the next table, be sure to clear the subset variable. An easy way to do this is to click the [Clear All] option on the cross-tabulation menu screen.

Data File:	**HOUSE108**
Task:	**Cross-tabulation**
➤ Row Variable:	**44) LCV RATE**
➤ Column Variable:	**11) PARTY**
➤ View:	**Table**
➤ Display:	**Column %**

16. Representatives' party affiliations are _____ related to their rankings from the League of Conservation Voters.

    a. strongly

    b. moderately

    c. weakly

    d. not

Let's see if representatives from the different regions of the country have diverse voting records as measured by the League of Conservation Voters' rankings.

> Data File: **HOUSE108**
>> Task: **Cross-tabulation**
> Row Variable: **44) LCV RATE**
> ➤ Column Variable: **13) REGION**
>> ➤ View: **Table**
>> ➤ Display: **Column**

17. Representatives from the East are most likely to fall into the _____ category.

    a. low

    b. moderately low

    c. moderately high

    d. high

18. A majority of representatives from which regions fall in the low category?

    a. East and Midwest

    b. Midwest and South

    c. South and West

    d. Midwest, South, and West

19. Representatives from the West

    a. show consensus, most fall in the high category.

    b. show consensus, most fall in the low category.

    c. are almost evenly divided between the high and low categories.

Are female members of Congress more or less likely to receive high ratings from the League of Conservation Voters?

> Data File: **HOUSE108**
>> Task: **Cross-tabulation**
> Row Variable: **44) LCV RATE**
> ➤ Column Variable: **4) SEX**
>> ➤ View: **Table**
>> ➤ Display: **Column %**

20. Female representatives are more likely than male representatives to be
rated highly by the League of Conservation Voters.   T   F

Two-thirds of the women in Congress are Democrats, while one-third are Republicans. Since party is related to these rankings by the League of Conservation Voters, let's subset the data to look at only Democratic members.

Data File:	**HOUSE108**
Task:	**Cross-tabulation**
Row Variable:	**44) LCV RATE**
Column Variable:	**4) SEX**
➤ *Subset Variable:*	**11) PARTY**
➤ *Subset Categories:*	**Include: 1) Democrat**
➤ *View:*	**Table**
➤ *Display:*	**Column %**

21. Female Democrats are no more likely than male Democrats to receive a high rating from the League of Conservation Voters.   T   F

<u>WHAT HAVE WE LEARNED?</u>

I.   What is the difference between an affinity group and an organized interest group? What are some of the instances where the opinions of members of an affinity group match the policy positions of the organized groups? What are some instances of dissimilarities?

II. Running for Congress is expensive. What proportion of members of Congress relies more heavily on PAC contributions than on contributions from individual citizens? Which members of Congress receive a greater proportion of their campaign funds from PACs?

III. Interest groups rank members of Congress by how often the representative's voting record matches the preferences of the interest group. In this exercise, we looked at the rankings from three interest groups. What is the most consistent finding about the rankings received from these groups? How do the characteristics of representatives or of their districts affect the rankings they receive from these interest groups?

WHAT ELSE CAN BE EXPLORED?

1. The GSS file can be used to explore more about affinity groups. Are there certain affinity groups that are more cohesive—sharing the same opinion on a number of issues? Are there other affinity groups whose members hold few opinions in common? The characteristics defining the affinity groups (e.g., gender or race) would be the independent variable and attitudes on the issues would be the dependent variable. How might the characteristics of these affinity groups affect organized interest groups in these areas?

2. The HOUSE108 file can be used to explore more about the patterns of campaign contributions to members of Congress. Are expensive campaigns financed in different ways than less expensive congressional campaigns? Either 26) CAMPAIGN $ or 32) $ PER VOTE can be used as an independent variable to separate more expensive from less expensive campaigns. What about campaigns without any real competition? Nearly one of five members of Congress faced no challenger from the other major party in the 2002 congressional elections. Variable 25) UNOPPOSED measures whether a race was contested by both major parties. Are the campaigns of members facing no challengers financed in a different manner from those facing competition?

3. The three interest group ratings in the HOUSE108 file can be explored further. One strategy would be to see how consistently a factor affects all three ratings. For example, one could test whether members of different racial or ethnic groups are ranked the same or differently by each of these interest groups. Keeping in mind the overlap between party affiliation and these interest group rankings, the effects of party can be held constant with either the "Control Variables" or "Subset Variables" option on the cross-tabulation menu screen.

Part IV

INSTITUTIONS

Exercise 12   **The Congress**

Exercise 13   **The Presidency**

Exercise 14   **The Bureaucracy**

Exercise 15   **The Courts**

Everyone talks about "the government." It's too big, too expensive, too conservative, too intrusive, too unresponsive—but, what *is* the government? Is it politicians, bureaucrats, judges, elected officials, or what? In the United States, it is all of these things.

The American government consists of three branches, or institutions: the legislative, the executive, and the judicial. The first consists of the Senate and the House of Representatives. The primary purpose of the legislative branch is to *enact* laws. The executive branch is headed by the president and includes all of the millions of employees who staff the government agencies. The primary purpose of the executive branch is to *administer* the laws. The judicial branch of government consists of federal courts, headed by the Supreme Court. Its primary purpose is to *interpret and apply* the laws.

In the next four exercises you will explore the institutions of our government.

THE CONGRESS

All legislative Powers herein granted shall be vested in a Congress of the United States . . .

ARTICLE I, UNITED STATES
CONSTITUTION

Tasks: Mapping, Univariate, Cross-Tabulation, Historical Trends
Data Files: STATES, HOUSE108, HISTORY, GSS

This table shows the number of members of the U.S. House of Representatives from each state beginning in 2003. California has the most, 53. Texas is second highest with 32, just barely ahead of New York with 29, followed by Florida (25), Pennsylvania (19), and Illinois (19).

➤ *Data File:* **STATES**
  ➤ *Task:* **Mapping**
➤ *Variable 1:* **59) HOUSE03**
  ➤ *View:* **List: Rank**

RANK	CASE NAME	VALUE
1	California	53
2	Texas	32
3	New York	29
4	Florida	25
5	Pennsylvania	19
5	Illinois	19
7	Ohio	18
8	Michigan	15
9	New Jersey	13
9	North Carolina	13

Membership in the House is based on population, so the more populous states have the most members. Because the number of seats in the House has been fixed at 435, and because states often grow or decline and their populations change relative to one another, seats are reapportioned every ten years. Reapportionment takes place the year after the census and goes into effect in the next election. The reapportionment from the 2000 census (listed above) starts with the 2002 elections. However, no state, no matter how small its population, may be denied at least one representative.

➤ *Data File:* **HISTORY**
  ➤ *Task:* **Historical Trends**
➤ *Variable:* **15) APPORTION**

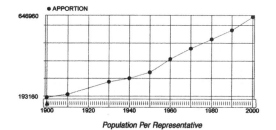

Population Per Representative

In 1790, each U.S. representative represented about 34,000 people. As the nation's population grew, the number of representatives increased until it was decided that no more representatives would be added. Thus, each representative today represents about 600,000 people.

CONGRESSIONAL MEMBERSHIP

In the following discussion, we'll look at certain features of the House of Representatives and use the members of the 108th Congress (elected in November 2002) to demonstrate these features.

➤ *Data File:* **HOUSE108**
➤ *Task:* **Univariate**
➤ *Primary Variable:* **11) PARTY**
➤ *View:* **Pie**

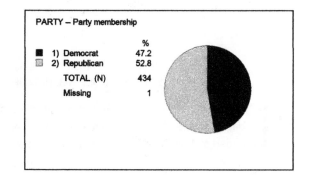

The first feature to note is that the House is currently split fairly evenly between Republicans and Democrats. Up until the 1994 election, Democrats had outnumbered Republicans in the House for 40 years—by substantial margins for most of that time. Then the 1994 election dramatically shifted power to the Republican Party. In the 108th Congress (2003–2004), Republicans held a 24-seat advantage over the Democrats.

Note that the numbers of Democrats and Republicans do not add up to 435. The 108th Congress had one independent: Bernard Sanders of Vermont. Sanders will be excluded from any analysis that compares political party with voting on House bills. Also, on almost any bill some representatives do not vote. Thus, the number of ayes and nays often does not add up to 435. Finally, during the two-year session of Congress a tiny number of representatives resign their position or die. New representatives are selected in special elections.

Data File: **HOUSE108**
Task: **Univariate**
➤ *Primary Variable:* **24) INCUMBENT**
➤ *View:* **Pie**

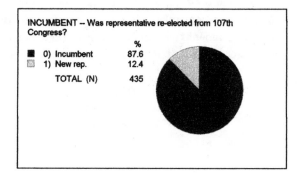

A second feature of Congress is the power of incumbency. We see here that 87.6 percent of the representatives in the 108th Congress were incumbents who were reelected. Thus, once a representative wins election to the House, the probability is extremely high that he or she can get reelected. One function of Congress is to represent the public, but "representation" has many definitions. One definition is **descriptive representation**. Under this definition, one asks, Do the members of Congress look like the American public? Are women and minorities as well represented as white males? Descriptive representation is argued to be important because underrepresented groups may hold distinctive positions on political issues, citizens may feel better represented by someone with a similar background, and government decisions will be more broadly accepted if all members of society see themselves represented in the decision-making process.

A second definition of representation is **substantive representation**. Under this definition, one asks what types of policy decisions are being made by Congress. Does Congress pass legislation that matches public preferences? Another question under this definition is to examine what factors lead some members of Congress to vote in support of a bill and the other group of representatives to vote against the bill. A third definition of representation is **service representation**. This definition focuses on the work of members of Congress in helping out individual constituents. For example, a constituent may contact a member of Congress for help in locating the necessary forms for a small business loan. Most members of Congress are quite good at such constituency services, which adds to the advantages of incumbents when seeking reelection.

DESCRIPTIVE REPRESENTATION

Let's first examine elements of descriptive representation. Women constitute half of the American population, but what are their numbers in Congress?

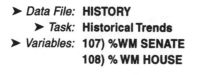

➤ *Data File:* **HISTORY**
➤ *Task:* **Historical Trends**
➤ *Variables:* **107) %WM SENATE**
108) % WM HOUSE

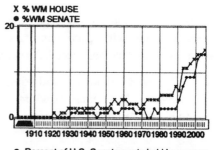

● Percent of U.S. Senate seats held by women
X Percent of U.S. House seats held by women

Notice that the scale on the vertical axis measures membership in Congress from 0 to 20 percent. Thus, at the start of the 21st century approximately 15 percent of the U.S. House of Representatives and Senate members are women. Very few women sat in Congress between 1920 and 1970. The number of women in the House increased in the 1980s, but the largest growth in women in both chambers occurred in the 1990s. Still, women remain underrepresented in Congress in terms of descriptive representation.

Let's next compare the religious beliefs of the American public to those of the members of Congress. We will look at the public's religious preferences with information from the GSS survey.

➤ *Data File:* **GSS**
➤ *Task:* **Univariate**
➤ *Primary Variable:* **14) RELIGION**
➤ *View:* **Pie**

RELIGION -- Respondent's religion: mainline Protestant, evangelical Protestant, Catholic, Jewish or none

		%
■	1) MAINL.PROT	22.1
▨	2) EVNGL.PROT	31.5
▦	3) CATHOLIC	28.4
☐	4) JEWISH	2.0
▨	5) NONE	16.0
	TOTAL (N)	2367
	Missing	398

Among the American public, one-third are evangelical Protestants (e.g., Baptists or Assemblies of God), who tend to hold more conservative religious beliefs. Another quarter are mainline Protestants (e.g., Methodists or Episcopalians). One out of four Americans is a Catholic, while 2 percent are Jewish.

➤ *Data File:* **HOUSE108**
➤ *Task:* **Univariate**
➤ *Primary Variable:* **7) RELIGION**
➤ *View:* **Pie**

RELIGION -- Religious Preference: Catholic, mainline Protestant, evangelical Protestant, Jew or other.

		%
■	1) Catholic	29.4
▨	2) Mainl.Prot	42.4
▦	3) Evngl.Prot	18.8
☐	4) Jew	6.4
▨	5) Other	3.1
	TOTAL (N)	425
	Missing	10

Comparing the percentages in this graph to those from the American public shows that Catholics and Jews are represented in Congress in numbers that generally match those found in the public. Evangelical Protestants are underrepresented in Congress, while mainline Protestants are overrepresented.

Finally, let's consider the racial and ethnic backgrounds of House members. The 2000 census indicated that 75 percent of Americans are white, 12 percent are African Americans, 4 percent are Asians, and 1 percent is Native Americans. In terms of ethnicity, 12 percent of Americans are Hispanics.

Data File: **HOUSE108**
Task: **Univariate**
➤ *Primary Variable:* **5) RACE/ETHNI**
➤ *View:* **Pie**

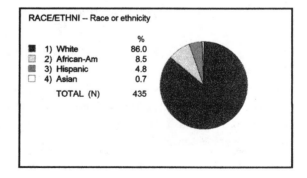

RACE/ETHNI -- Race or ethnicity

		%
■	1) White	86.0
▨	2) African-Am	8.5
▦	3) Hispanic	4.8
☐	4) Asian	0.7
	TOTAL (N)	435

Most racial and ethnic minority groups remain underrepresented in Congress while whites are over, represented.

Part IV: Institutions

Data File: **HOUSE108**
➤ Task: **Cross-tabulation**
➤ Row Variable: **33) TAXACT**
➤ Column Variable: **11) PARTY**
➤ View: **Table**
➤ Display: **Column %**

TAXACT by PARTY
Cramer's V: 0.963**

TAXACT		PARTY			
		Democrat	Republican	Missing	TOTAL
	No	198	1	1	199
		96.6%	0.4%		46.3%
	Yes	7	224	0	231
		3.4%	99.6%		53.7%
	Missing	0	4	0	4
	TOTAL	205	225	1	430
		100.0%	100.0%		

Another feature of Congress is that party affiliation is a very important determinant of how representatives vote on many bills. While there are many routine, noncontroversial bills in Congress on which Republicans and Democrats are not different from one another, there is a substantial percentage of bills that find a majority of Republicans on one side and a majority of Democrats on the other side. Here we see that almost all Democrats voted against this tax bill and every Republican except one voted for it. The differences between Democrats and Republicans are not this sharp on most bills, but there are definite patterns.

Data File: **HOUSE108**
Task: **Cross-tabulation**
➤ Row Variable: **38) TAXBRK_04**
➤ Column Variable: **11) PARTY**
➤ View: **Table**
➤ Display: **Column %**

TAXBRK_04 by PARTY
Cramer's V: 0.482**

TAXBRK_04		PARTY			
		Democrat	Republican	Missing	TOTAL
	No	75	1	0	76
		37.7%	0.5%		18.2%
	Yes	124	217	1	341
		62.3%	99.5%		81.8%
	Missing	6	11	0	17
	TOTAL	199	218	1	417
		100.0%	100.0%		

On this vote to permanently extend the 10 percent tax bracket for the federal income tax, a majority of members from both parties voted for the bill. All but one Republican voted for the bill along with two-thirds of the Democrats. This bill does not fit the classic definition of a party-line vote, where a majority of one party votes for the bill and a majority of the other party votes against the bill. Yet, party is still an important factor in how House members voted on this bill. Notice that Cramer's V is statistically significant, and the value of Cramer's V indicates a fairly strong relationship.

Data File: **HOUSE108**
Task: **Cross-tabulation**
➤ Row Variable: **42) SPC SHTTL**
➤ Column Variable: **11) PARTY**
➤ View: **Table**
➤ Display: **Column %**

SPC SHTTL by PARTY
(Only one row or column -- summary not available)

SPC SHTTL		PARTY			
		Democrat	Republican	Missing	TOTAL
	Yes	192	218	1	410
		100.0%	100.0%		100.0%
	Missing	13	11	0	24
	TOTAL	192	218	1	410
		100.0%	100.0%		

Exercise 12: The Congress

Here we see that every member who voted cast a vote in favor of the resolution of support for the families of the astronauts killed in the crash of the space shuttle *Columbia*. Congress makes a number of such resolutions each year: praising the good works of various groups, honoring famous Americans upon their death, and even congratulating winning sports teams. Such commemorations are mostly uncontroversial and thus receive unanimous or near unanimous votes.

Rather than continuing to look at voting patterns for individual bills, let's look at a measure that summarizes the overall voting records of House members. In Exercise 11 we saw how interest groups select a few votes from each session of Congress and use these votes to rank how favorable members are to the interest group's preferences. The selection of a small number of votes does not tell the whole story about a member's voting record. Political science professors Keith Poole and Howard Rosenthal, however, have devised a method to rank members' overall voting records. From their rankings, we can see which members of Congress are the most liberal in their voting records and which members are the most conservative. Let's begin by looking at how these voting records match up with the two parties.

	Data File:	**HOUSE108**
	Task:	**Cross-tabulation**
➤	Row Variable:	**46) IDEOLOGY**
➤	Column Variable:	**11) PARTY**
➤	View:	**Table**
➤	Display:	**Column %**

IDEOLOGY by PARTY
Cramer's V: 0.953**

		PARTY			
		Democrat	Republican	Missing	TOTAL
IDEOLOGY	Liberal	104	0	1	104
		50.7%	0.0%		24.0%
	Mod. Lib.	101	11	0	112
		49.3%	4.8%		25.8%
	Mod. Cons.	0	113	0	113
		0.0%	49.3%		26.0%
	Conserv.	0	105	0	105
		0.0%	45.9%		24.2%
	TOTAL	205	229	1	434
		100.0%	100.0%		

A very strong pattern exists between members' overall voting records and their party. The value of Cramer's V is nearly a perfect 1.000, and the pattern is statistically significant. Democrats and Republicans in Congress vote in distinctly different ways.

Are there any patterns in members' voting records beyond the influence of party? Does the type of constituency matter? We know that on a number of issues minorities are more liberal than whites. Thus a natural question is whether the number of minority residents in a district affects the voting patterns of House members beyond the influence of party. To test for this possibility, we need to control for party when looking for the effects of constituency type on members' voting records. We will look at one table for Democratic House members and a second table for Republican House members.

	Data File:	**HOUSE108**
	Task:	**Cross-tabulation**
	Row Variable:	**46) IDEOLOGY**
➤	Column Variable:	**16) DIST.AFR**
➤	Control Variable:	**11) PARTY (Democrat)**
➤	View:	**Table**
➤	Display:	**Column %**

IDEOLOGY by DIST.AFR
Controls: PARTY: Democrat
Cramer's V: 0.234**

		DIST.AFR				
		50% or +	15%-49.9%	6%-14.9%	0-5.9%	TOTAL
IDEOLOGY	Liberal	19	21	25	39	104
		79.2%	38.2%	51.0%	50.6%	50.7%
	Mod. Lib.	5	34	24	38	101
		20.8%	61.8%	49.0%	49.4%	49.3%
	TOTAL	24	55	49	77	205
		100.0%	100.0%	100.0%	100.0%	

The option for selecting a control variable is located on the same screen you use to select other variables. For this example, select 11) PARTY as a control variable and then click [OK] to continue as usual. Separate tables showing the relationship between ideology ratings and percent African American in district will be shown for Democrats and Republicans.

For Democratic representatives, the greater the percentage of African Americans in the district the more liberal the representative's voting record. In districts with more than 50 percent African Americans, 79.2 percent of Democratic House members fall in the most liberal category. In districts with the fewest African American residents, 50.6 percent of the Democratic House members fall in the most liberal category.

> **To look at the pattern for Republican House members, click the right arrow under the heading "Control 1 of 3" in the lower left-hand corner of the screen. The heading will change to "Control 2 of 3."**

Data File:	**HOUSE108**		
Task:	**Cross-tabulation**		
Row Variable:	**46) IDEOLOGY**		
Column Variable:	**16) DIST.AFR**		
➤ Control Variable:	**11) PARTY (Republican)**		
➤ View:	**Table**		
➤ Display:	**Column %**		

IDEOLOGY   by   DIST.AFR
Controls: PARTY: Republican
Cramer's V: 0.091

	DIST.AFR			
	15%-49.9%	6%-14.9%	0-5.9%	TOTAL
Mod. Lib.	1	2	8	11
	3.6%	3.2%	5.8%	4.8%
Mod. Cons.	11	28	74	113
	39.3%	45.2%	53.2%	49.3%
Conserv.	16	32	57	105
	57.1%	51.6%	41.0%	45.9%
TOTAL	28	62	139	229
	100.0%	100.0%	100.0%	

This table shows no pattern between the number of African Americans living in a district and the voting records of Republican House members. (We will ignore the third table, which consists of the one House member who is neither a Democrat nor a Republican.)

Does the wealth of a district affect the voting patterns of a House member beyond the influence of party? We might suspect that in wealthier districts the public would support lower taxes and fewer government programs in such a manner as to increase the conservatism of their representatives. On the other hand, the district's preferences for taxes and government services may influence which candidates are elected, such that once House members' party affiliations are held constant, no additional influence is seen for district wealth.

Data File:	**HOUSE108**		
Task:	**Cross-tabulation**		
Row Variable:	**46) IDEOLOGY**		
➤ Column Variable:	**19) DIST.FAM$**		
➤ Control Variable:	**11) PARTY (Democrat)**		
➤ View:	**Table**		
➤ Display:	**Column %**		

IDEOLOGY   by   DIST.FAM$
Controls: PARTY: Democrat
Cramer's V: 0.141

	DIST.FAM$			
	Low	Medium	High	TOTAL
Liberal	37	32	35	104
	42.5%	56.1%	57.4%	50.7%
Mod. Lib.	50	25	26	101
	57.5%	43.9%	42.6%	49.3%
TOTAL	87	57	61	205
	100.0%	100.0%	100.0%	

The wealth of a district has no effect on the voting record of Democratic House members. The same is true for Republican House members.

	Data File:	HOUSE108
	Task:	Cross-tabulation
	Row Variable:	46) IDEOLOGY
	Column Variable:	19) DIST.FAM$
➤	Control Variable:	11) PARTY (Republican)
➤	View:	Table
➤	Display:	Column %

IDEOLOGY   by   DIST.FAM$
Controls: PARTY: Republican
Cramer's V: 0.090

IDEOLOGY	DIST.FAM$	Low	Medium	High	TOTAL
	Mod. Lib.	3	3	5	11
		5.1%	3.9%	5.3%	4.8%
	Mod. Cons.	35	36	42	113
		59.3%	47.4%	44.7%	49.3%
	Conserv.	21	37	47	105
		35.6%	48.7%	50.0%	45.9%
	TOTAL	59	76	94	229
		100.0%	100.0%	100.0%	

Your turn.

REVIEW QUESTIONS

Based on the first part of this exercise, answer True or False to the following items:

1. In the earlier history of the United States, as the population increased the
    number of members in the House of Representatives increased.   T   F

2. Republicans have outnumbered Democrats in the House since the elections
    of 1952.   T   F

3. In the 108th Congress (2003–2004), Republicans outnumber Democrats in
    the House.   T   F

4. If a person gets elected to Congress, the probability is roughly 90 percent that he
    or she will get reelected the next time.   T   F

5. Political party affiliation is only weakly related to how members vote on bills in
    the House of Representatives.   T   F

6. Democratic members of Congress are very likely to be liberal, and Republican
    members are very likely to be conservative.   T   F

EXPLORIT QUESTIONS

DESCRIPTIVE REPRESENTATION AND CONGRESSIONAL ELECTIONS

We saw in the first section of this exercise that less than 10 percent of House members are African
Americans and less than 5 percent are Hispanics. Let's look at which districts elect these members
to Congress. In an attempt to increase the number of minority representatives, some congressional
district lines have been drawn to include a large number of minority voters in what are called majority-
minority districts. Has this strategy been successful?

> **If you created the tables for the beginning section of this exercise, you will need to clear the
> control variable. On the cross-tabulation command screen, click the [Clear All] option
> before proceeding with the next set of commands.**

➤ *Data File:*   **HOUSE108**
➤ *Task:*   **Cross-tabulation**
➤ *Row Variable:*   **5) RACE/ETHNI**
➤ *Column Variable:*   **16) DIST.AFR**
➤ *View:*   **Table**
➤ *Display:*   **Column %**

7. In congressional districts with a population that is 50 percent or more African American, all of the House members elected from these districts are African Americans.   T   F

8. All of the African Americans elected to Congress are from congressional districts where 50 percent or more of the residents are African Americans.   T   F

Data File: **HOUSE108**
Task: **Cross-tabulation**
Row Variable: **5) RACE/ETHNI**
➤ *Column Variable:*   **17) DIST.HIS**
➤ *View:*   **Table**
➤ *Display:*   **Column %**

9. In congressional districts with a population that is 50 percent or more Hispanic, most of the House members elected from these districts are Hispanic.   T   F

10. All of the Hispanics elected to Congress are from congressional districts where 50 percent or more of the residents are Hispanic.   T   F

11. Majority-minority districts have been a successful strategy for the election of minorities to Congress. African American and Hispanic members of the House are the most likely candidates to be elected from these districts.   T   F

Some regional patterns exist in where individuals of different faiths live. The largest proportion of Catholics is found in the eastern states with the smallest proportion living in southern states. Jews are more likely to live in eastern states than in other parts of the country. Evangelical Protestants are more often found in the South. Let's see if these regional patterns appear in the election of members to Congress.

Data File: **HOUSE108**
Task: **Cross-tabulation**
➤ *Row Variable:*   **7) RELIGION**
➤ *Column Variable:*   **13) REGION**
➤ *View:*   **Table**
➤ *Display:*   **Column %**

12. Catholic members of the House are most likely to be elected from

   a.   Eastern states.
   b.   Western states.
   c.   Midwestern states.
   d.   Southern states.
   e.   All areas of the country in equal numbers.

13. Mainline Protestant members of the House are most likely to be elected from

   a.   Eastern and Midwestern states.
   b.   Midwestern and Southern states.
   c.   Southern and Western states.
   d.   Western and Eastern states.
   e.   All areas of the country in equal numbers.

14. Evangelical Protestant members of the House are most likely to be elected from

   a.   Eastern states.
   b.   Western states.
   c.   Midwestern states.
   d.   Southern states.
   e.   All areas of the country in equal numbers.

15. Jewish members of the House are most likely to be elected from

   a.   Eastern and Midwestern states.
   b.   Midwestern and Southern states.
   c.   Southern and Western states.
   d.   Western and Eastern states.
   e.   All areas of the country in equal numbers.

16. Members of Congress often match the racial, ethnic, and religious backgrounds
    of the constituents in their districts.   T   F

EXPLORING THE VOTING PATTERNS OF HOUSE MEMBERS

In the opening section of this exercise, we looked at votes on various tax bills and found party to be a very important factor. Let's examine a different kind of bill. In February of 2004, the House passed the Unborn Victims of Violence Act after the publicity surrounding the murder of Laci Peterson and her unborn son. This act, which was subsequently passed by the Senate and signed into law by President Bush, made it a federal offense to cause harm to a fetus separate from the harm caused to the pregnant woman. This act provoked controversy because it was the first time that federal law granted legal status to a fetus, which some abortion rights activists feared could undermine *Roe v. Wade.* The bill passed the House on a strong party-line vote, with 94 percent of Republicans supporting the bill and 76 percent of Democrats opposing the bill. Let's see if any factors other than party can explain representatives' votes on this bill.

Data File: **HOUSE108**
Task: **Cross-tabulation**
➤ Row Variable: **36) UNBORN_VCT**
➤ Column Variable: **7) RELIGION**
➤ Control Variable: **11) PARTY (Democrat)**
➤ View: **Table**
➤ Display: **Column %**

Keep in mind that if the relationship shown in a table is statistically insignificant (i.e., no asterisks attached to Cramer's V), you must report no pattern between the two variables. So look at the statistical significance of each table before answering the questions.

17. Among Democratic members of the House, which religious group was most likely to vote against this bill?

    a.   Catholics

    b.   Mainline Protestants

    c.   Evangelical Protestants

    d.   Jews

    e.   There are no statistically significant differences across the religious groups.

Data File: **HOUSE108**
Task: **Cross-tabulation**
Row Variable: **36) UNBORN_VCT**
Column Variable: **7) RELIGION**
➤ Control Variable: **11) PARTY (Republican)**
➤ View: **Table**
➤ Display: **Column %**

18. Among Republican members of the House, which religious group was most likely to vote against this bill?

    a.   Catholics

    b.   Mainline Protestants

    c.   Evangelical Protestants

    d.   Jews

    e.   There are no statistically significant differences across the religious groups.

Data File: **HOUSE108**
Task: **Cross-tabulation**
Row Variable: **36) UNBORN_VCT**
➤ Column Variable: **4) SEX**
➤ Control Variable: **11) PARTY (Democrat)**
➤ View: **Table**
➤ Display: **Column %**

19. Female Democrats were more likely than male Democrats to vote against this bill.   T   F

> *Data File:* **HOUSE108**
> *Task:* **Cross-tabulation**
> *Row Variable:* **36) UNBORN_VCT**
> *Column Variable:* **4) SEX**
> ➤ *Control Variable:* **11) PARTY (Republican)**
> ➤ *View:* **Table**
> ➤ *Display:* **Column %**

20. Female Republicans were more likely than male Republicans to vote against this bill.   T   F

> *Data File:* **HOUSE108**
> *Task:* **Cross-tabulation**
> *Row Variable:* **36) UNBORN_VCT**
> ➤ *Column Variable:* **13) REGION**
> ➤ *Control Variable:* **11) PARTY (Democrat)**
> ➤ *View:* **Table**
> ➤ *Display:* **Column %**

21. Democrats from which region of the country were most likely to vote against this bill?
    a. East
    b. Midwest
    c. South
    d. West
    e. There are no statistically significant differences across the regional groups.

> *Data File:* **HOUSE108**
> *Task:* **Cross-tabulation**
> *Row Variable:* **36) UNBORN_VCT**
> *Column Variable:* **13) REGION**
> ➤ *Control Variable:* **11) PARTY (Republican)**
> ➤ *View:* **Table**
> ➤ *Display:* **Column %**

22. Republicans from which region of the country were most likely to vote against this bill?
    a. East
    b. Midwest
    c. South
    d. West
    e. There are no statistically significant differences across the regional groups.

23. While party is the major factor influencing House members' voting on the Unborn Victims of Violence Act, representatives' religion, home region, and gender also influenced their votes.   **T F**

In the opening section of this exercise, we explored the overall pattern of voting by House members by using the Poole and Rosenthal measure, which ranks members from the most liberal to the most conservative. We saw that this ideological ranking overlaps by large margins with the party affiliation of House members. We also tested for any influence of constituency characteristics on these voting patterns. In this section, we will test for the effects of the characteristics of the House members, when controlling for the effects of party.

Data File:	**HOUSE108**
Task:	**Cross-tabulation**
➤ *Row Variable:*	**46) IDEOLOGY**
➤ *Column Variable:*	**5) RACE/ETHNI**
➤ *Control Variable:*	**11) PARTY (Democrat)**
➤ *View:*	**Table**
➤ *Display:*	**Column %**

24. Looking at the first row in this table, among Democrats which ethnic or racial group is most likely to have a liberal voting record?
    a. Whites
    b. African Americans
    c. Hispanics
    d. Asians
    e. There are no statistically significant differences across the ethnic and racial groups.

Data File:	**HOUSE108**
Task:	**Cross-tabulation**
Row Variable:	**46) IDEOLOGY**
Column Variable:	**5) RACE/ETHNI**
➤ *Control Variable:*	**11) PARTY (Republican)**
➤ *View:*	**Table**
➤ *Display:*	**Column %**

25. Looking at the third row in this table, among Republicans which ethnic group is most likely to have a conservative voting record?
    a. Whites
    b. Hispanics
    c. There are no statistically significant differences between whites and Hispanics.

        Data File: **HOUSE108**
        Task: **Cross-tabulation**
     Row Variable: **46) IDEOLOGY**
➤ *Column Variable:* **7) RELIGION**
➤ *Control Variable:* **11) PARTY (Democrat)**
      ➤ *View:* **Table**
    ➤ *Display:* **Column %**

26. Looking at the first row in this table, among Democrats which religious group is most likely to have a liberal voting record?

    a.   Catholics

    b.   Mainline Protestants

    c.   Evangelical Protestants

    d.   Jews

    e.   There are no statistically significant differences across the religious groups.

        Data File: **HOUSE108**
        Task: **Cross-tabulation**
     Row Variable: **46) IDEOLOGY**
   Column Variable: **7) RELIGION**
➤ *Control Variable:* **11) PARTY (Republican)**
      ➤ *View:* **Table**
    ➤ *Display:* **Column %**

27. Looking at the third row in this table, among Republicans which religious group is most likely to have a conservative voting record?

    a.   Catholics

    b.   Mainline Protestants

    c.   Evangelical Protestants

    d.   Jews

    e.   There are no statistically significant differences across the religious groups.

        Data File: **HOUSE108**
        Task: **Cross-tabulation**
     Row Variable: **46) IDEOLOGY**
➤ *Column Variable:* **13) REGION**
➤ *Control Variable:* **11) PARTY (Democrat)**
      > *View:* **Table**
    ➤ *Display:* **Column %**

28. Looking at the first row in this table, Democrats from which region are least likely to have a liberal voting record?

   a. East

   b. Midwest

   c. South

   d. West

   e. There are no statistically significant differences across the regions.

Data File:	**HOUSE108**
Task:	**Cross-tabulation**
Row Variable:	**46) IDEOLOGY**
Column Variable:	**13) REGION**
➤ *Control Variable:*	**11) PARTY (Republican)**
➤ *View:*	**Table**
➤ *Display:*	**Column %**

29. Looking at the third row in this table, Republicans from which region are least likely to have a conservative voting record?

   a. East

   b. Midwest

   c. South

   d. West

   e. There are no statistically significant differences across the regions.

Data File:	**HOUSE108**
Task:	**Cross-tabulation**
Row Variable:	**46) IDEOLOGY**
➤ *Column Variable:*	**4) SEX**
➤ *Control Variable:*	**11) PARTY (Democrat)**
➤ *View:*	**Table**
➤ *Display:*	**Column %**

30. Female Democrats are more likely than male Democrats to have a liberal voting record.   T   F

Data File:	**HOUSE108**
Task:	**Cross-tabulation**
Row Variable:	**46) IDEOLOGY**
Column Variable:	**4) SEX**
➤ *Control Variable:*	**11) PARTY (Republician)**
➤ *View:*	**Table**
➤ *Display:*	**Column %**

31. Female Republicans are less likely than male Republicans to have a conservative voting record.   T   F

WHAT HAVE WE LEARNED?

I.   Advocates of descriptive representation feel that it is important for members of Congress to mirror the demographic patterns found in the American public. How much does Congress look like the American public? What types of congressional districts are more likely to elect racial or ethnic minorities? What are the patterns for the election of representatives from the different religious faiths? Finally, do you think that descriptive representation is important? Why or why not?

II. How did Congress's consideration of the Unborn Victims of Violence Act become intertwined with the debate over abortion? How did this affect the factors that shaped House members' votes on this bill?

III. The voting patterns of House members can be summarized along a liberal to conservative scale. This ideology scale is strongly associated with the party affiliations of the members. Beyond the influence of party, which traits of members or characteristics of their districts also influence voting patterns in Congress?

WORKSHEET

WHAT ELSE CAN BE EXPLORED?

1. Is there a gender gap inside Congress? On how many issues do male and female representatives have distinctively different voting patterns? Does the type of issue matter? Keep in mind that two-thirds of the women in Congress are Democrats, so a control for party may be needed to uncover any true gender differences in voting records.

2. One third of the members of Congress are lawyers. Using 10) LAWYER? as the independent (i.e., column) variable, tests can be conducted on whether lawyers vote differently on specific issues or on the various rankings of voting patterns.

3. With 15) POWER as the independent variable, a study can be conducted of whether Republicans in leadership roles are distinctive from rank-and-file Republicans. Since only members of the majority party can hold the powerful positions of committee and subcommittee chairs, the HOUSE108 file needs to be subdivided to include only Republican members. Use the "Subset Variables: 11) Party" and "Include: 2) Republican" commands on the cross-tabulation menu screen to accomplish this.

THE PRESIDENCY

[S]hould my administration prove to be a very wicked one, or what is more probable, a very foolish one, if you, the people, are but true to yourselves and to the Constitution, there is but little harm I can do, thank God!

ABRAHAM LINCOLN, 1861

Tasks: Mapping, Univariate, Cross-Tabulation
Data Files: STATES, USPRES

The American presidency was invented by the Constitutional Convention. Never before had a nation been led by a freely elected chief executive with powers independent of the legislative branch of government. In all other democracies at that time, and nearly all of them since, executive power was vested in the leader of the legislature; if we were to adopt that system, the Speaker of the House of Representatives would be the chief executive. Only a handful of nations, all of them in North and South America, follow the American model of an elected, independent executive who is in charge of the entire executive branch of government.

Because the American presidency has so much authority and so many independent resources, the delegates at the Constitutional Convention were very worried about the wrong sort of person gaining office. That's why they created the electoral college. They never meant for presidents to be elected by popular vote. Instead, they wanted presidents to be selected by a few of the nation's most informed and concerned leaders. Thus, Alexander Hamilton explained in 1788 that the process of selection by the electoral college "affords a moral certainty, that the office of president will never fall to the lot of any man who is not in an eminent degree endowed with the requisite qualifications."

While vestiges of the electoral college remain, these days the popular vote pretty much decides who becomes president, with the 2000 election being a major exception. Over the previous 100 years, the electoral college vote mirrored the popular vote, but even when this occurred, the electoral college still had subtle effects on who became president. So, let's see how well the system has worked.

> *Data File:* **STATES**
> > *Task:* **Mapping**
> *Variable 1:* **56) PRESIDENTS**
> > *View:* **List: Rank**

RANK	CASE NAME	VALUE
1	New York	7
1	Ohio	7
3	Virginia	5
4	Massachusetts	4
5	Texas	3
5	California	3
5	Tennessee	3
8	Pennsylvania	1
8	Louisiana	1
8	Kansas	1

Here we see the home states of each of the 43 presidents, from George Washington to George W. Bush (although Bush was the 42nd person to hold the office, the record books refer to him as the 43rd president because they count Grover Cleveland twice since his two terms of office were not consecutive).

The eastern bias is clear. More than half of all presidents have come from four states: Ohio (7), New York (7), Virginia (5), and Massachusetts (4). Eleven states have had only one president, and 32 have had none. Two major factors have played a role: population size and when states entered the union. In the beginning, only a few states *could* produce presidents because there were only 14 states. Thus, New York, Virginia, and Massachusetts were electing presidents long before most other states existed. Moreover, even in the days when the electoral college actually met and chose a president, population size mattered a lot since each state's votes were proportionate to its population. In 1790 Virginia was by far the most populous state being twice as large as second-place Pennsylvania, hence its many presidents—including George Washington and Thomas Jefferson. New York's many presidents can be traced to the fact that it too was one of the original states and soon became by far the most populous state (it was not until the early 1960s that California had more people than New York, and Texas did not pass New York until the 1990s).

That leaves Ohio. How did it elect seven presidents? There are three factors: age, population, and location. Ohio is an old state, having entered the union in 1803, and it soon became one of the most populous states, ranking fourth largest in the latter 19th century. But of even greater importance is location. Ohio is the most eastern state of the Midwest, so its politicians often mediated conflicts between the East and the more westerly areas, which was an advantage for its presidential candidates. They were acceptable to all regions—so much so that in the 1920 election the winner was the Republican senator from Ohio (Harding) and the loser was the governor of Ohio (Cox).

Data File: **STATES**
Task: **Mapping**
Variable 1: **56) PRESIDENTS**
> *Variable 2:* **10) POPULATION**
> > *Views:* **Map**

PRESIDENTS – Number of United States Presidents

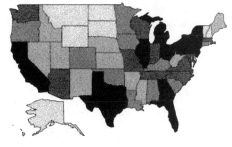

POPULATION – 2000: Resident Population (In Millions)(Census)

r = 0.560**

Even though populations have changed a lot through the decades, there still is a strong and significant correlation between the number of presidents a state has produced and its population.

Now, let's see what sorts of people have been president. For one thing, they all have been males. A woman ran for vice president in 1984, but as yet no woman has been nominated for president by a major party. But what about other features of the American presidency?

➤ *Data File:* **USPRES**
➤ *Task:* **Univariate**
➤ *Primary Variable:* **6) PARTY**
➤ *View:* **Pie**

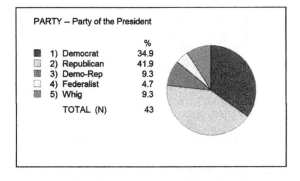

PARTY -- Party of the President

		%
■	1) Democrat	34.9
▨	2) Republican	41.9
▨	3) Demo-Rep	9.3
▢	4) Federalist	4.7
▨	5) Whig	9.3
	TOTAL (N)	43

This data file consists of the 43 presidents. Here we see their party affiliations. There have been 15 Democrats and 18 Republicans. But that leaves 10 others. The Federalists were an antiparty party. The name was applied to the opponents of political parties as divisive "factions," including George Washington, who devoted much of his farewell address to condemning parties: "Let me . . . warn you in the most solemn manner against the baneful effects of the spirit of party, generally."

The Federalist name was adopted by Alexander Hamilton to clarify opposition to the party formed by Thomas Jefferson, who was as ardently in favor of parties as Washington was against them. Jefferson's party was called the Democratic-Republicans and they elected four early presidents, including Jefferson himself. When Andrew Jackson became a presidential candidate, the party shortened its name to the Democratic Party. Meanwhile, the name Federalist disappeared; the new opposition party came to be known as the Whigs, and they elected four presidents. During the 1850s the issue of slavery split both the Whigs and the Democrats, and the antislavery factions of each withdrew to form the Republican Party, whose first successful presidential candidate was Abraham Lincoln. Since 1853, all U.S. presidents have been either Democrats or Republicans.

Data File: **USPRES**

Task: **Univariate**

➤ Primary Variable: **17) YRS IN OFF**

➤ View: **Pie**

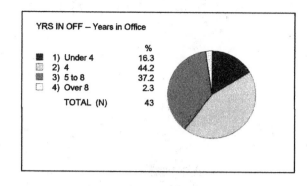

A presidential term in office is four years. Here we see that seven presidents served fewer than four years. These were either presidents who died in office or vice presidents who succeeded and then did not serve a term of their own. Nineteen presidents served but a single term, and 16 more began a second term (and most completed it). For 150 years no president ever sought a third term, modeling themselves on George Washington, who declined a third term. Indeed, as the Democratic Party platform put it in 1896, "We declare it to be the unwritten law of this Republic, established by custom and usage of 100 years . . . that no man should be eligible for a third term of the Presidential office."

After Franklin D. Roosevelt ran for and won third and fourth terms, the 22nd Amendment to the Constitution was adopted:

> No person shall be elected to the office of the President more than twice, and no person who has held the office of President, or acted as President, for more than two years of a term to which some other person was elected President shall be elected to the office of President more than once.

PRESIDENTS AND CONGRESS: THE POLITICS OF VETOES

Presidents have many formal and informal powers. One of their formal powers is the ability to veto legislation passed by Congress. President Washington vetoed only two pieces of legislation during his two terms in office. President Franklin Delano Roosevelt cast the most vetoes—at 635. He, however, was president for 14 years. Dividing 635 by 14 reveals that Roosevelt cast an average of 45 vetoes for each year in office.

Data File: **USPRES**

Task: **Univariate**

➤ Primary Variable: **18) VETOES**

➤ View: **Pie**

VETOES -- Average Number of Vetoes for Each Year in Office (CWP)

		%
■	0) 0 to 1	32.6
▨	1) 2 to 5	23.3
▨	2) 6 to 12	30.2
▢	3) Over 12	14.0
	TOTAL (N)	43

Here we see that about one-third of the presidents cast no more than one veto for each year in office, one-quarter of the presidents cast between two and five vetoes each year, another third vetoed six to twelve pieces of legislation each year, and 14 percent vetoed twelve or more bills for every year in office.

Data File: **USPRES**
➤ Task: **Cross-tabulation**
➤ Row Variable: **18) VETOES**
➤ Column Variable: **35) ERA**
➤ View: **Table**
➤ Display: **Column %**

VETOES by ERA
Cramer's V: 0.768**

		ERA		
		Pre CW	Post CW	TOTAL
VETOES	**0 to 1**	12	2	14
		75.0%	7.4%	32.6%
	2 to 5	4	6	10
		25.0%	22.2%	23.3%
	6 to 12	0	13	13
		0.0%	48.1%	30.2%
	Over 12	0	6	6
		0.0%	22.2%	14.0%
	TOTAL	16	27	43
		100.0%	100.0%	

Presidents up until the time of the Civil War were quite reluctant to use the veto power. As mentioned previously, George Washington cast only two vetoes. John Adams, Thomas Jefferson, John Quincy Adams, William Harrison, Zachary Taylor, and Millard Fillmore did not veto any legislation. Three-quarters of the pre–Civil War presidents cast either no vetoes or less than one veto for each year in office. None of these presidents averaged more than five vetoes per year. Since the Civil War, half of the presidents have cast between six and twelve vetoes for each year in office.

Presidential vetoes may be considered a sign of a strong presidency or a weak presidency. Franklin Delano Roosevelt was one of the strongest presidents in U.S. history, convincing Congress to pass his New Deal programs. Yet, Roosevelt often resorted to using vetoes as well. Thus, some great presidents use the veto power to further increase their influence. On the other hand, vetoes also may be a sign of presidential weakness. A stronger president should be able to influence Congress during the early stages of the legislative process, such that bills the president finds objectionable do not pass Congress. Gerald Ford succeeded to the presidency after the resignation of President Richard Nixon. Ford was never elected president and thus could not claim a popular mandate. He also faced a Congress controlled by the opposition party. Ford had little influence over Congress and used the presidential veto 66 times. Many of Ford's vetoes, additionally, were overturned by Congress.

Congress can vacate a presidential veto with two-thirds votes in both the U.S. House of Representatives and the Senate. With a super-majority vote required in both houses of Congress, overrides of presidential vetoes are rare. Less than 5 percent of vetoes are overturned by Congress. Perhaps a surer sign of presidential weakness is the percent of vetoes overridden by Congress.

Data File: **USPRES**
➤ Task: **Univariate**
➤ Primary Variable: **29) OVERRIDE**
➤ View: **Pie**

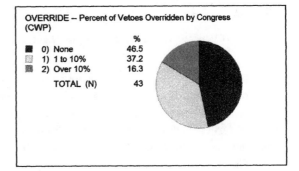

OVERRIDE – Percent of Vetoes Overridden by Congress (CWP)

		%
■	0) None	46.5
▨	1) 1 to 10%	37.2
▨	2) Over 10%	16.3
	TOTAL (N)	43

This chart shows that nearly half (46.5 percent) of presidents have had no vetoes overridden. But remember that a number of early presidents cast no vetoes and therefore could have no vetoes overridden. A more appropriate chart would examine only presidents from the post–Civil War era, when vetoes, and overrides of vetoes, are more common.

Data File: **USPRES**	
Task: **Univariate**	
Primary Variable: **29) OVERRIDE**	
➤ *Subset Variable:* **35) ERA**	
➤ *Subset Categories:* **Include: 1) Post CW**	
➤ *View:* **Pie**	

OVERRIDE -- Percent of Vetoes Overridden by Congress (CWP)

		%
■	0) None	22.2
▨	1) 1 to 10%	59.3
▨	2) Over 10%	18.5
	TOTAL (N)	27

[Subset]

Looking only at presidents since the Civil War, we see that presidents can expect that between 1 and 10 percent of their vetoes will be overridden by Congress. Only six presidents have been able to sustain all of their vetoes, while five other presidents have seen more than 10 percent overturned.

PRESIDENTS AND THE COURTS: APPOINTMENT POWERS

Presidents attempt to influence the legislative process by proposing legislation, molding the national agenda, and signing or vetoing legislation. They influence the judicial branch through their appointment of judges. Presidents nominate potential judges, and the Senate typically confirms these nominees. Presidents nominate judges both to the Supreme Court and for all other federal courts. Once confirmed, these judges serve lifetime appointments. Thus, one of the legacies of any president is in the number of judges appointed. Let's first look at Supreme Court appointments.

Data File: **USPRES**	
Task: **Univariate**	
➤ *Primary Variable:* **25) SUP CT**	
➤ *View:* **Pie**	

SUP CT -- Number of Supreme Court Appointments (COURT)

		%
■	0) None	11.6
▨	1) One	23.3
▨	2) 2 - 3	34.9
☐	3) 4 or more	30.2
	TOTAL (N)	43

If you are replicating this pie chart, be sure to delete the subset variable from the previous example.

Four presidents were unable to appoint any Supreme Court judges, because no vacancies occurred on the Court during that president's term in office. President Jimmy Carter was one of these presidents who never had the opportunity to appoint a Supreme Court justice. President George W. Bush during his first term also did not have a chance to make a Supreme Court nomination. Of the nine justices on the Supreme Court in April 2005, President Reagan appointed four, Presidents George H. Bush and Bill Clinton each appointed two, and one was appointed by President Ford. As the pie chart shows, most presidents can expect to appoint between one and three Supreme Court justices, but one-third of the presidents have been able to appoint four or more justices.

Data File: **USPRES**
Task: **Univariate**
➤ *Primary Variable:* **26) TOT JUDGES**
➤ *View:* **Pie**

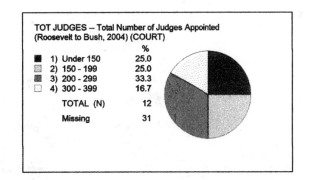

Presidents make many more judicial appointments to federal district courts or to the federal court of appeals. The pie chart above indicates the total number of judges appointed by presidents since Franklin Delano Roosevelt's presidency. As shown, presidents make hundreds of judicial appointments. Because presidents tend to appoint judges from their own political party, these presidential appointments shape the future decision making of the judicial branch.

Your turn.

REVIEW QUESTIONS

Based on the first part of this exercise, answer True or False to the following items:

1. More presidents are from California than from any other state.   T   F

2. Most democracies have copied the American institution of the presidency.   T   F

3. The 22nd Amendment limits presidents to two terms.   T   F

4. Abraham Lincoln was the first Republican to be elected president.   T   F

5. Most presidents can expect that over 10 percent of their vetoes will be overridden
    by Congress.   T   F

6. Every president has been able to appoint at least one Supreme Court justice.   T   F

EXPLORIT QUESTIONS

PRESIDENTS' PRIOR OFFICES

The experience and background of a candidate becomes an issue in every presidential election. Vice presidents benefit, or suffer, based on the public's view of the current administration.Senators have experience in national politics, but may have no executive experience. Governors, and others with no experience in Washington D.C., may benefit from being outsiders, but may also be accused of lacking experience in national and international affairs. Candidates from appointed positions or nongovernment positions may be attacked for not having served in an elective office, but may benefit from having broad experience in cabinet, diplomatic, or other nongovernment positions.

Let's see if past presidents shared common backgrounds.

> *Data File:* **USPRES**
> *Task:* **Univariate**
> *Primary Variable:* **21) GOV?**
> *View:* **Pie**

7. What percentage of past presidents had been governors?   _____%

> *Data File:* **USPRES**
> *Task:* **Univariate**
> ➤ *Primary Variable:* **22) SEN?**
> ➤ *View:* **Pie**

8. What percentage of past presidents had been senators?   _____%

> *Data File:* **USPRES**
> *Task:* **Univariate**
> ➤ *Primary Variable:* **23) VEEP?**
> ➤ *View:* **Pie**

9. What percentage of past presidents had been vice presidents?   _____%

In Exercise 10, the term "minority" president was introduced. Rather than referring to the ethnic or racial background of a president, this term referred to presidents who were elected by less than 50 percent of the popular vote. President George W. Bush is a minority president, since he lost the popular vote to Democratic candidate Al Gore, but won the presidency with a majority of the electoral college vote. President Bill Clinton also was a minority president, because the strong showing of third-party candidate Ross Perot split the popular vote three ways, leaving Clinton to win the presidency with 43 percent (1992) and 49 percent (1996) of the popular vote. How many U.S. presidents have been minority presidents, elected with less than 50 percent of the popular vote? (The ten missing cases in the pie chart occur because no popular vote was recorded for the first five presidents and five presidents succeeded to the office from the vice presidency and never won the presidency on their own.)

> *Data File:* **USPRES**
> *Task:* **Univariate**
> ➤ *Primary Variable:* **34) MINOR**
> ➤ *View:* **Pie**

10. Nearly half of the U.S. presidents have been minority presidents, receiving less
    than half of the popular vote.   T   F

EXPLAINING PRESIDENTIAL VETOES

In the opening section of this exercise, we saw that the rate at which presidents veto legislation varied. Early presidents rarely vetoed legislation. Since the Civil War, some presidents have cast many vetoes, while others have vetoed very little legislation. Let's see if we can uncover any patterns in the use of the veto power by presidents.

Since the veto power was not used frequently by presidents prior to the Civil War, we will use the subsetting facility of MicroCase to look only at post–Civil War presidents. Once you select 35) ERA as the subset variable, a menu will appear with categories to select. Use your mouse to check off the category for post–Civil War presidents. Make sure that the option of "Include Selected Categories" has a black dot in the circle. If this option is not selected, click on it with your mouse. The remainder of the questions in this exercise will use only post–Civil War presidents. Once you have selected this subset of cases, it will remain in force as long as you use the arrow key (rather than the menu key) to return to the cross-tabulation menu.

Another factor to keep in mind when looking at post–Civil War presidents is that there are only 26 people who have been the nation's chief executive during this time period. With so few cases, patterns in the data have to be very strong before we can assume that these patterns have not occurred by random chance. Thus, differences in percentages across categories will need to be very large to reach statistical significance. However, if we find patterns which are statistically significant, they also will be substantively important. Let's first examine whether Democratic or Republican presidents have cast more vetoes.

Data File:	**USPRES**
➤ *Task:*	**Cross-tabulation**
➤ *Row Variable:*	**18) VETOES**
➤ *Column Variable:*	**6) PARTY**
➤ *Subset Variable:*	**35) ERA**
➤ *Subset Categories:*	**Include: 1) Post CW**
➤ *View:*	**Table**
➤ *Display:*	**Column %**

11. What is the value of V for this table?   V = _____

12. Is V statistically significant?   Yes   No

13. The pattern in this table is strong enough to exceed random chance, and thus we can conclude that Republican presidents cast more vetoes than Democratic presidents.   T   F

Presidential success with Congress may depend on the strength of the presidential party in Congress. A Republican president will have more natural allies, who would vote to sustain the president's vetoes, if the Republican party was the majority party in Congress. Variable 28) PTY-CONG measures the strength of the president's party in Congress by the number of years the president's party is the majority party in one or both houses of Congress. Does the strength of the president's party in Congress influence the rate at which presidents veto legislation?

Data File:	**USPRES**
Task:	**Cross-tabulation**
Row Variable:	**18) VETOES**
➤ *Column Variable:*	**28) PTY-CONG**
➤ *Subset Variable:*	**35) ERA**
➤ *Subset Categories:*	**Include: 1) Post CW**
➤ *View:*	**Table**
➤ *Display:*	**Column %**

14. What is the value of V for this table?   V = _____

15. Is V statistically significant?   Yes   No

16. We can be certain, beyond a reasonable doubt, that when the president's party is stronger in Congress the president will cast fewer vetoes.   T   F

Do "minority" presidents, elected by less than 50 percent of the popular vote, have less influence over Congress and thus need to resort to casting more presidential vetoes?

Data File:	**USPRES**
Task:	**Cross-tabulation**
Row Variable:	**18) VETOES**
➤ *Column Variable:*	**34) MINOR**
➤ *Subset Variable:*	**35) ERA**
➤ *Subset Categories:*	**Include: 1) Post CW**
➤ *View:*	**Table**
➤ *Display:*	**Column %**

17. What is the value of V for this table?   V = _____

18. Is V statistically significant?   Yes   No

19. We can be certain, beyond a reasonable doubt, that presidents elected by less than a majority of the popular vote will cast more vetoes.   T   F

We might expect that presidents who served as senators may better understand Congress and thus have to resort to a veto less often, whereas presidents who served as governors may be less acquainted with the ways of Washington D.C. and have to cast more vetoes.

Data File:	**USPRES**
Task:	**Cross-tabulation**
Row Variable:	**18) VETOES**
➤ *Column Variable:*	**22) SEN?**
➤ *Subset Variable:*	**35) ERA**
➤ *Subset Categories:*	**Include: 1) Post CW**
➤ *View:*	**Table**
➤ *Display:*	**Column %**

20. What is the value of V for this table?   V = _____

21. Is V statistically significant?   Yes   No

22. We can be certain, beyond a reasonable doubt, that presidents who previously served in the Senate will cast fewer vetoes.   T   F

       Data File: **USPRES**
          Task: **Cross-tabulation**
   Row Variable: **18) VETOES**
➤ *Column Variable:* **21) GOV?**
➤ *Subset Variable:* **35) ERA**
➤ *Subset Categories:* **Include: 1) Post CW**
       ➤ *View:* **Table**
   ➤ *Display:* **Column %**

23. What is the value of V for this table?   V = _____

24. Is V statistically significant?   Yes   No

25. We can be certain, beyond a reasonable doubt, that presidents who
      previously served as governors will cast more vetoes.   T   F

26. It is easy to predict the number of vetoes a president will cast based on
      prior political experience, president's electoral strength, and the strength of
      the president's party in Congress.   T   F

EXPLAINING VETO OVERRIDES

In the beginning of this exercise, we also saw that presidents vary in their success in sustaining their vetoes. While few vetoes are overridden by Congress, some presidents had none of their vetoes overturned; other presidents have more than 10 percent overridden by Congress. Once again, we will confine our analysis to post–Civil War presidents, who have been more likely to issue vetoes and thus have presented Congress with more opportunities to overturn these vetoes. Do Democratic or Republican presidents have more of their vetoes overridden by Congress?

       Data File: **USPRES**
          Task: **Cross-tabulation**
➤ *Row Variable:* **29) OVERRIDE**
➤ *Column Variable:* **6) PARTY**
➤ *Subset Variable:* **35) ERA**
➤ *Subset Categories:* **Include: 1) Post CW**
       ➤ *View:* **Table**
   ➤ *Display:* **Column %**

27. What is the value of V for this table?   V = _____

28. Is V statistically significant?   Yes   No

29. The pattern in this table exceeds random chance; thus we can conclude that
      Republican presidents have more of their vetoes overridden by Congress.   T   F

Next let's test whether the strength of the president's party in Congress influences the rate at which presidential vetoes are overridden.

Data File: **USPRES**
Task: **Cross-tabulation**
Row Variable: **29) OVERRIDE**
➤ Column Variable: **28) PTY-CONG**
➤ Subset Variable: **35) ERA**
➤ Subset Categories: **Include: 1) Post CW**
➤ View: **Table**
➤ Display: **Column %**

30. What is the value of V for this table?   V = _____

31. Is V statistically significant?   Yes   No

32. The pattern in this table exceeds random chance; thus we can conclude
     that when the presidential party is stronger in Congress, presidential
     vetoes are overturned less often.   T   F

Next let's once again examine the effect of winning the presidency with less than a majority of the popular vote.

Data File: **USPRES**
Task: **Cross-tabulation**
Row Variable: **29) OVERRIDE**
➤ Column Variable: **34) MINOR**
➤ Subset Variable: **35) ERA**
➤ Subset Categories: **Include: 1) Post CW**
➤ View: **Table**
➤ Display: **Column %**

33. What is the value of V for this table?   V = _____

34. Is V statistically significant?   Yes   No

35. The pattern in this table exceeds random chance; thus we can conclude
     that presidents elected with less than a majority of the popular vote will
     see more of their vetoes overturned by Congress.   T   F

Let's return to prior service as senators versus governors to see if either is more successful in sustaining their vetoes.

> Data File: **USPRES**
> Task: **Cross-tabulation**
> Row Variable: **29) OVERRIDE**
> ➤ Column Variable: **22) SEN?**
> ➤ Subset Variable: **35) ERA**
> ➤ Subset Categories: **Include: 1) Post CW**
> ➤ View: **Table**
> ➤ Display: **Column %**

36. What is the value of V for this table?   V = _____

37. Is V statistically significant?   Yes   No

38. The pattern in this table exceeds random chance; thus we can conclude
    that presidents with prior service in the Senate have their vetoes overridden
    less often by Congress.   T   F

> Data File: **USPRES**
> Task: **Cross-tabulation**
> Row Variable: **29) OVERRIDE**
> ➤ Column Variable: **21) GOV?**
> ➤ Subset Variable: **35) ERA**
> ➤ Subset Categories: **Include: 1) Post CW**
> ➤ View: **Table**
> ➤ Display: **Column %**

39. What is the value of V for this table?   V = _____

40. Is V statistically significant?   Yes   No

41. The pattern in this table exceeds random chance; thus we can conclude
    that presidents with prior service as governors have their vetoes overridden
    more often by Congress.   T   F

42. It is easier to explain the number of presidential vetoes overridden than it is
    to explain the number of presidential vetoes originally cast.   T   F

WORKSHEET   EXERCISE 13

WHAT HAVE WE LEARNED?

I.   Who is likely to become a U.S. president? Do presidents tend to come from certain states? What previous offices have they held?

II.   One of the checks and balances written into the Constitution is the president's right to veto legislation counterbalanced by Congress's ability to override these vetoes. How often do Presidents' veto legislation? How often are these vetoes overridden by Congress? What, if any, factors can explain the number of presidential vetoes or the number of congressional overrides?

III.   Presidents appoint judges, who are usually confirmed by the Senate. How likely is a president to make an appointment to the Supreme Court? How often do presidents appoint judges to other federal courts? Why are these court appointments considered to be one of the lasting legacies of presidents?

WHAT ELSE CAN BE EXPLORED?

1. With the USPRES file you can explore more about the backgrounds of presidents. You can see how many were lawyers or military leaders, how many had a college education, how old they were when elected, and their religious and ethnic backgrounds. You could also explore whether differences exist in these traits between presidents from the 18th and 19th centuries versus those from the 20th and 21st centuries by using 27) CENTURY to distinguish between these two eras.

2. The USPRES file contains a variable 24) RATING which lists whether a president was ranked high, medium, or low by a group of political scientists and historians. Can you explain which presidents were ranked more highly by looking at some of their background factors or behavior in office?

3. With the STATES file you can explore the presidential elections from 1920 to 2004. For each election, a variable (e.g., STATES'20) is included that maps the states won by each presidential candidate, while a second set of variables (e.g., HARDING'20) lists the popular vote in each state for the winning candidate (and sometimes additional contestants). In an earlier chapter we looked at how support has changed in the South for Democratic versus Republican presidential candidates. Can you find any other regional changes (e.g., northeastern, western, or midwestern states) in support for each party's presidential candidates?

THE BUREAUCRACY

The President . . . may require the Opinion, in writing, of the principal Officer in each of the executive Departments, upon any Subject relating to the Duties of their respective Offices . . . and by and with the Advice and Consent of the Senate, shall appoint Ambassadors, other public Ministers and Consuls, Judges of the supreme Court, and all other Officers of the United States, whose Appointments are not herein otherwise provided for, and which shall be established by Law; but the Congress may by Law vest the Appointment of such inferior Officers, as they think proper, in the President alone, in the Courts of Law, or in the Heads of Departments.

SECTION 2, ARTICLE II, UNITED STATES CONSTITUTION

Tasks: Mapping, Univariate, Cross-Tabulation, Historical Trends, Scatterplot
Data Files: STATES, GSS, HISTORY, NATIONS

The section of the Constitution quoted above is *everything* the founders bothered to say about the executive branch of government, aside from the presidency. Nothing is said about a cabinet, about a State Department, or about any of the thousands of agencies that today constitute the federal government and often are referred to collectively as the bureaucracy. The reason the Constitution said so little about this aspect of government is that in those days the government was so little.

In traditional agrarian societies, such as those in Europe during medieval times, the government was nothing more than the king's or queen's household and court. Needed functionaries such as clerks, accountants, and tax collectors were servants of the crown, equal in status to the cooks, grooms, and butlers making up the royal household. When the ruler needed a general, an advisor, a chief justice, or an administrator of the treasury, one of the noble members of the court was asked to do the job. The nobles did not regard a government post as an occupation or even a full-time activity. Often they had no special qualifications beyond their noble birth and their social graces.

This system worked because governments in those days did very little. Beyond extracting taxes from the populace, maintaining a minimum of public order, and defending the realm against invaders, there was little to do. After all, more than 90 percent of the population led quiet rural lives without schools, post offices, roads, hospitals, or fire departments. Laws were simple. There were no regulatory agencies, no inspectors, and no *paperwork*—tax collectors used carts, not forms.

As the world became modern, this system could not suffice. With rapidly growing populations and the rise of industry, the demands on government grew. As a result, governments got much larger. And, as more and more people were needed to staff the government, the old selection methods became obsolete.

When George Washington took office as the first president of the United States, his first task was to appoint people to fill all of the jobs in the federal government including postmasters to manage all the local post offices. In making these appointments, Washington *personally* evaluated each person. How could he? Easily, there being fewer than 700 of them! For years, each time the political party in control of the American government changed, nearly all government employees were discharged and replaced with supporters of the new administration. Thus, when Thomas Jefferson took office, he fired hundreds of Federalists appointed by Presidents Washington and Adams and replaced them with his supporters. This practice was known as the **spoils system**: the spoils (or benefits) of public office go to the supporters of winning politicians. This system reached its height in American history when Andrew Jackson was elected and thousands of government employees were terminated.

Aside from corruption and other abuses, the spoils system was undesirable because it meant that many technical or otherwise complex jobs were continually being turned over to beginners. Eventually, the civil service system was introduced whereby people are hired and promoted on the basis of merit, not political connections, and they may be terminated only for sufficient cause.

Today, governments, like all *large organizations*, are **bureaucracies**. All bureaucracies have certain key features. They consist of a set of positions, each with very specific and often very specialized duties. These positions are administered on the basis of clearly specified lines of authority. Hiring and promotion are done on the basis of qualifications and training. Finally, and very important, careful, written records are kept of all communications and transactions.

Bureaucracies exist because they are the most efficient solution to the problems of coordinating and controlling the actions of large numbers of people involved in some common enterprise, whether it be managing General Motors or running the Department of Commerce.

The problem is that bureaucracies often develop goals of their own, and these may put them in conflict with the purposes for which the organization was created or with the interests of those whom it was intended to serve. This is why the words *bureaucrat* and *bureaucracy* carry unpleasant connotations, suggesting meddlesome people and muddled organizations. This is especially true when people speak of government bureaucracies. From all parties and nearly all candidates, complaints are directed toward government agencies and their millions of employees—the bureaucracy. It is too big, too wasteful, too arrogant, too powerful, and too inefficient.

Let's pursue some of these concerns.

GOVERNMENT WORKERS

> ➤ *Data File:* **STATES**
> ➤ *Task:* **Mapping**
> ➤ *Variable 1:* **79) FEDEMPLOY**
> ➤ *View:* **List: Rank**

RANK	CASE NAME	VALUE
1	Maryland	244.0
2	Alaska	218.4
3	Hawaii	201.5
4	Virginia	196.2
5	Connecticut	144.6
6	Utah	142.3
7	New Mexico	140.4
8	Montana	131.9
9	South Dakota	131.6
10	North Dakota	126.2

Here we see that the federal bureaucracy is not confined to Washington D.C. Among the states, Maryland and Virginia have among the highest proportions of federal employees because so many agencies have moved to suburbs near Washington. Their employees often become residents of these two states which surround the District. However, many other states far from Washington are high in federal employees. One reason is that they have many military installations. Members of the armed forces are not counted in these personnel figures, but military bases always employ a lot of civilians.

Obviously, the federal payroll has grown incredibly since the days of George Washington. Every state has many times more federal employees than made up the total number in 1789. Let's examine this growth.

> ➤ *Data File:* **HISTORY**
> ➤ *Task:* **Historical Trends**
> ➤ *Variables:* **53) NON-D EMP**

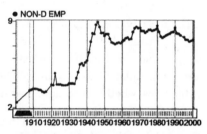

Non-defense executive branch employees per 1000 population

In 1900 there were slightly over 2 government employees per 1,000 population. Since the mid-sixties, this rate has been about 8 per 1,000. (Those employed in national defense are not included in these numbers.)

TRUST IN THE EXECUTIVE BRANCH

> ➤ *Data File:* **GSS**
> ➤ *Task:* **Univariate**
> ➤ *Primary Variable:* **52) FED.GOV'T?**
> ➤ *View:* **Pie**

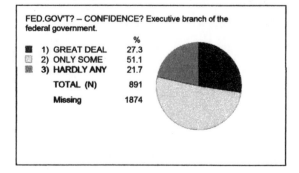

Exercise 14: The Bureaucracy

233

Here we see that although a fifth (21.7 percent) of Americans say they have only a low level of confidence in the executive branch of the federal government, a majority of Americans (51.1 percent) say they have at least some confidence. Another quarter (27.3 percent) say they have a "great deal" of confidence. That is not a very powerful vote of confidence. What about public evaluations of other branches of government?

Data File: **GSS**
➤ Task: **Cross-tabulation**
➤ Row Variable: **52) FED.GOV'T?**
➤ Column Variable: **55) SUP.COURT?**
➤ View: **Table**
➤ Display: **Total %**

FED.GOV'T? by SUP.COURT?
Cramer's V: 0.327**

	SUP.COURT?				
	GREAT DEAL	ONLY SOME	HARDLY ANY	Missing	TOTAL
GREAT DEAL	155	73	10	5	238
	17.8%	8.4%	1.1%		27.4%
ONLY SOME	132	278	34	11	444
	15.2%	32.0%	3.9%		51.0%
HARDLY ANY	31	99	58	5	188
	3.6%	11.4%	6.7%		21.6%
Missing	3	4	2	1865	1874
TOTAL	318	450	102	1886	870
	36.6%	51.7%	11.7%		

Note first that the instructions ask MicroCase to calculate total percents. Total percents are calculated by dividing the number in each cell by the total number of respondents answering both questions (in this example, 1,865). Total percents are helpful when we are not looking for a cause and effect pattern between two variables, but only whether two attitudes might overlap. Thus, the number in the upper left corner indicates what percent of all respondents ranked both the executive branch and the Supreme Court in the highest category.

About one in five Americans (17.8 percent) rank both the executive branch and the Supreme Court highly. The most typical response, however, is to have some confidence in both institutions, with one-third of Americans (32.0 percent) falling into this category. Less than 10 percent of Americans (6.7 percent) give both institutions the lowest ranking of hardly any confidence. The answers for these three groups fall along the diagonal of the table—these are the people who have the same opinion of both institutions, whether it is high, medium or low.

Respondents who fall in the categories to the left and below the diagonal are those who rank the executive branch lower than the Supreme Court. Adding together the totals for these three cells (15.2, 3.6, 11.4) reveals that one-third (30.2 percent) of Americans rank the Supreme Court as more trustworthy than the executive branch. Respondents in the three cells above and to the right of the diagonal constitute those who rank the executive branch more highly than the Supreme Court. Only 13.4 percent of respondents fall into these categories. Thus, while most Americans (56.5 percent on the table diagonal) have an identical rating of these two branches of the government, one-third ranks the Supreme Court higher and only one in 10 ranks the executive branch higher.

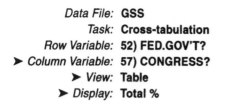

Data File:	GSS
Task:	Cross-tabulation
Row Variable:	52) FED.GOV'T?
➤ Column Variable:	57) CONGRESS?
➤ View:	Table
➤ Display:	Total %

FED.GOV'T?   by   CONGRESS?
Cramer's V: 0.376**

| | | CONGRESS? | | | | |
		GREAT DEAL	ONLY SOME	HARDLY ANY	Missing	TOTAL
F E D . G O V ' T ?	GREAT DEAL	85	125	33	0	243
		9.6%	14.2%	3.7%		27.6%
	ONLY SOME	27	342	79	7	448
		3.1%	38.8%	9.0%		50.8%
	HARDLY ANY	5	79	107	2	191
		0.6%	9.0%	12.1%		21.7%
	Missing	0	7	3	1864	1874
	TOTAL	117	546	219	1873	882
		13.3%	61.9%	24.8%		

This table looks at respondents' confidence in the executive branch compared to Congress. Once again, the most typical response (38.8 percent) is to rank both institutions in the some confidence category. One in four (21.7 percent) ranks both institutions the same but either in the high (9.6 percent) or low (12.1 percent) categories. Another quarter (26.9 percent) rate the executive branch more highly than Congress (cells above and to the right of the diagonal), while only one in ten (12.7 percent) ranks Congress more highly than the executive branch (cells below and to the left of the diagonal).

Many Americans rank all three institutions the same. Among those who distinguish among the three, the Supreme Court tends to receive the highest rankings, followed by the executive branch. Congress receives the least confidence from American public. The next figure shows trends in these evaluations across the last 30 years.

➤ Data File:	HISTORY
➤ Task:	Historical Trends
➤ Variables:	38) CONF CONG
	39) CONF COURT
	40) CONF GOV

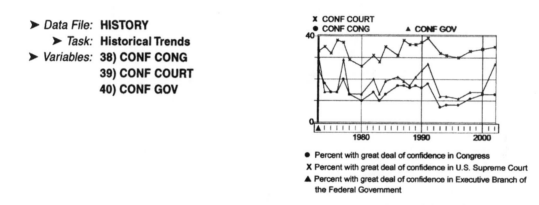

● Percent with great deal of confidence in Congress
X Percent with great deal of confidence in U.S. Supreme Court
▲ Percent with great deal of confidence in Executive Branch of the Federal Government

Across the entire time span, public confidence is highest for the Supreme Court. Evaluations of Congress and the executive branch are lower but tend to move together. One exception is the last entry, for 2002, where public confidence in the executive branch was 10 percentage points higher for the executive branch than for Congress. The recent events of 9/11 in 2001 may have increased public confidence in the executive branch in this 2002 survey. National crises produce the rally-around-the-flag phenomena, where the public increases its support of the president. As the president is the head of the executive branch, some of the increased support for the president may spill over to influence opinions about the executive branch as well.

Your turn.

WORKSHEET

NAME:

COURSE:

DATE:

EXERCISE

14

REVIEW QUESTIONS

Based on the first part of this exercise, answer True or False to the following items:

1. The civil service system also is called the spoils system. T F

2. The secretary of agriculture is the only cabinet member mentioned in the Constitution. T F

3. Thomas Jefferson participated in the spoils system. T F

4. The principal defect of bureaucracies is that promotion usually is based on who you know. T F

5. Large business organizations manage not to become bureaucracies. T F

EXPLORIT QUESTIONS

FEDERAL EMPLOYMENT

According to the preliminary discussion, a sizable proportion of federal employees are used to staff military installations. Let's look at the relationship between the per capita Defense Department expenditures and the federal employment rate across states.

> ➤ Data File: **STATES**
> ➤ Task: **Scatterplot**
> ➤ Dependent Variable: **79) FEDEMPLOY**
> ➤ Independent Variable: **87) MILITARY $**
> ➤ View: **Reg. Line**

6. What is the value of the Pearson correlation coefficient? r = _____

7. Is the relationship statistically significant? Yes No

8. This result fails to support the idea that the greater the military presence in a state, the higher the federal employment rate. T F

Many people are concerned about the growth of government. Let's look at government growth in more detail.

> ➤ *Data File:* **HISTORY**
> > ➤ *Task:* **Historical Trends**
> ➤ *Variables:* **49) FED EMP RT**

9. Government employment seems to

    a. have increased at a relatively constant rate.

    b. have spikes at certain short periods.

    c. have had little change over time.

10. Scrolling through the events listed at the bottom, which of the following events seem to have had the greatest impact on the government employment rate?

    a. presidential elections

    b. wars

    c. new inventions

    d. constitutional amendments

Let's separate defense employment from nondefense government employment.

> *Data File:* **HISTORY**
> *Task:* **Historical Trends**
> ➤ *Variables:* **50) DEF EMP RT**
> **53) NON-D EMP**

11. Wars affect defense employment but have relatively little impact on other types of government employment.   T   F

12. Since the Vietnam War ended in 1974, the defense employment rate has slowly declined.   T   F

13. The nondefense government employment rate has remained fairly constant since the mid-sixties.   T   F

14. Except for wartime, nondefense employment is higher than defense employment.   T   F

FEDERAL SPENDING

Government outlays over time also reflect the relative growth of various segments of government. Of course, one area of spending for the government is for defense. Another general area of spending assists individual Americans. These are human resource programs. Many American families are touched by these programs, which include Social Security and Medicare for the elderly, Food Stamps and Head Start programs for the poor, and government guarantees for student loans for college students. Let's look at spending levels for defense and human resources over time (controlling for the size of the U.S population).

> Data File: **HISTORY**
>> Task: **Historical Trends**
> ➤ Variables: **54) DEF$/POP**
>> **55) HR$/POP**

15. Spending on human resources has been growing since the late sixties.   T   F

16. Since the mid-eighties, spending on national defense was fairly stable between the mid-1980s and 2000.   T   F

In the 1930s, when the Social Security program was first enacted, only 5.4 percent of Americans were over the age of 65. In the 1960s, when Medicare, the health insurance program for the elderly, was passed, 9.3 percent of Americans were over the age of 65. The 2000 census showed 12.4 percent of Americans over 65. How has this increase in the elderly affected government spending on these programs?

> Data File: **HISTORY**
>> Task: **Historical Trends**
> ➤ Variables: **56) S.S.$/POP**
>> **58) MED$/POP**

17. Federal spending has increased on Social Security and Medicare since the 1970s.   T   F

18. The federal government spends more money on Medicare than on Social Security.   T   F

HANDLING HEALTH CARE

The federal government is not the only level of government that has bureaucracies. State and local governments also have bureaucracies and provide many complementary services to the federal government. Both levels of government have agencies responsible for schools, transportation, crime prevention, and a host of other government functions. Let's examine health care spending by the 50 state governments. The specific variable in the STATES file looks at health care spending per capita, that is, the dollar amount spent per state resident.

> ➤ Data File: **STATES**
> ➤ Task: **Mapping**
> ➤ Variable 1: **112) ST HEALTH**
> ➤ View: **List: Rank**

19. Which state spends the highest dollar amount per state resident?   _____

20. How much money does this state spend per resident? $ _____

21. Which state spends the lowest dollar amount per state resident?   _____

22. How much money does this state spend per resident? $ _____

One reason states may vary in health expenditures is the types of preferences found in the population. In general, Democrats tend to prefer more government spending on social welfare programs, whereas Republicans tend to prefer less government spending on such programs. Let's add a measure of the partisanship of each state's residents to see if this can explain variations in state expenditures on health programs.

> Data File: **STATES**
> Task: **Mapping**
> ➤ Variable 1: **112) ST HEALTH**
> ➤ Variable 2: **49) POP-DEM**
> ➤ View: **Map**

                                                                                          ___

23. What is the correlation between Democratic citizenry and state spending on
    health programs?   r = _____

24. Is it statistically significant?   Yes   No

25. Do these results support the notion that states with more Democratic
    citizens spend more money on health care?   Yes   No

Nations also vary in their level of government support for health care. Many of the industrialized nations provide their citizens with health insurance. In the United States, health insurance is privately funded. Let's see how the United States compares to other industrial countries in total spending (both private and government spending) per capita on health care.

> ➤ Data File: **NATIONS**
> ➤ Task: **Mapping**
> ➤ Variable 1: **41) HEALTH**
> ➤ View: **List: Rank**

                                                                                        RANK

26. U.S. ranking on total (private and public) spending on health care as a
    percentage of GDP (gross domestic product)   _____

Now let's look at how the United States ranks on government spending on health care. The variable in the NATIONS data set calculates the percentage of total health care spending which comes from government sources.

> Data File: **NATIONS**
> Task: **Mapping**
> ➤ Variable 1: **42) GOVT-HLT**
> ➤ View: **List: Rank**

                                                                                        RANK

27. U.S. ranking on government spending on health care   _____

CHARACTERITICS AND ATTITUDES OF GOVERNMENT WORKERS

More than 21 million Americans work for a government agency. About one in ten of these government workers are employed by the **federal government**, while nearly 90 percent work for a state or local government. Government employees are a diverse workforce. There are social workers and teachers, accountants and lawyers, chemists and geologists, clerks and janitors, bus drivers and mechanics, and police officers and firefighters. The list goes on to include almost every profession and job type in the U.S. today. Nevertheless, all these individuals work for one of the many U.S. governments. As a group, do government workers have any characteristics that distinguish them from other Americans? To explore this possibility, we can use a question from the GSS which asks respondents if they work for the government. Let's start with seeing if people with different characteristics are more or less likely to become a government employee.

> ➤ *Data File:* **GSS**
> ➤ *Task:* **Cross-tabulation**
> ➤ *Row Variable:* **19) WORK GOVT**
> ➤ *Column Variable:* **3) EDUCATION**
> ➤ *View:* **Table**
> ➤ *Display:* **Column %**

Be sure to look at the percentages in the table, the value of Cramer's V, and whether the relationship is statistically significant when answering the following series of questions.

28. College graduates are more likely than those from other levels of
    education to become government workers.   T   F

> *Data File:* **GSS**
>   *Task:* **Cross-tabulation**
> *Row Variable:* **19) WORK GOVT**
> ➤ *Column Variable:* **7) RACE**
> ➤ *View:* **Table**
> ➤ *Display:* **Column %**

29. Africans Americans are more likely than whites to become
    government workers.   T   F

> *Data File:* **GSS**
>   *Task:* **Cross-tabulation**
> *Row Variable:* **19) WORK GOVT**
> ➤ *Column Variable:* **21) PARTY**
> ➤ *View:* **Table**
> ➤ *Display:* **Column %**

30. Democrats are more likely than Republicans to become government workers.   T   F

Now let's consider whether government workers hold different attitudes from other Americans. This requires a change in the variable ordering. Working for the government now becomes the independent variable, and attitudes become the dependent variables.

Data File:	**GSS**
Task:	**Cross-tabulation**
➤ Row Variable:	**33) POOR$**
➤ Column Variable:	**19) WORK GOVT**
➤ View:	**Table**
➤ Display:	**Column %**

31. Government workers are more likely than other Americans to feel that
    the government is spending too little money on the poor.   T   F

Data File:	**GSS**
Task:	**Cross-tabulation**
➤ Row Variable:	**28) DEFENSE$**
➤ Column Variable:	**19) WORK GOVT**
➤ View:	**Table**
➤ Display:	**Column %**

32. Government workers are less likely than other Americans to feel
    that too much money is being spent on defense.   T   F

Data File:	**GSS**
Task:	**Cross-tabulation**
➤ Row Variable:	**52) FED.GOV'T?**
➤ Column Variable:	**19) WORK GOVT**
➤ View:	**Table**
➤ Display:	**Column %**

33. Government workers are more likely than other Americans to have a
    great deal of confidence in the federal government.   T   F

WHAT HAVE WE LEARNED?

I.   What are the patterns in government employment? How has the number of government employees changed over time? What factors might explain these changes? Also, describe the types of agencies and levels of government where large numbers of government employees are found. How might the politics of an area be affected if it is home to a large number of government employees?

II.   What are the traits of government employees? How are they similar to or different from other Americans? How might these similarities or differences influence the operation of the numerous American governments and affect politics at the national, state, or local levels?

III.   How does the federal government spend its money? What are the patterns of spending on defense versus spending to assist individuals? Describe how spending on programs for the elderly has changed over time and what might be the future for these programs. Finally, governments have many choices when deciding whether and how to assist individuals with their medical needs. What have been the decisions of the U.S. federal and state governments in this area? How does this contrast to the decisions of other governments across the world?

WHAT ELSE CAN BE EXPLORED?

1. The GSS data file allows for further exploration of possible similarities or differences between government workers and other Americans. One strategy would be to try to discover other characteristics associated with becoming a government employee (i.e., government employment as the dependent variable), while another strategy would be to pursue further whether government employees have distinctive opinions on political issues (i.e., government employment as the independent variable).

2. Government spending can be investigated with the HISTORY file. One set of variables reveals the American public's preferences for government spending on the environment, defense, welfare, health, aid to minorities, and drug addition. Another set of variables contains additional information on government spending in specific categories. A final set of variables examines the federal government's revenue, deficit, and debt over time. Each of these three sets of variables are measured on different scales (percent public holding an opinion, federal spending controlled for population size, and revenue and debt as a percent of the size of the economy), so they cannot be placed on the same graph. However, historical trends could be compared across a series of graphs.

3. With the GSS file, Americans' confidence in the executive branch of the federal government can be investigated. Using 52) FED.GOV'T? as the dependent variable, a variety of individual traits and attitudes can be tested as potential causes (i.e., independent variables) for these evaluations of the executive branch.

THE COURTS

The judicial Power of the United States shall be vested in one supreme Court, and in such inferior Courts as the Congress may from time to time ordain and establish. The Judges, both of the supreme and inferior Courts, shall hold their Offices during good Behaviour, and shall, at stated Times, receive for their Services, a Compensation, which shall not be diminished during their Continuance in Office.

ARTICLE III, UNITED STATES
CONSTITUTION

Tasks: Mapping, Univariate, Cross-Tabulation, Historical Trends, Auto-Analyzer
Data Files: STATES, GSS, NES, HISTORY

The Supreme Court consists of nine justices, one of whom serves as chief justice. Justices are nominated by the president, and their appointment is confirmed (or rejected) by the Senate. Because all federal judges are appointed for life, the average term on the Court is quite long. Since the first justices were appointed in 1789, only 106 men and 2 women have served on the Court (Sandra Day O'Connor was appointed to the Court in 1981 by President Ronald Reagan, and Ruth Bader Ginsburg was appointed in 1993 by President Bill Clinton) and William Rehnquist is only the 15th chief justice.[1] Lifetime appointments also result in a relatively older Court—the average age was 71 in 2005.

➤ *Data File:* **STATES**
➤ *Task:* **Mapping**
➤ *Variable 1:* **57) # S. COURT**
➤ *View:* **List: Rank**

RANK	CASE NAME	VALUE
1	New York	14
2	Ohio	9
2	Massachusetts	9
4	Virginia	8
5	Tennessee	6
5	Pennsylvania	6
7	Kentucky	5
8	Georgia	4
8	Maryland	4
8	California	4

---

[1] In 1795, John Rutledge served for four months while Congress recessed. The Senate rejected his nomination when Congress reconvened. Thus, some scholars say Rehnquist is the 16th chief justice.

Here we see the number of justices from each state. Understandably, the oldest states have more justices since they have had much greater opportunity. Nevertheless, the South has been somewhat overrepresented on the Court, five of the top twelve states being southern or border states. A total of 19 states never have had a justice.

The Constitution says nothing about the courts having the power to overrule Congress and to reject laws as unconstitutional. Rather, those who wrote the Constitution assumed that the courts would confine themselves to applying existing law to specific cases, and they never anticipated judges asserting new "laws" or discarding old ones. Thus, in *The Federalist Papers*, Alexander Hamilton characterized the courts as the "least dangerous" and "the weakest" branch of government. However, in deciding a case in 1803, Chief Justice of the Supreme Court John Marshall asserted the right of the courts "to say what the law is." He further claimed that "a law repugnant to the Constitution is void." This position went unchallenged in Congress at that time and soon became the accepted view of Court power.

The Supreme Court often tackles the most controversial items of the day. The Court is the arbiter when different values conflict. For example, is burning the American flag a protected form of free speech or is it an unacceptable desecration of the flag? The Supreme Court ruled flag burning is a protected form of political speech. Do school vouchers, tuition assistance to students from poorly performing public schools to attend private schools, violate the separation of church and state when most of these private schools are affiliated with religious organizations? The Supreme Court ruled vouchers do not constitute state support for religion. The Supreme Court makes many such decisions about our civil liberties and civil rights. Lower courts make decisions about crime and punishment. While most of these decisions follow legal precedents, the discretion of judges in sentencing, for example, has provoked controversy in recent years.

AMERICAN PUBLIC OPINION TOWARD THE COURTS

➤ *Data File:* **GSS**
➤ *Task:* **Univariate**
➤ *Primary Variable:* **45) SCH.PRAY**
➤ *View:* **Pie**

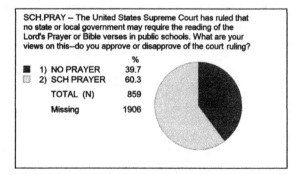

Although it has been more than 40 years since the Supreme Court prohibited government-sponsored prayer in the public schools, in 1962, this decision still has not gained general public acceptance. A large majority (60.3 percent) favor prayer in public schools. This is true even though the wording of the survey question maximizes support for the Court position since it does not deal with *allowing* prayer or Bible reading, but rather with laws *requiring* prayer or Bible reading.

Among the most controversial rulings are those interpreted by many as favoring the rights of criminals over those of victims of crimes. These concerns are not limited to the Supreme Court but are directed against the court system in general.

Data File: **GSS**
Task: **Univariate**
➤ Primary Variable: **42) COURTS?**
➤ View: **Pie**

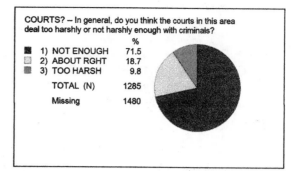

COURTS? – In general, do you think the courts in this area deal too harshly or not harshly enough with criminals?

		%
■	1) NOT ENOUGH	71.5
▨	2) ABOUT RGHT	18.7
▩	3) TOO HARSH	9.8
	TOTAL (N)	1285
	Missing	1480

Americans overwhelmingly accuse the courts of not being sufficiently harsh in their treatment of criminals.

Data File: **GSS**
Task: **Univariate**
➤ Primary Variable: **55) SUP.COURT?**
➤ View: **Pie**

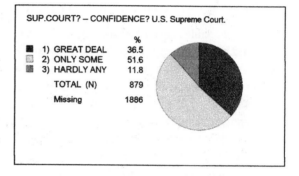

SUP.COURT? – CONFIDENCE? U.S. Supreme Court.

		%
■	1) GREAT DEAL	36.5
▨	2) ONLY SOME	51.6
▩	3) HARDLY ANY	11.8
	TOTAL (N)	879
	Missing	1886

Given these results, it is not surprising that Americans are somewhat ambivalent about the Supreme Court. While about one in three expresses a great deal of confidence in the Court, more than half (51.6 percent) say they have "only some" confidence and 11.8 percent say they have "hardly any" confidence in the Court.

But, whatever they feel about the Court, what do Americans actually *know* about it? For example, how many even know the name of the chief justice?

➤ Data File: **NES**
➤ Task: **Univariate**
➤ Primary Variable: **94) CHIEF J.ID**
➤ View: **Pie**

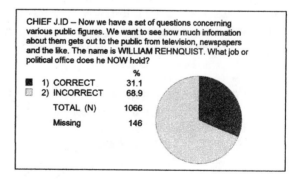

CHIEF J.ID – Now we have a set of questions concerning various public figures. We want to see how much information about them gets out to the public from television, newspapers and the like. The name is WILLIAM REHNQUIST. What job or political office does he NOW hold?

		%
■	1) CORRECT	31.1
▨	2) INCORRECT	68.9
	TOTAL (N)	1066
	Missing	146

When asked to name the job or political office held by William Rehnquist, only about one in three could correctly identify him as the chief justice of the Supreme Court, thus revealing him to be one of the least-known major public officials.

Data File: **NES**
➤ *Task:* **Cross-tabulation**
➤ *Row Variable:* **94) CHIEF J.ID**
➤ *Column Variable:* **113) NEWS TYPE**
➤ *View:* **Table**
➤ *Display:* **Column %**

CHIEF J.ID   by   NEWS TYPE
Cramer's V: 0.315**

| | NEWS TYPE | | | | | |
	TV & PAPER	NEWSPAPER	TV	NEITHER	Missing	TOTAL
CORRECT	84	78	47	122	1	331
	60.4%	47.6%	25.0%	21.3%		31.1%
INCORRECT	55	86	141	451	1	733
	39.6%	52.4%	75.0%	78.7%		68.9%
Missing	16	20	24	86	0	148
TOTAL	139	164	188	573	2	1064
	100.0%	100.0%	100.0%	100.0%		

How do we learn the names of public officials? Obviously it's from the news media. Here we see a clear example of the differential impact of TV and newspapers in informing citizens. People who read newspapers every day, but do not watch TV news that often, are twice as likely to have correctly identified William Rehnquist than are those who rely only on TV for their daily news. And those who rely on both TV and newspapers are even more likely to know Rehnquist than those who rely entirely on printed news.

A very plausible reason for the failure of TV to inform the public on many matters is that it is well known that TV scrimps on coverage of events for which it has no video and gives extra coverage, even to rather unimportant events, if it has good video. There is no video of the Supreme Court, so TV cannot let us see Rehnquist or other Court members in their official roles. Instead, important Supreme Court decisions usually are reported on TV by a reporter standing on the steps of the Court building and summarizing what the Court has done. Further, TV reports always are much shorter than the coverage given the same stories in newspapers—news stories usually contain many times more words than do the equivalent TV stories. As a result, the names of judges are mentioned far less often on TV than the names of other important officials.

SUPREME COURT DOCKET

The U.S. Supreme Court has many powers. It interprets laws and, occasionally, declares laws unconstitutional. But before the Supreme Court can issue a ruling on a case, it must first decide to hear that case. The Supreme Court selects to hear only a few cases from the thousands of cases appealed to it each year. Foremost the Supreme Court justices have time to hear only a select number of cases, as each case involves a number of stages from oral arguments, to preliminary discussion of decisions, to a final written opinion. By selecting among cases, the Court also demonstrates its power to decide what are the most important legal questions facing the nation. Let's examine both the number of cases appealed to the Supreme Court and the number of cases that conclude with a written opinion.

➤ *Data File:* **HISTORY**
➤ *Task:* **Historical Trends**
➤ *Variables:* **61) #CASE,S.CT**
         67) #S.C.DEC

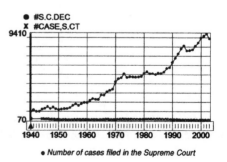

● *Number of cases filed in the Supreme Court*

✱ *Number of Supreme Court cases decided by signed opinions*

As you can see, the number of cases appealed to the Supreme Court has risen dramatically over the years, from slightly less than 1,000 in the 1940s to between 7,000 and 8,000 in the past decade. Yet, the number of cases on which the Supreme Court issues a written opinion has varied only from 79 to 199. The Supreme Court simply refuses to hear more than 95 percent of the cases appealed to it. Since 1993, the Supreme Court has issued fewer than 100 written opinions each year, exercising even more control over its docket.

Your turn.

REVIEW QUESTIONS

Based on the first part of this exercise, answer True or False to the following items:

1. There are 12 justices on the Supreme Court.   T   F

2. Bill Clinton was the first president to appoint a woman to the Supreme Court.   T   F

3. A majority of Americans feel courts deal too harshly with criminals.   T   F

4. Federal judges are appointed for life.   T   F

5. Most Americans oppose prayer in public schools.   T   F

6. The Supreme Court issues a written opinion on 95 percent of the cases
   appealed to it.   T   F

EXPLORIT QUESTIONS

CONFIDENCE IN THE SUPREME COURT

In the opening section of this exercise we saw that one-third of Americans have a great deal of confidence in the Supreme Court, about half have only some confidence, and the remainder have little confidence. Can we explain which citizens have more trust toward the Court and which have less?

Using the AUTO-ANALYZER task, let's see what demographic characteristics affect confidence in the Supreme Court.

> *Data File:* **GSS**
>> *Task:* **Auto-Analyzer**
> *Variable:* **55) SUP.COURT?**
>> *View:* **Univariate**

Remember, if the relationship is not statistically significant, you must report no differences in evaluations of the Supreme Court by each of the groups.

     ➤ *View:* **Sex**

7. Men are more likely than women to have a great deal of confidence in the Supreme Court.   T   F

     ➤ *View:* **Race**

8. Whites are more likely than African Americans to have a great deal of confidence in the Supreme Court.   T   F

     ➤ *View:* **Income**

9. The higher the income the more likely an individual is to have a great deal of confidence in the Supreme Court.   T   F

     ➤ *View:* **Education**

10. College graduates are more likely than others to have a great deal of confidence in the Supreme Court.   T   F

     ➤ *View:* **Religion**

11. Individuals from mainline Protestant churches are more likely than those from other religious groups to have a great deal of confidence in the Supreme Court.   T   F

The Supreme Court has ruled on many controversial issues, and the ruling of the Court is not always popular. Perhaps an individual's attitude on these issues affects his or her confidence in the Court.

        Data File: **GSS**
       ➤ *Task:* **Cross-tabulation**
  ➤ *Row Variable:* **55) SUP.COURT?**
➤ *Column Variable:* **45) SCH.PRAY**
       ➤ *View:* **Table**
    ➤ *Display:* **Column %**

12. One's attitude toward school prayer has an effect on one's confidence in the Supreme Court.   T   F

        Data File: **GSS**
          Task: **Cross-tabulation**
    Row Variable: **55) SUP.COURT?**
➤ *Column Variable:* **62) ABORT ANY**
       ➤ *View:* **Table**
    ➤ *Display:* **Column %**

13. One's attitude toward abortion has an effect on one's confidence in the Supreme Court.   T   F

> *Data File:* **GSS**
> *Task:* **Cross-tabulation**
> *Row Variable:* **55) SUP.COURT?**
> ➤ *Column Variable:* **40) EXECUTE?**
> ➤ *View:* **Table**
> ➤ *Display:* **Column %**

14. One's attitude toward the death penalty has an effect on one's confidence in the Supreme Court.   T   F

15. Taken together, these results suggest that confidence in the Supreme Court is generally based on more than one issue.   T   F

Let's see if one's basic attitudes, such as partisanship and ideology, influence attitudes toward the Supreme Court.

> *Data File:* **GSS**
> *Task:* **Cross-tabulation**
> *Row Variable:* **55) SUP.COURT?**
> ➤ *Column Variable:* **21) PARTY**
> ➤ *View:* **Table**
> ➤ *Display:* **Column %**

16. Republicans are the most likely to have a great deal confidence in the Supreme Court.   T   F

> *Data File:* **GSS**
> *Task:* **Cross-tabulation**
> *Row Variable:* **55) SUP.COURT?**
> ➤ *Column Variable:* **23) LIB./CONS.**
> ➤ *View:* **Table**
> ➤ *Display:* **Column %**

17. Moderates are the least likely to have confidence in the Supreme Court.   T   F

18. Basic attitudes, such as partisanship and ideology, strongly influence one's opinion of the Supreme Court.   T   F

CASE LOADS OF FEDERAL DISTRICT COURTS

In the opening section of this exercise, we saw how the number of cases appealed to the Supreme Court has risen dramatically over the years. The Supreme Court, however, has control over its docket and can select to hear only a small fraction of these cases. The lowest level of the federal court system, the federal district court, does not have such discretionary control over the cases it hears. District courts are the starting point for criminal cases involving the violation of federal laws, though most criminal cases are heard in state courts. Federal district courts also hear civil cases, where one private party (e.g., an individual or a business) sues another private party for damages. Civil cases are heard in federal court if they involve parties from different states and seek damages over $75,000. Let's examine the number of criminal and civil cases heard in federal district court in the past 60 years.

> ➤ *Data File:* **HISTORY**
>   ➤ *Task:* **Historical Trends**
> ➤ *Variables:* **64) #CIV COM**
>   **65) #CRIM COM**

19. The workload (combined total of criminal and civil cases) before the federal district court has risen dramatically over the past 60 years.   T   F

20. The change in the workload of the federal district court is due mainly to a large change in the number of criminal cases.   T   F

STATE COURTS

Most criminal and civil cases are heard in state courts, not federal courts. More than 100 million cases are heard each year in courts across the 50 states. State courts differ from the federal courts in some rules and procedures and in the existence of a greater variety of courts. State courts also differ from the federal courts in the methods for choosing judges. All federal judges, whether for the Supreme Court or one of the district courts, are nominated by the president and confirmed by the Senate. Once confirmed, federal judges have "life tenure," i.e., serving until they decide to retire. Some state court judges are appointed by the governors; some are appointed by legislatures. Many state court judges are elected, but some in partisan and others in nonpartisan elections. In a number of states, judges are appointed for an initial term and then subject to a retention election. In the retention election only the sitting judge's name is listed on the ballot with a question of whether or not this judge should continue to serve. In almost all cases, state judges are subject to periodic review (and possible removal) by the electorate or other state officials. A single state may use different selection methods for different types of courts. Let's look at the methods used by the states to select judges for their version of the Supreme Court.

> ➤ *Data File:* **STATES**
>   ➤ *Task:* **Mapping**
> ➤ *Variable 1:* **248) ST JUDGE**
>   ➤ *View:* **Map**
>   ➤ *Display:* **Legend**

21. Which method for selecting judges is used by the largest number of states? [*Hint:* Look at the values listed in the legend box.]

    a. partisan elections

    b. nonpartisan elections

    c. retention elections

    d. commission appointment

22. Which method for selecting judges is found primarily in the eastern states?

    a. partisan elections

    b. nonpartisan elections

    c. retention elections

    d. commission appointment

23. Which method for selecting judges occurs across a wide variety of states in many regions of the country?

    a. partisan elections

    b. nonpartisan elections

    c. retention elections

    d. all of the above

WORKSHEET   **EXERCISE 15**

WHAT HAVE WE LEARNED?

I.   What is the American public's evaluation of the Supreme Court? Who holds a higher opinion of the Court, and who is more likely to have hardly any confidence in the Court? Does the public's attitudes on issues matter for evaluations of the Court? Are the patterns that explain confidence in the Supreme Court mostly strong, moderate, or weak?

II.   What is the difference between the docket of the Supreme Court and that of lower federal courts? Which type of case has been most responsible for the increasing workload of the courts?

III.   What are the differences between the way judges are selected for the federal court versus the 50 state court systems? Do you think it matters how judges are selected for the types of decisions they might make?

<u>WHAT ELSE CAN BE EXPLORED?</u>

1. In this exercise we examined factors that could explain why some Americans had higher evaluations of the Supreme Court. Lower courts make many more decisions than the Supreme Court. The GSS question, 42) COURTS?, provides information on whether the public views courts in their area as too lenient in dealing with criminals. What factors might explain opinions on this issue?

2. One of the controversies that the Supreme Court has ruled on over the past 40 years is capital punishment. In 1972, the Supreme Court overturned all of the state laws on capital punishment for being too arbitrary. States responded by rewriting their death penalty laws. In recent years, the Supreme Court has tackled questions of execution of the moderately mentally retarded and defendants who were under 18 when the crime was committed. By using the GSS question 40) EXECUTE?, one can explore which types of Americans are more likely to approve of the death penalty.

3. In 2002, the U.S. Supreme Court in *Zelman v. Simmons-Harris* ruled in favor of the school voucher plan used in the Cleveland, Ohio, school system. Vouchers are a system of government assistance that facilitates children from poorly performing public schools to attend private schools. In the Cleveland case, 60 percent of the vouchers went to children from poor families. Yet, more than 90 percent of the children receiving vouchers attended religiously affiliated schools. The Supreme Court ruled the voucher system as having a valid secular purpose of assisting poor families with school tuition. Thus, the program did not constitute government support for religion. What is the American public's opinion on school vouchers? By using the NES survey question 83) SCH VCHR as the dependent variable, one can explore which Americans favor and which oppose school voucher programs.

APPENDIX: VARIABLE NAMES AND SOURCES

◆ DATA FILE: COLONIAL ◆

1) CASE ID
2) POP 1790
3) %BRITISH
4) % PROT.
5) # SLAVES
6) %SLAVES 90
7) #FREE AFR.

8) % FREE
9) # AFRI.-AM
10) %BLACK 90
11) CHURCHED76
12) WHITE CH76
13) %R CATH 76
14) %ENGLISH90

15) %SCOTCH 90
16) %P.IRISH 90
17) %C.IRISH90
18) %GERMAN90
19) %DUTCH 90
20) %FRENCH 90
21) %SWEDISH90

◆ DATA FILE: COUNTY ◆

1) NAME
2) POPULATION
3) POPCHNG
4) %URBAN
5) %RURAL
6) DENSITY
7) %<5
8) %>64
9) MED_AGE
10) %WHITE
11) %BLACK
12) %AMER.IN
13) %AMER.IND2
14) %ASIAN
15) %ASIAN2
16) RACE2+
17) %MALE
18) %FEMALE
19) SEX RATIO
20) BRTH RATE
21) DTH RATE
22) INFANT DTH
23) %ARAB
24) %CZECH
25) %DANISH
26) %DUTCH
27) %ENGLISH
28) %FRENCH
29) %FR.CAN
30) %GERMAN
31) %GREEK

32) %HUNGAR
33) %IRISH
34) %ITALIAN
35) %LITHU
36) %NORWEG
37) %POLISH
38) %PORTEG
39) %RUSSIAN
40) %SCT.IRH
41) %SCOTTISH
42) %SLOVAK
43) %S.AFRIC
44) %SWEDISH
45) %SWISS
46) %UKRAN
47) %WELSH
48) %W.INDIA
49) %CHINESE
50) %FILIPINO
51) %JAPANESE
52) %INDIAN
53) %KOREAN
54) %VIETNAM
55) %THAI
56) %PAKISTANI
57) %INDONES
58) %HISPANIC
59) %HISPANIC2
60) %MEXICAN
61) %PUERTO RC
62) %CUBAN

63) %NON-ENG
64) %FRGN BRN
65) NO MOVE
66) %VETERANS
67) %DISABLE
68) %HSGRAD
69) %COLLEGE
70) INCOME
71) POVERTY
72) CHLD POV
73) MANAGEMENT
74) SERVICE
75) SALES
76) FARM
77) CONSTRUCT
78) TRANSPORT
79) AGRICULTUR
80) MANUFACTUR
81) GVT WRKER
82) WORKING
83) FEM WORK
84) UNEMPLOY
85) PRIV SCH
86) NEW HOUSE
87) FAMIL SIZE
88) CHILDREN
89) FEM HEAD
90) FEDFUND
91) SOC SECUR
92) CRIME RATE

◆ DATA FILE: GSS ◆

1) MARITAL
2) # CHILDREN
3) EDUCATION
4) DAD EDUC.
5) MOM EDUC.
6) SEX
7) RACE
8) HISPANIC
9) AGE
10) PAR. BORN
11) INCOME
12) EVER UNEMP
13) UNIONIZED?
14) RELIGION
15) RELPERSN
16) ATTEND
17) PRAY
18) BIBLE
19) WORK GOVT
20) REGION
21) PARTY
22) DEM/REP
23) LIB./CONS.
24) VOTED 00
25) WHO IN 00?
26) BIG CITY$
27) BLACK$
28) DEFENSE$
29) FOR. AID$
30) WELFARE $
31) SOC.SEC.$
32) MASS TRAN$
33) POOR $
34) EQUALIZE$
35) TAXES?

36) ATHEIST SP
37) RACIST SP
38) COMMUN.SP
39) FR.SPEECH
40) EXECUTE?
41) GUN LAW?
42) COURTS?
43) GRASS?
44) WAR
45) SCH.PRAY
46) INTERMAR.?
47) AFFRM. ACT
48) HAPPY?
49) BIG BIZ?
50) RELIGION?
51) EDUCATION?
52) FED.GOV'T?
53) LABOR?
54) PRESS?
55) SUP.COURT?
56) SCIENCE?
57) CONGRESS?
58) MILITARY?
59) MEN BETTER
60) ABORT.WANT
61) ABORT.HLTH
62) ABORT ANY
63) SEX ED?
64) PREM.SEX
65) HOMO.SEX
66) PORN.LAW?
67) EUTHANASIA
68) SUIC.WISH
69) OWN GUN?
70) HUNT?

71) NEWSPAPER?
72) WATCH TV
73) MOTH.WORK?
74) WIFE@HOME
75) HELP POOR?
76) MUCH GOVNT
77) GOV.MED.
78) GOV.BLACK
79) ETHNIC HAR
80) COP HIT
81) DISC MAN
82) DISC WOMAN
83) MOTHR WRK
84) MEN OVRWRK
85) AIDKIDS
86) TEEN BC
87) GOODLIFE
88) HELPFUL
89) GET AHEAD
90) SEX OF SEX
91) VOL CHRTY
92) GIV CHRTY
93) BOYCOTT
94) SIGN PET
95) PROTEST
96) CON OFFCL
97) GIV CHNG
98) HELP NEEDY
99) PART THON
100) USE WEB?
101) CHAT POL
102) WEB POL
103) REV.DISCRM
104) DISCUSS

◆ DATA FILE: HOUSE108 ◆

1) NAME
2) STATE
3) DISTRICT
4) SEX
5) RACE/ETHNI
6) AGE
7) RELIGION
8) EDUCATION
9) MARITAL

10) LAWYER?
11) PARTY
12) # TERMS
13) REGION
14) SOUTH DEM
15) POWER
16) DIST.AFR
17) DIST.HIS
18) DIST.ASIAN

19) DIST.FAM$
20) DIST.POV
21) DIST.ELD
22) DIST.CHLD
23) %OF VOTE
24) INCUMBENT
25) UNOPPOSED
26) CAMPAIGN $
27) OPPONENT $

Appendix: Variable Names and Sources

◆ DATA FILE: HOUSE108 (cont'd) ◆

28) CANOPP
29) %PAC CONTR
30) %IND CONTR
31) INDPAC
32) $ PER VOTE
33) TAXACT
34) KID_TAX

35) MARR_PEN
36) UNBORN_VCT
37) AMT_TAX
38) TAXBRK_04
39) INDECENCY
40) FOOD_TORT
41) DOD$05

42) SPC SHTTL
43) NTU RATE
44) LCV RATE
45) ACLU RATE
46) IDEOLOGY

◆ DATA FILE: USPRES ◆

1) namyear
2) NAME
3) YEAR
4) ELECTVOTE
5) POPVOTE
6) PARTY
7) EARLY
8) PRESNUMBER
9) ELECT AGE
10) HEIGHT
11) EDUCATION
12) LAWYER

13) MILITARY
14) MIL FAME
15) RELIGION
16) HOW RELIG
17) YRS IN OFF
18) VETOES
19) ASSASSIN
20) ETHNICITY
21) GOV?
22) SEN?
23) VEEP?
24) RATING

25) SUP CT
26) TOT JUDGES
27) CENTURY
28) PTY-CONG
29) OVERRIDE
30) UNELECT
31) # VPRES
32) SEC ELEC C
33) SEC POP VT
34) MINOR
35) ERA

◆ DATA FILE: NATIONS ◆

1) COUNTRY
2) POP98
3) P.INTEREST
4) TALK POL.
5) PERSUASION
6) PETITION?
7) INTEREST G
8) SIT-INS
9) REVOLUTION
10) LEFT/RIGHT
11) ANTI-RACE
12) ANTI-FORGN
13) ANTI-JEW
14) ANTI-GAY
15) %FEM LEGIS

16) %FEM HEADS
17) WOMEN WANT
18) DEMOCRACY
19) CIVIL LIBS
20) VERY HAPPY
21) NATL PRIDE
22) PRESS?
23) PARLIAMENT
24) UNIONS?
25) WORK PRIDE
26) CHEAT TAX
27) TAKE BRIBE
28) CARS/CAP
29) % URBAN
30) NEWSPAPERS

31) TELEVISION
32) LITERACY
33) ABRT.UNWED
34) A.UNWANT
35) GDP/CAP
36) # PARTIES
37) %BIG PARTY
38) % VOTED
39) FIGHT COPS
40) EDUC EXPTD
41) HEALTH
42) GOVT-HLT
43) MIL-GNP
44) MIL-PC

◆ DATA FILE: NES ◆

1) SEX
2) RACE
3) INCOME
4) EDUCATION
5) PARTY
6) MARITAL
7) AGE
8) RELIGION
9) REGION
10) HISPANIC
11) UNION
12) CHURCH
13) BIBLE
14) PRAY
15) RELIG IMP
16) IDEOLOGY
17) PRES 00
18) ELEC FAIR
19) TV NEWS?
20) READ PAPER
21) BUSH APP
22) CONG APP
23) BUSH THERM
24) KERRY THRM
25) CHNY THERM
26) EDWRD THRM
27) LBUSH THRM
28) MCCN THERM
29) DIV GOVT
30) BUSH IDEO
31) KERRY IDEO
32) ECONOMY
33) INTL POLCY
34) PRTY ECON
35) PRTY TERRO
36) PRTY PEACE
37) ISOLAT
38) AFGHAN WAR

39) IRAQ WAR
40) TERRORISM
41) GOVT SPEND
42) DEMS GVSP
43) REPS GVSP
44) TAX CUT
45) INSURANCE
46) GOVJOBS
47) ABORT$LAW
48) PBIRTH ABO
49) ENVRG
50) BUSH ER
51) KERRY ER
52) DEATH PEN
53) GUN CNTRL
54) EQL ROLE
55) FLAG FEEL
56) GAY MARR
57) INFORMED?
58) HSE TYPE
59) SENTYPE
60) INTEREST?
61) MEDIA TRST
62) PRTY TALK
63) TALK POL?
64) BUTTON
65) CONTRIBUTE
66) CONT$PARTY
67) VOTED
68) EARLY VOTE
69) PRESVOTE
70) VOTE HOUSE
71) VOTE SEN
72) HSE CNTRL
73) SEN CTRL
74) INCUM APP
75) GEN INT
76) GOV BLKHLP

77) IMPORTS?
78) IMMIGRANTS
79) ABORTION
80) ABORT BUSH
81) ABRT KERRY
82) SS REFORM?
83) SCH VCHR
84) POL DISC
85) TALK RADIO
86) WEB POL
87) GAY JOB
88) GAY MIL
89) GAY ADOPT
90) PRTY_DIFFS
91) SPEAKER ID
92) VPRES_ID
93) BRITISH ID
94) CHIEF J.ID
95) CONTACT
96) CIV INVOLV
97) VOLUNTR
98) FAMILY VAL
99) BLK_MOBIL
100) BLK_HISTOR
101) TRUST GOV
102) BIG INTERS
103) GOVT WASTE
104) CROOKED?
105) DON'T CARE
106) GOVT ATTN
107) ELECT ATTN
108) AFFIRM ACT
109) DEMOC SAT
110) PRTY VIEW
111) KNOW
112) CONG KNOW
113) NEWS TYPE

◆ DATA FILE: STATES ◆

1) STATE NAME
2) BIG REGION
3) SUNBELT
4) THE WEST
5) THE SOUTH
6) UNION/CONF

7) SLAVE/FREE
8) UN/CONF SL
9) %SLAV ST
10) POPULATION
11) POP2003
12) POPGROW90

13) POPGROW00
14) URBAN00
15) URBAN1900
16) MOBILE HOM
17) NEW HOMES
18) MALE HOMES

19) FEM HOMES	67) STLEG REP	115) ST HWY
20) FAMILY$	68) STLEG CMP	116) WELF'96
21) HIGH $	69) HOUSE DEM	117) TOUGH LOVE
22) %POOR	70) HOUSE REP	118) STATE DEBT
23) PERCAP$	71) SEN DEM	119) $PER PUPIL
24) %FOREIGN	72) SEN REP	120) HIGH ED%
25) %WHITE	73) CONG DEM	121) HIGH ED PP
26) %AFRIC.AM	74) CONG REP	122) CLLG COST
27) %ASIAN	75) CONG CMP	123) TOXIC
28) %AMER.IN	76) INCOME TAX	124) GUN WAIT
29) %HISPANIC	77) FED$ RATIO	125) GUN LIC
30) %SPAN.SPK	78) %FED LAND	126) GUN RECORD
31) %COLLEGE	79) FEDEMPLOY	127) VIOL.CRIME
32) %HIGH SCH	80) SOC SEC #	128) MURDER
33) %HS DROP	81) SOC SEC $	129) RAPE
34) AGE	82) UNMP INS #	130) ROBBERY
35) AVE PAY	83) UNMP INS $	131) ASSAULT
36) UNEMPLOY	84) FOODSTMP #	132) BURGLARY
37) %UNION	85) TANF #	133) LARCENY
38) MARR RATE	86) TANF $	134) PROP CRIME
39) DIVORCE	87) MILTARY $	135) HATE CRIME
40) BIRTH	88) MILITARY #	136) DTH LAW
41) ABORT RATE	89) VETERANS #	137) EXCTD 30
42) WEIGHT	90) FED FUND	138) EXCTD 77
43) EXERCISE	91) FED AID	139) DTH ROW
44) SMOKERS	92) FED FOOD	140) PRISONERS
45) NO INSUR	93) FED EDUC	141) POLICE
46) LIBERAL	94) FED HOUSE	142) ST LOC EMP
47) MODERATE	95) FED LABOR	143) LOC GOVTS
48) CONSER	96) FED HUMAN	144) LOC$/CAP
49) POP-DEM	97) FED TRAN	145) LOC EXP
50) POP-IND	98) HIGHWAY	146) LOC DBT
51) POP-REP	99) SPEED	147) LOC FED
52) PROCHOICE	100) ST TOT TAX	148) LOC STATE
53) PROLIFE	101) ST INC TAX	149) LOC LOC
54) DTH OPIN	102) SALES TAX	150) LOC PROP
55) N.R./NAT	103) INC VS SLS	151) LOC SALE
56) PRESIDENTS	104) ALCHL TAX	152) STATES1860
57) # S. COURT	105) TBCO TAX	153) STATES'20
58) HOUSE93	106) CIG TAX	154) HARDING'20
59) HOUSE03	107) LOTTERY	155) LEFT'20
60) HSE CHG	108) LTTRY $	156) STATES'24
61) INITIATIVE	109) LTTRY PC	157) COOL'24
62) REFERENDUM	110) ST SPND	158) LAFOLL'24
63) BLK OFF	111) ST EDUC	159) STATES'28
64) HISP OFF	112) ST HEALTH	160) HOOVER'28
65) WOMEN LEG	113) ST WELFARE	161) STATES'32
66) STLEG DEM	114) ST CORR	162) FDR'32

163) STATES'36	192) CARTER'80	221) THRD PTY04
164) FDR'36	193) ANDERSN'80	222) BLK REG'60
165) STATES'40	194) STATES'84	223) WHT REG'60
166) FDR'40	195) REAGAN'84	224) BLK REG'76
167) STATES'44	196) STATES'88	225) WHT REG'76
168) FDR'44	197) BUSH'88	226) MOTOR VOT
169) STATES'48	198) STATES'92	227) VOTED'92
170) TRUMAN'48	199) CLINTON'92	228) REGIST'92
171) DEWEY'48	200) BUSH'92	229) VOTED'96
172) THURMND'48	201) PEROT'92	230) REGIST'96
173) WALLACE'48	202) STATES'96	231) VOTED'00
174) STATES'52	203) CLINTON'96	232) REGIST'00
175) IKE'52	204) DOLE'96	233) VOTED'02
176) STATES'56	205) PEROT'96	234) VOTED'04
177) IKE'56	206) STATES'00	235) ELECTOR'40
178) STATES'60	207) GWBUSH'00	236) ELECTOR'60
179) KENNEDY'60	208) GORE'00	237) ELECTOR'90
180) STATES'64	209) NADER'00	238) ELECTOR'00
181) JOHNSON'64	210) BUCHANN'00	239) ECGAIN'602
182) STATES'68	211) THRD PTY00	240) EC GAIN'00
183) NIXON'68	212) MARGINP	241) BSH-VIS'00
184) HUMPH'68	213) MARGIN	242) GOR-VIS'00
185) WALLACE'68	214) GORENADER	243) BSH-VIS'04
186) STATES'72	215) GWB ECVOTE	244) KER-VIS'04
187) NIXON'72	216) GORE ECVOT	245) CMPTV'92
188) STATES'76	217) STATES'04	246) CMPTV'96
189) CARTER'76	218) GWBUSH'04	247) CMPTV'00
190) STATES'80	219) KERRY'04	248) ST JUDGE
191) REAGAN'80	220) NADER'04	

◆ TREND FILE: HISTORY ◆

1) Date	16) %DEM HOUSE	31) %F F.PRES
2) POPULATION	17) D.PRES %	32) % BLK PRES
3) %<5	18) M.D.PRES %	33) GOV.CROOK?
4) %65&OVER	19) F.D.PRES %	34) TRUST GOV
5) % URBAN	20) W.D.PRES%	35) WASTE TAX
6) %HS	21) B.D.PRES %	36) CONF.TV
7) %COLLEGE	22) %HH TELE	37) CONF.PRESS
8) %NO HS	23) TV VIEW	38) CONF CONG
9) LAWYER/CAP	24) READ PAPER	39) CONF COURT
10) DOCTOR/CAP	25) NEWS/100	40) CONF GOV
11) CPI(1967)	26) TV/100 HH	41) CONF MED
12) VOTER PART	27) SOUTH.DEM	42) CONF MIL
13) % DEM	28) CIVLIB INX	43) ENVIR $
14) % REP	29) %FEM PRES	44) DEFENSE $
15) APPORTION	30) %M F.PRES	45) WELF $

46) HEALTH $
47) BLACK $
48) DRUG $
49) FED EMP RT
50) DEF EMP RT
51) LEG EMP RT
52) JUDG EMP R
53) NON-D EMP
54) DEF$/POP
55) HR$/POP
56) S.S.$/POP
57) I.S.$/POP
58) MED$/POP
59) HEAL$/POP
60) ED$/POP
61) #CASE,S.CT
62) #CASE COMM
63) #CRIM CASE
64) #CIV COM
65) #CRIM COM
66) RACE SEG
67) #S.C.DEC

68) HSE-OTH
69) SEN-OTH
70) %REP HOUSE
71) DEM$
72) REP$
73) %BLACK
74) %WHITE
75) %AMER IND
76) %ASIAN
77) %HISPANIC
78) %FOREIGN B
79) MEDIAN AGE
80) #BILLS
81) #BILLS PAS
82) SCH PRAY
83) ABORT ANY
84) FED-REC
85) FED EXP
86) DEFICIT
87) FED REC G
88) FED EXP G
89) DEFICIT G

90) DEBT
91) DEBT GDP
92) INCOME TAX
93) CORP TAX
94) SOCSEC TAX
95) EXCISE TAX
96) WM SENATE
97) WM HOUSE
98) WM ST LEG
99) SEN DEM
100) SEN REP
101) INC TAX GD
102) CORP TX GD
103) SOC SEC GD
104) EXCISE GD
105) HSE SIZE
106) SEN SIZE
107) %WM SENATE
108) % WM HOUSE
109) C DEM IDEO
110) C REP IDEO

SOURCES

NES—National Election Study

The NES data file is based on selected variables from the 2004 American National Election Study provided by the National Election Studies, Institute for Social Research at the University of Michigan and the Inter-university Consortium for Political and Social Research. The principal investigators are Nancy Burns, Donald R. Kinder, and the National Election Studies.

GSS—General Social Survey

The GSS data file is based on selected variables from the National Opinion Research Center (University of Chicago) General Social Surveys for 2002, distributed by The Roper Center and the Inter-university Consortium for Political and Social Research. The principal investigators are James A. Davis, Tom W. Smith, and Peter V. Marsden.

STATES—The Fifty States of the U.S.

The data in the STATES file are from a variety of sources. The variable description for each variable uses the following abbreviations to indicate the source.

ABC: *Audit Bureau of Circulation Blue Book.*
BJS: Bureau of Justice Statistics.
CAWP: Courtesy of Center for American Women and Politics, Eagleton Institute of Politics, Rutgers University, http://www.cawp.rutgers.edu.
CENSUS: The summary volumes of the U.S. Census.
DES: U.S. Dept. of Education, *Digest of Education Statistics.*
FEC: Federal Election Commission.
NCHS: National Center for Health Statistics.
HHS: Department of Health and Human Services.
HIGHWAY: Federal Highway Administration, Highway Statistics.
INS: Immigration and Naturalization Service.
OMB: Office of Management and Budget.
SA: *Statistical Abstract of the United States* for the indicated year.
SNES: Senate National Election Study, 1988–1992.
SOS: Secretary of State web pages for the 50 state governments.
S.R.: State Rankings (Morgan Quitno Corp., Lawrence, KS).
UCR: *Uniform Crime Reports.*

NATIONS—Nations of the World

The data in the NATIONS file are from a variety of sources. The variable description for each variable uses the following abbreviations to indicate the source.

ABC: *Blue Book*, Audit Bureau of Circulation
DES: *Digest of Education Statistics*, U.S. Dept. of Education
ES: Electoral Studies
FITW: *Freedom in the World*, 1995, Freedom House
HDR: *Human Development Reports*, United Nations Development Program

PRB: *World Population Data Sheet*, 1994, Population Research Council

SA: *Statistical Abstract of the United States*

TWF: *The World Fact Book, 1994–1995*, Central Intelligence Agency

WABF: *The World Almanac and Book of Facts*, 1995

WVS: World Values Survey, Institute for Social Research, Inter-university Consortium for Political and Social Research

USPRES—Presidents of the United States

Data in the USPRES file are from a variety of readily available sources, such as a world almanac or an encyclopedia, the U.S. Census, or other government publications. The variable description for each variable uses the following abbreviations to indicate the source.

NARA: National Archives and Records Administration, http://www.archives.gov/

CWP: Web pages of the U.S. House of Representatives and U.S. Senate, http://www.house.gov and http://www.senate.gov.

COURT: Federal judiciary web page, http://www.uscourts.gov.

COLONIAL—The Thirteen Colonies plus Georgia and Maine

The data in the COLONIAL file are from a variety of readily available sources, such as a world almanac or an encyclopedia, the U.S. Census, or other government publications.

HOUSE108—U.S. House of Representatives, 108th Congress

Data in the HOUSE108 file are from a variety of readily available sources, such as the U.S. Census, the U.S. House of Representatives and U.S. Senate websites, the Federal Election Commission, or other government publications.

ACLU RATE: Courtesy of the American Civil Liberties Union, ACLU Scorecard, 108th Congress, U.S. House of Representatives, http://www.aclu.org.

NTU RATE: Courtesy of the National Taxpayers Union, NTU Rates Congress, 108th Congress, 2nd Session, http://www.ntu.org.

LCV RATE: Courtesy of the League of Conservation Voters, National Environmental Scorecard, 108th Congress, http://www.lcv.org.

IDEOLOGY: Courtesy of Keith Poole, Poole-Rosenthal DW-NOMINATE Scores, 108th Congress, http://voteview.com.

HISTORY—Historical Information on the United States and its Citizens

The data in the HISTORY file are from a variety of readily available sources, such as a world almanac or an encyclopedia, the U.S. Census, or other government publications. The variable description for each variable uses the following abbreviations to indicate the source.

CAWP: Courtesy of Center for American Women and Politics, Eagleton Institute of Politics, Rutgers University, http://www.cawp.rutgers.edu.

COURT: Federal Judiciary web page, http://www.uscourts.gov.

FEC: Federal Election Commission web page, http://www.fec.gov.

GSS: General Social Survey.

HWP, HOUSE: U.S. House of Representatives web page, http://www.house.gov.

OMB: Office of Management and Budget, http://www.whitehouse.gov/omb/

PR: Poole-Rosenthal DW-NOMINATE scores, courtesy of Keith Poole.

SA: *Statistical Abstract of the United States*, various years.

SWP, SENATE: U.S. Senate web page, http://www.senate.gov.

COUNTY—Counties in the United States

This file contains data from the U.S. Census Bureau's 2000 release of the *County and City Data Book*.